Enforcing Order on the Border

Enforcing Order on the Border

Race, Policing, and Immigration
Enforcement in South Texas

Eric Gamino

The University of Georgia Press
ATHENS

Sociology of Race and
Ethnicity web page

All photographs are by the author.

© 2025 by the University of Georgia Press
Athens, Georgia 30602
www.ugapress.org
All rights reserved
Designed by Kaelin Chappell Broaddus
Set in 10.5/13.5 Garamond Premier Pro Regular
by Mary McKeon

Most University of Georgia Press titles are
available from popular e-book vendors.

Printed digitally

Library of Congress Control Number: 2025007458
ISBN: 9780820373928 (hardback)
ISBN: 9780820373935 (paperback)
ISBN: 9780820373942 (epub)
ISBN: 9780820373959 (PDF)

CONTENTS

ILLUSTRATIONS

ABBREVIATIONS

BP	Border Patrol
DHS	Department of Homeland Security
DMCSO	Del Monte County Sheriff's Office
DPS	Texas Department of Public Safety
DREAM	Development, Relief, and Education for Alien Minors Act
ESL	English as a second language
FEMA	Federal Emergency Management Agency
IA	illegal alien
ICE	U.S. Immigration and Customs Enforcement
IIRIRA	Illegal Immigration Reform and Immigrant Responsibility Act of 1996
LAPD	Los Angeles Police Department
OLS	Operation Lone Star
OPSG	Operation Stonegarden
OSS	Operation Strong Safety
RGV	Rio Grande Valley
SSI	Supplemental Security Income
UA	undocumented alien
USBP	U.S. Border Patrol

ACKNOWLEDGEMENTS

The realization of this book has been accomplished primarily due to the many contributions of guidance and support received in my life's journey over the years from respected mentors, colleagues, friends, and family. Certainly, I owe much gratitude to my high school math teacher, Mr. David "Black Rooster" Nava, for his willingness on occasion to stray off-topic from linear and quadratic equations long enough to provide me and my classmates life-lesson lectures filled with hard truths about what it takes to succeed in the real world and advice about how to unlock the potential within each one of us. His encouraging words inspired me to attend college, even though my high school guidance counselor was convinced I needed to either learn a trade or join the military in order to become successful in life.

I also thank Kelly F. Himmel, who sparked my interest in qualitative methodology, for his support and words of encouragement as I pursued a doctoral degree. Moreover, I thank my friend Rubén Farías for his help and support while we were in graduate school together. To Dan Kiniry, thank you for your friendship; for introducing me to the local immigrant community in Bryan/College Station, Texas, while I lived there; and for including me in your humanitarian efforts. Thanks also to Holly Foster, Pat Rubio Goldsmith, Kathryn Henderson, Edward Murguia, and William Alex McIntosh for serving on my graduate committee. To my friend and colleague, Omar Camarillo, thank you for always being there for me and for lending a helping hand when I have needed it the most. In addition, I'm forever indebted to the late Juan José Bustamante for his mentorship, guidance, and, most importantly, his friendship. He took me under his wing and was instrumental in helping me navigate academia, often serving as my guiding light. I miss

Juan dearly, but I take solace in knowing that I have followed in his footsteps by helping others and paying it forward—*Descansa en paz*, Juan.

I extend my gratitude to everyone who participated in the research that comprises the data presented in the book and to the staff from University of Georgia Press, especially Mick Gusinde-Duffy, for their dedication and support. I also thank David L. Brunsma and David G. Embrick for supporting this project.

Thanks to Daryl Herring, who has served as my editor since my graduate school days and has helped refine my writing style and voice. The book has benefited immensely from his editorial guidance. I also owe a great debt to my late colleague Anthony "Tony" Bouza for both his honest and candid conversations with me and for helping me understand the complexities of the policing profession and the difficulties associated with police reform—R.I.P., Tony.

I thank my uncle Mario García for his unwavering support of my brothers and me, and I thank my brothers, Graciano and Hugo, for always being there for me and for their words of encouragement. Growing up, we experienced our fair share of tough times, but we have always stayed the course and been there for each other through the good and bad times—I love you guys. To my mother, Micaela, I know it was not easy being a single mother of three boys, but know that I appreciate all the sacrifices you made for us. It did not go unnoticed, and I love you with all my heart, *Ma*. To my daughter, Victoria Guadalupe, and son, Mario Angelo, you are the best writing partners anyone could ever ask for. You were literally and figuratively by my side as I wrote and worked on the book—I love you both so much.

My journey in academia has been challenging; however, my lovely wife Dora has always been there to encourage me to press forward. Thank you, Dora, for your enduring love and support, for holding down the fort while I worked on the book, and for being a great mother to our children. I love you so much.

Finally, I thank God, *La Virgen de Guadalupe*, Saint Michael the Archangel, *Santo Toribio Romo* (the patron saint of migrants), and my nephew Graciano Gael for their guidance and protection.

Enforcing Order on the Border

INTRODUCTION

The 2020 U.S. presidential election surprised many individuals and not just because of the controversy created by then president Donald Trump. Rather, what surprised individuals—in particular, political pundits and commentators—is what transpired in South Texas during the 2020 presidential election. Former president Trump almost flipped the entire South Texas region, traditionally a Democratic stronghold, and nearly emerged with a Republican win. That is, President Joe Biden narrowly won in certain counties in the Rio Grande Valley (RGV) of South Texas—and by smaller margins than 2016 former presidential candidate Hillary Clinton, who received overwhelming support in the RGV in opposition to then presidential candidate Trump. People were amazed at how President Trump was able to increase his support in the RGV from the 2016 presidential election to the 2020 presidential election.

Those results surprised many because the RGV is a majority-minority Mexican-origin community and because Trump made it clear that he holds an anti-immigrant nativistic view toward Mexican-origin individuals, as evidenced by what he said when he announced his 2016 presidency: "When Mexico sends its people, they're not sending their best. . . . They're bringing drugs. They're bringing crime. They're rapists. And some, I assume, are good people."[1] The RGV results of the 2020 presidential election, however, did not surprise me one bit. As someone who was raised in and spent more than thirty years living in the RGV, I know that even though the region is predominantly Mexican origin, the residents of this area are not the rigid, monolithic society many individuals unfamiliar with the borderlands area presume them to be. Though it may be perplexing to some that President Trump made inroads in the RGV with Mexican Americans who bore the

brunt of his aforementioned anti-Mexican-origin, nativistic verbal attack, some
Mexican Americans in the RGV share a similar ideology.

Subsequently, two years later on June 21, 2022, a local Republican female poli-
tician in the RGV made U.S. political history by becoming the first Mexican-born
congresswoman elected to serve in the U.S. Congress.[2] Her platform aligned with
the mainstream Republican Party: pro-God, pro-life, pro-family, pro-America,
and so forth. In November of that same year, another local Republican female pol-
itician from the RGV was elected to serve in the U.S. Congress. She too shared the
same anti-immigrant beliefs as President Trump and supported the completion of
a border wall on the U.S.-Mexico border.[3] When asked whether she felt insulted
by President Trump's anti-immigrant rhetoric (the aforementioned 2016 anti-
Mexican-origin disparaging comments) since she is a third-generation Mexican
American, she said she was unfazed by his comments.[4] Despite President Trump's
vitriolic comments about Latino immigrants, these two Latina politicians, similar
to other Mexican Americans in the RGV, share the same anti-immigrant view, even
though it may seem like a paradoxical phenomenon to those unfamiliar with the
borderlands.

Residents of the RGV, similar to other borderland communities along the entire
southwestern U.S.-Mexico border, are diverse in terms of gender, religion, social
class, age, education, immigration history, and especially political ideology, even
though the majority of residents are predominantly Mexican origin.[5] The same
can be said about Mexican-origin individuals who do not reside in the borderlands.[6] As someone raised amid this diversity, I am always shocked by how others
who are removed from the region want to pigeonhole and stereotype these residents who have literally been there for generations. Thus, my academic interest lies
in exploding some of the myths many pundits hold regarding this important segment of society within the United States.

Enforcing Order on the Border thus focuses on my experiences as a police officer serving in the RGV to illustrate the intersection between race, policing, and
immigration enforcement from an institutional perspective. Moreover, as a former resident of the RGV, I have always been curious why some U.S.-born Latinos,
in particular, Mexican Americans, are antagonistic toward Latino immigrants, especially since both groups live within the same majority-minority Latino-origin
community.[7] Previous academic scholarship by David G. Gutiérrez exemplified
the ambivalent relationship that evolved over time between Mexican Americans
and Mexican immigrants. His study revealed that Mexican American community leaders and activists' political ideology associated with immigration policy
and immigrants changed from one of antipathy and nativism to Mexican-origin
ethnic solidarity over the years.[8] Moreover, in her study of intraethnic relations in

the predominantly Mexican-origin community of La Puente, California, Gilda L. Ochoa found that some of her Mexican American participants derided Mexican immigrants, while others assisted them. The study illustrated how some Mexican Americans may do both, thus revealing the nuanced relationship between both groups. This scholarship elucidated how ultimately Mexican Americans end up forming intraethnic solidarity with their Mexican immigrant counterparts.[9]

I was born in Illinois but raised in a small, impoverished, criminogenic community located in the RGV. Throughout my time in the borderlands, I witnessed the anti-immigrant sentiment experienced by immigrants at the hands of U.S.-born Latinos. This experience prompted me to question how such animosity toward immigrants can exist, given that the sentiment comes from fellow Latinos.[10] As a former police officer, I witnessed my fair share of social misery, encountered many disturbing incidents (including death and violence), and saw the worst in humanity. Certainly, I could have written a book about those disturbing aspects of police work, but my interests lie more in how the concept of race and racism operates in a majority-minority community. This book, a chronicle of my lived experiences as a Mexican American residing in the RGV, includes an autoethnographic examination of my life as a resident of the RGV coupled with my experience as a police officer for two different police departments in the RGV.

The book moves beyond the Black/white binary and reveals how the concept of race/racism functions within a predominantly Latino-origin community, the RGV. The chapters expose the interplay between local police, federal immigration officials (U.S. Border Patrol [USBP]), and civilians (U.S. citizens, documented immigrants, undocumented immigrants, and permanent residents) regarding immigration. In particular, *Enforcing Order on the Border* illustrates the process of intraracial/intraethnic conflict within the RGV from a police officer's perspective by examining the relationship among and between civilians and police officers. Beyond the examination of intraracial/intraethnic conflict in the RGV, this book also provides insight into local police participation in federal immigration enforcement practices—the "crimmigration" phenomenon.[11]

Several studies examine immigration enforcement between local police and U.S. Immigration and Customs Enforcement (ICE) in the form of 287(g) agreements.[12] A recent study conducted in Nashville, Tennessee, succeeded in illustrating the manner in which local police departments participated in the federal deportation regime through traffic stops and immigrant processing at the county jail as part of the 287(g) program.[13] Moreover, Doris Provine and colleagues provided a comprehensive examination of local immigration policing by illustrating the vastly different responses among several local police departments in the United States to immigrants.[14] That is, while some police departments embrace welcoming approaches toward immigrants, others participate in stringent immigration enforcement practices, and others choose to do nothing at all regarding immigrants. The findings illustrate the complex and nuanced responses regarding local police participation in immigration enforcement according to local-context factors.

Immigration enforcement practices can be detrimental to police-community relations in regard to police legitimacy.[15] In particular, these practices can have negative consequences for the lives of undocumented adolescent youths and their family members by causing anxiety, distress, and fears of deportation.[16] That is, for undocumented immigrants, immigration enforcement practices are often considered forms of legal violence.[17] Social scientists further note that immigration enforcement practices in the United States equate to a gendered racial removal project, since immigration enforcement practices primarily target working-class men of color.[18]

Moreover, the vast majority of crimmigration scholarship offers insight into the collaborative efforts between local police and federal immigration officials regarding interior immigration enforcement in the United States.[19] However, *Enforcing Order on the Border* shifts the focus of police-immigration collaborations to my institutional perspective as a police officer. I provide an examination of the long-standing history of local police participation in immigration enforcement in the borderlands and demonstrate how this practice still occurs during routine work activities.

For example, during a June 2023 ride-along with a deputy from the Maverick County Sheriff's Office, located on the Texas-Mexico border, one local journalist experienced firsthand local police officers engaged in immigration enforcement practices.[20] While on routine patrol, a deputy spotted a shirtless male walking on the roadway, and when the deputy made a U-turn, the shirtless male began to run. The deputy caught up with the male and detained him for questioning. During the questioning, the male, who was identified as an eighteen-year-old Honduran immigrant, admitted to the deputy that he had entered clandestinely into the United States. When the journalist asked the deputy about such encounters, the deputy replied, "A lot of these illegal immigrants that are crossing come with weapons, such as knives, some type of bats."[21] Eventually, the deputy transported the Honduran immigrant to the USBP station for processing. As surprising and/or alarming as this immigration enforcement incident might seem, the process of local police partaking in such immigration enforcement practices is all too common in the borderlands. Thus, I explain how systemic racism is historically deeply rooted in the criminal justice system, particularly in law enforcement agencies, as a result of racialized institutional practices on the U.S.-Mexico border to contextualize the aforementioned incident that the journalist experienced while on the ride-along.

This book explores the central topics of how undocumented Latino immigrants become racialized by their coracial/coethnic counterparts, how undocumented Latino immigrants are affected by racialized immigration enforcement practices, and to what extent the racialization process and racialized immigration enforcement practices reveal evidence of racism in the RGV. Michael Omi and Howard Winant define "racialization" as a fluid and changing entity. Further, they define this racialization process as "the sociohistorical process by which racial categories are created, inhabited, transformed, and destroyed."[22] Thus, racialization entails the organization of the social order along racial lines by the interaction between microlevel processes, such as personal interactions among individuals, and macrolevel processes, such as social structures or social relations.

Enforcing Order on the Border is an examination of how Latinos on the South Texas–Mexico border racialize each other through the use of derogatory terminology and of how Latino undocumented immigrants are primary targets of racialized immigration enforcement initiatives by local police and federal immigration authorities, particularly the USBP. Consequently, this collaborative effort in the South Texas–Mexico borderlands creates a distinctive method of policing that I refer to as "Constitution-free policing" (see chapter 2). In sum, this book reveals that the intraracial/intraethnic conflict among Latinos, particularly Mexican Americans, in the RGV serves as a method to maintain white supremacy by pitting coracials/coethnics against each other.

Why the Police?

My policing experience began when I was in my early twenties, soon after I obtained my undergraduate degree and began my career as a police officer for the Le Grand, Texas, Police Department.[23] My four-year tenure with that department ended when I was accepted into graduate school at Texas A&M University in College Station, Texas. Even though I was accepted into graduate school, I still had a desire to continue serving as a police officer. Therefore, before moving to College Station, I maintained active status of my State of Texas police officer license by becoming a reserve deputy with the Del Monte County Sheriff's Office (DMCSO). Thus, during the time that I lived in College Station, I was a reserve deputy with the sheriff's office.

After successfully completing my preliminary examinations, I moved back to the RGV and began my fieldwork. For the first three months of my fieldwork, I continued in my reserve deputy status; however, after those three months, I began full-time employment with the sheriff's office, serving as a deputy sheriff for about a year and a half. I then reverted back to reserve deputy status with the sheriff's office for the remainder of the fieldwork. *Enforcing Order on the Border* emerged from my experiences serving as a deputy with the DMCSO both full-time and as a reserve. *Enforcing Order on the Border*, a qualitative examination of police-community relations on the South Texas–Mexico border in the RGV, is based on my fieldwork, during which I used a combination of participant observation and autoethnography as the principal research methods. I collected the findings discussed in this book between 2012 and 2015 during calls for service as I conducted my ethnographic fieldwork as a police officer for the DMCSO.

Participant Observation

The methodology of participant observation is appropriate for research dealing with virtually every aspect of human existence.[24] During participant observation, a researcher takes part in the daily activities, rituals, interactions, and events of a research subject's life and collects data in the form of field notes.[25] I observed interactions among my colleagues, other law enforcement officials, and civilians as we responded to calls for service during our routine daily work activities.

By using participant observation, "it is possible to illustrate what goes on, whom or what is involved, when and where things occur, and how they transpire."[26] Utilizing participant observation as a data collection method allowed me the opportunity to illustrate what transpired during calls for service, since police work is known as low-visibility work.[27] That is, most police-civilian contacts are made in intimate settings, such as the residence of the 911 caller. Participant observation is appropriate when certain minimal conditions are met: "The researcher is granted access to a setting, research is observable within an everyday life situation or setting, and the research problem is concerned with human meanings and interactions viewed from the insiders' perspective."[28] By utilizing participant observation, *Enforcing Order on the Border* reveals from an insider perspective the complexities of policing on the U.S.-Mexico border—which at times involves immigration enforcement—and how officers make sense of their enforcement duties.

Moreover, participant observation seeks to unveil, make accessible, and demonstrate the meanings people use to make sense out of their daily lives. For instance, Danielle Egan was a participant observer in two strip clubs in New England; her goal was to illustrate the everyday life experiences of female exotic dancers and their male clients from the perspective of the dancers.[29] Peter Moskos described the experiences and meanings of being a police officer in Baltimore, Maryland, from an insider's viewpoint.[30] Danny Jorgensen asserted that "the world of everyday life is for the methodology of participant observation the ordinary, usual, typical, routine, or natural environment of human existence."[31] Consequently, *Enforcing Order on the Border* focuses on the everyday, work-related experiences of Mexican American police officers who work along the South Texas–Mexico border and their interactions with civilians.

According to Moskos, "Prolonged participant observation research is the best and perhaps only means of gathering valid data on job-related police behavior."[32] Moreover, according to Michael Agar, participant observation implies that "the raw material of ethnography lies out there in the daily activities of the individuals one is interested in, and the only way to access those activities is to establish relationships with individuals, to participate alongside them in what they do, and to observe interactions."[33] By employing this method, I was able to observe the interactions between the DMCSO deputies and the civilians they came in contact with, along with the interactions I had with civilians and other law enforcement officials during routine calls for service. I was also able to observe the interactions between my fellow deputies while we were at the police department. Furthermore, as previously mentioned, I used autoethnography as a research method for *Enforcing Order on the Border*.

Autoethnography in Sociological Research

Autoethnography uses the self as both subject and object; its inquiry arises out of several layers of consciousness connecting the personal with the cultural.[34] Autoethnography has a double meaning: it refers either to the ethnography of one's own group (e.g., police officers) or to the autobiographical writing that has ethnographic interest. Moreover, autoethnography is defined as a form of self-narrative that situates "the self within a social context."[35] Thus, this method allowed me to illustrate what was occurring within the research setting from my own perspective as a researcher conducting research with the police.

Autoethnography is defined as "autobiograph[y] that self-consciously explore[s] the interplay of the introspective, personally engaged self with cultural descriptions mediated through language, history, and ethnographic explanation."[36] *Enforcing Order on the Border* is an illustration of my experiences as a Latino male who was raised in the RGV and who eventually worked as a police officer and doubled as an ethnographic researcher. Autoethnography focuses on connecting the self to the cultural (in this case, police officers). Autoethnography asks its readers to "become co-participants and to feel the truth of the researchers' stories by engaging the storyline on a moral, emotional, and intellectual level."[37] In the following chapters, I am going to take you on a ride-along with me so you can take a look behind the "blue wall of silence" and become a coparticipant experiencing police work on the South Texas–Mexico border.

Autoethnography also entails a blurring between the researcher and the re-searched, and the findings are illustrated through the chronology of fieldwork events, drawing attention not only to the culture under study but also to the ex-periences that are important to the cultural description and interpretation.[38] Autoethnography is a method of qualitative research writing in which the re-searcher illustrates his or her own experiences.[39] Similar to ethnography, "auto-ethnography pursues the vital objective of cultural understanding underlying au-tobiographical experiences."[40] By utilizing autoethnography, I was able to illustrate my unique positionality of being a police officer and researcher at the same time. Autoethnography allowed me to demonstrate my findings in a way that made my experiences meaningful with regard to the culture under study.

Observing the Observers: Going Native and Taking Field Notes

Because I was a member of the DMCSO, I had to "go native" while I conducted my fieldwork. Going native implies that the fieldworker is "immersed in the field to such an extent that the fieldworker becomes a member."[41] In addition, the concept of going native suggests that the researcher has knowingly become a member of the group under study. It was inevitable that I would go native in order to conduct my research, particularly since I was already a member of one of the researched groups, police officers. Some will criticize my lack of objectivity, and, similar to other Latinos who have conducted ethnographic research within a police depart-ment, I make no claim to objectivity.[42] In particular, as Moskos, who is the only other person to conduct autoethnographic research as a police officer, argued, "Being on the inside, I made little attempt to be objective. I did not pick, much less randomly pick, my research site or research subjects. I researched where I was assigned."[43] I can make no claim to objectivity in my work for similar reasons.

Even though I was a police officer who doubled as a researcher, the complex-ities of police work sometimes influenced the way I navigated my researcher role while going native. That is, the dangers that come along with a profession such as police work dictate that one must be security conscious first and a researcher sec-ond.[44] I had to keep in mind that "the official work role in these cases must super-sede, when the situation arises, research interests."[45]

The practice of going native is considered problematic because it may result

in the researcher ignoring the research and becoming a member of the group under study instead.[46] However, writing field notes reminds researchers that they are
conducting research within their group of membership. As Robert Emerson and
Melvin Pollner argue, "Writing field notes provides one concrete method for reminding and recommitting to research purposes. The fieldworker may get caught
up in the moment-by-moment, day-after-day experience of living in the field. . . .
Taking up the task of writing field notes draws the fieldworker back into the space
of research and observation."[47] Because I was a fellow police officer similar to the
police officer participants in this book, critics may argue that I lost sight of my researcher role; however, the data collection process of writing field notes served as a
daily reminder of my other role—that of a researcher.

I collected the data for this book in two social settings: either while at a call for
service or while inside the roll call room at the police department. I wrote detailed
field notes of my observations between fellow deputies, other law enforcement officials, and civilians while responding to particular calls for service. Moreover, because *Enforcing Order on the Border* is autoethnographical, I also wrote detailed
field notes of my interactions with civilians when I responded to particular calls
for service by myself. I followed the same data collection techniques when I responded to a call for service alone as when I had a partner. In addition, conversations between me and my partner and the language used by police officers to char-
acterize Latino undocumented immigrants provided important data for my field
notes. These interactions are illustrated in subsequent chapters.

My field notes varied in length and detail; some days I wrote more than others
depending on how busy I was during that particular workday. Perhaps one of the
most difficult tasks of doubling as a police officer and researcher occurred when
I left work tired and had to force myself to expand my field notes in full detail at
home. I knew that if I did not write out my notes for that particular work shift
right away, I would eventually forget most of what had been said during the calls
for service. My field notes resulted in several hundred single-spaced typed pages.
Importantly, "when taking notes for a book, it helps that pen and paper are required for police officers."[48] Consequently, pen and pad, along with routine patrol work, simplified the data collection process because I was able to write down
my observations during my routine work activities without raising suspicion. Although I made every effort to note the exact phrasing participants used during our
conversations and my observations, I did not use an audio recorder, so I acknowledge that I have had to paraphrase some comments. I note when the quotes are
nonverbatim by including the explanation "paraphrased from field notes."[49]

Data Collection Sites: Routine Patrol
Work and the Roll Call Room

Routine patrol work involves handling different calls for service.[50] Each call is an isolated incident that a police officer handles accordingly. Moreover, calls for service vary from one extreme, such as violent and dangerous calls that might feature armed murderers, to the other, such as mundane domestic disputes and general assistance.[51] Calls for service are either officer initiated, such as when an officer makes contact with a civilian regarding a certain issue without being dispatched to the particular location, or civilian initiated, such as when the 911 communications center of the police department receives a phone call from a civilian needing police intervention. The latter occurs when "the communication center receives incoming calls from citizens, makes a series of discretionary decisions about how to handle those calls, and in many but not all cases dispatches police cars to the scene of the incident."[52]

Patrol work is associated with the monotony of paperwork, and, contrary to popular belief, the policing profession is writing intensive. Police officers have to write reports for most calls for service they respond to during their workday; indeed, police work is about 80 percent writing related.[53] That fact was one of many eye-opening experiences for me as a police officer. Once I obtained my undergraduate degree, I figured that my days of writing a lot were over, since I assumed police work did not require constant writing. However, I quickly realized through my daily policing duties that police work is writing intensive: most calls for service require written documentation, and police reports need to be detailed and thorough, since they are considered official narratives of an incident that will eventually be scrutinized by defense attorneys in a court setting. During routine patrol work, I also wrote field notes that resulted from candid conversations I had with my squad mates while we spoke with each other in between calls for service.

I collected many observational field notes about my fellow deputies inside the roll call room, specifically, what was said during briefings.[54] Collecting field notes in this setting allowed me to illustrate police officers' behavior behind the scenes and, more importantly, to illustrate what is said among police officers when they are away from the public. My notes illustrate typical conversations shared within this intimate space among police officers at the police department.[55] Importantly, the roll call room is the center hub of all police activity in the police department because it is the location where briefings are conducted and where officers are shielded from civilian access.[56]

In sum, I followed a threefold step analysis during my collection of data: coding, thematic analysis, and description. I utilized the qualitative software ATLAS. ti6.[57] In order to contextualize the findings that resulted from my field notes, what follows is a discussion of the theoretical frameworks guiding the subsequent chapters of *Enforcing Order on the Border*.

Theories of Racial Conflict

THE RACIAL CONTRACT

To provide an understanding and context for the actions in the subsequent chapters, this book is guided theoretically by Charles Mills's racial contract theory, Joe Feagin's white racial frame theory, and racist nativism. These theoretical conceptions can aid in understanding the creation and maintenance of white supremacy, particularly as it relates to this book, in the U.S.-Mexico borderlands. Most notably, Mills argues that "white supremacy is the unnamed political system that has made the modern world what it is today."[58] Aside from existing for several hundred years and being thought of as a political system, "white supremacy can illuminatingly be theorized as based on a 'contract' between whites, a Racial Contract" that serves to ensure the enduring legacy of white supremacy.[59] Moreover, racial categories and racial differences are a social construction and therefore are contingent on the meanings that individuals and institutions give them.[60] Mills further argues that "the Racial Contract establishes a racial polity, a racial state, and a racial juridical system. And the purpose of this state . . . [serves] to maintain and reproduce this racial order, securing the privileges and advantages of the full white citizens and maintaining the subordination of nonwhites."[61] The racial formation of Latinos—Mexican-origin individuals in particular—is viewed as a paradox, because Mexicans were *legally* constructed as being racially white even though they were *socially* constructed as being nonwhite and thus a racially inferior group.[62]

Mills argues that the racial contract is another way of theorizing about and critiquing the state and that the white supremacist state was established and is reproduced by two methods of coercion: physical violence and ideological conditioning. In regard to physical violence, white supremacy has been maintained through various means, such as slave patrols, racial segregation (Jim Crow laws), lynchings, and other forms of violence that have targeted different racial groups in nuanced ways. Recent scholarship by David Embrick reveals that not only have Blacks and Latinos historically been the primary targets of the racial contract through physical violence (lynchings), but they continue to disparately experience the enforcement of the racial contract in comparison to other racial groups, as evidenced by officer-involved shootings resulting in the deaths of Blacks and Latinos.[63] Mills elaborates on how systemic racism is a central component of the criminal justice system, thus disproportionately impacting people of color: "The coercive arm of the state, then—the police, the penal system, the army—need to be seen as in part the enforcers of the Racial Contract, working both to keep the peace . . . and to maintain the racial order."[64]

In essence, the police have two primary functions in society—keeping the peace and maintaining order—even though most associate the police with the ethos of protecting and serving.[65] Moreover, policing practices that are intended to keep the peace and maintain order in society overwhelmingly impact people of color, as evidenced by the enforcement of the racial contract through physical violence. Thus, as noted by Mills, in order to understand the long history of police deviance toward people of color, "one has to recognize it not as excesses by individual racists but as an organic part of this political enterprise."[66] Mills observes that one must look beyond the actions of a "few bad apples" and grasp the long-standing history of systemic racism prevalent in the criminal justice system. Consequently, it is no surprise that the police are often viewed as an occupying army in communities of color.[67] Policing expert Anthony Bouza points out, "When cops deal with the poor (Blacks, Hispanics, the homeless, and the street people), the rubber of power meets the road of abuse."[68] Bouza further argues, "The police are an instrument of the rich to control the poor," or, simply put, the police maintain a racial polity through enforcement of the racial contract.[69]

According to Mills, the other method by which the white supremacist state is established and reproduced is through ideological conditioning. He reveals that this requires labor and involves the development of a depersonalizing apparatus through which people of color must learn to see themselves and ultimately accept their subpersonhood. Moreover, "racism as an ideology needs to be understood as aiming at the minds of nonwhites as well as whites, inculcating subjugation."[70] In particular, the succeeding chapters of this book illustrate how some Latinos on the South Texas–Mexico border ensure the maintenance of white supremacy as a result of ideological conditioning—internalized racism.[71] Feagin's theoretical conception of the white racial frame provides the framework to establish a common understanding of how some Latinos serve as enforcers of white supremacy through ideological conditioning.

THE WHITE RACIAL FRAME

Over the years, the white racial frame has been imposed on the minds of most Americans—specifically, white elite men—and has become the dominant "frame of reference" in the United States in regard to racial matters.[72] More specifically, most white Americans have combined at least three important features that influence this racial framing of society. White Americans' racial frame includes (1) negative racial stereotypes, (2) images, and (3) metaphors involving people of color along with positive or superior views of whites. In essence, this dominant racial frame is both negative and ethnocentric toward people of color.

Similar to other aspects of everyday life, the dominant white racial frame is learned through everyday socializing aspects of human interaction, and once inculcated in the mind, the white racial frame is durable and opposed to change. As Feagin argues, "Frames as entrenched as the dominant white frame are hard to counter or uproot."[73] Therefore, the internalization of the white racial frame can pose serious consequences for people of color because, once internalized, it is difficult to counter such racist thinking.[74] As is illustrated in this book, some Latinos advocate the white racial frame as a means through which to distance and differentiate themselves from their coracial/coethnic immigrant counterparts. By doing so, Latinos maintain the white frame because of their inability to oppose it, leading to the maintenance of white supremacy by pitting coracial/coethnics against each other. Moreover, the dominant racial frame overlaps with and is connected to other related frames or subframes.

THE CREATION OF SUBFRAMES

According to Feagin, the dominant white racial frame overlaps and connects with other collective subframes to help individuals view and make sense of social worlds. The white racial frame consists of racialized emotions, images, and stories of people of color along with racial ideology. Specifically, once a person operates out of the white racial frame, it in turn triggers related subframes. These subframes are differentiated ways to understand and interpret society. That is, individuals can integrate new items into the dominant white racial frame and apply its stereotypes, images, and interpretations through discriminatory actions to marginalize and oppress certain individuals.[75]

For example, with regard to the racial framing of Mexicans, Hilario Molina II argued that the white racial frame is "something that predates the Mexican and American War, and as a result, two important subframes emerge from this racial frame: (1) a subframe that views Mexican-origin individuals from an old racial perspective of inferiority—the anti-Mexican subframe; and (2) a contemporary subframe that centers on anti-Mexican immigrant sentiment—the anti-Mexican immigrant subframe."[76] The next section details how some Latinos internalize the dominant white racial frame to create new subframes with regard to their anti-immigrant sentiments about Latino immigrants.

THE SUBFRAME OF RACIALIZED OPPRESSION: ANTI-LATINO IMMIGRANTS

The dominant framing of Latinos consists of differing stereotypes that include a belief in Latino criminality, welfare dependency, hyperfertility, and the like.[77] Moreover, the use of racialized terminology when referring to Latino immigrants also contributes to the dominant framing of Latinos.[78] Feagin notes how the Spanish language is also the target of anti-Latino framing and argues that "mocking Spanish involves whites, especially in the middle and upper classes, [creating] derisive terms . . . [and] such mock Spanish by white English speakers generates, overtly or subtly, a negative view of Spanish, those who speak it, and their culture."[79] Accordingly, I expand on Feagin's theoretical framework of the white racial frame by illustrating how the anti-Latino immigrant subframe operates within a majority-minority community that serves to maintain and reproduce white supremacy. That is, as do all other subframes, the anti-Latino immigrant subframe derives from the white racial frame and entails anti-Latino immigrant sentiment with regard to "racial ideas, terms, images, emotions, and interpretations."[80]

Latinos are under constant pressure to adopt the dominant white frame on racial matters, and when they do, they help reinforce the maintenance of white supremacy.[81] As noted by Feagin, some Latinos "often accept significant parts of the dominant white racial framing—sometimes including negative framing that whites have historically directed at their own group."[82] *Enforcing Order on the Border* seeks to problematize and shed light on the overlooked aspect of intraracial/intraethnic conflict in order to address the maintenance of white supremacy. Similar to Mills, Feagin makes note that as of today, the system of racial oppression continues to be highly organized and institutionalized and still operates in conjunction with the modern economy of the United States, governmental bureaucracies, and the complex legal system.[83]

RACIST NATIVISM

Given the long-standing history of anti-immigrant sentiment and local police participation in immigration enforcement initiatives, are actions and incidents that target racial and ethnic immigrant groups racist, nativist, or both? To answer this question, Cameron Lippard argues that scholars and the general public alike should utilize "racist nativism" as a theoretical framework to examine how both racism and nativism work in conjunction with each other to maintain white supremacy.[84] The combination of both factors to illustrate the second-class treatment of immigrants in the United States emerged as a theoretical framework during the 1950s, as noted in John Higham's theoretical conception of racial nativism, which argued that early twentieth-century immigrants such as Italians encountered both nativistic hostility and racist ideologies—racialization—that then served to distinguish foreigners from natives.[85] Several years later, Lindsay Perez Huber and her colleagues further extended Higham's theoretical conception of racial nativism to document the immigrant experience in the twenty-first century as it relates to Latino immigrants and people of color.

Huber and her colleagues define racist nativism as "the assigning of values to real or imagined differences, in order to justify the superiority of the native, who is to be perceived white, over that of the non-native, who is perceived to be people and immigrants of color, and thereby defend the right of whites, or the natives, to dominance."[86] Thus, Huber and colleagues' conception of racist nativism encompasses racialization and anti-immigrant beliefs that manifest as an ideology evident within institutional practices such as immigration enforcement that ultimately serve to ensure white supremacy.[87] As previously mentioned, *Enforcing Order on the Border* explores how undocumented Latino immigrants become racialized by other Latinos on the South Texas–Mexico border through discriminatory language, how undocumented Latino immigrants become the targets of racialized immigration enforcement practices, and to what extent this racialization reveals evidence of racism and nativism.

Similar to the social construction of race that has negatively affected Blacks and their experiences with the criminal justice system, Latino immigrants have been the targets of racist and nativistic immigration enforcement initiatives. Thus, as Lippard notes, "Today's racist and nativist targets and goals have become very similar in that they both look to people of color to oppress and exploit to sustain" white supremacy.[88] The following chapter illustrates how a long-standing history of racial and nativistic attacks on Latino immigrants has existed, as noted by local police participation in immigration enforcement with immigration authorities such as the USBP. Huber and her colleagues note that racist nativism affects not only Mexican immigrants on a daily basis but also other Latino immigrants in general, such as Central Americans. Moreover, Huber and her colleagues argue that racist nativism, as a racial conflict theoretical framework, calls for "a methodological consideration grounded in qualitative research that can better describe and analyze the draconian effects of policy and practice on [Latino] communities."[89] These effects are precisely what the subsequent chapters reveal; the chapters also provide further insight into the collaborative efforts between local and state police with federal immigration authorities such as the USBP that lead to such harmful effects. Consequently, all three racial conflict theoretical perspectives (the racial contract, the white racial frame, and racist nativism) provide the theoretical foundation to contextualize the actions illustrated in *Enforcing Order on the Border*.

PHOTO 1. Two wooden-framed houses on separate properties.

PHOTO 2. Wooden-framed house with an attached travel trailer.

PHOTO 3. Wooden-framed house with the refrigerator outside.

Research Location: The Rio Grande
Valley of Texas (Del Monte County)

The location of this study was the RGV of South Texas, which consists of four counties and borders the Mexican state of Tamaulipas to the south. Mexican-origin individuals represent the largest racial/ethnic group in the borderland, constituting approximately 80 percent of the total population.[90] Moreover, most of the residents served by the DMCSO reside in neighborhoods known as *colonias*. According to Joachim Singlemann, Tim Slack, and Kayla Fontenont, colonias are "unincorporated subdivisions with small plots and little infrastructure, where houses often lack such basic amenities as electricity and plumbing. Residents in the colonias are both socially and geographically isolated."[91] Colonias consist of many houses and mobile homes that are often dilapidated and more than likely do not meet building codes.[92] In addition, colonia residents' "homes are a mixture of trailers and self-built constructions, with the long-term goal of achieving a fully consolidated brick-built dwelling."[93] Unfortunately, this long-term goal is rarely achieved due to financial constraints. Thus, most houses within colonias consist of small trailers, mobile homes, or wooden-framed homes.

The residents of colonias epitomize the adage "out of sight, out of mind." Colonias are hidden from the public eye, since they are located away from major highways and roads and situated between rural farm fields of cotton, sorghum, and corn.[94] If one drives through a colonia, one cannot help but notice the poverty of these rural locations of the county. Generally, for the RGV as a whole, poverty is the norm among its Latino residents. That is, "to live in the Valley and to be Hispanic is almost by definition to be in or close to poverty."[95] The majority of Latinos in the RGV who experience high levels of poverty reside within colonias as immigrants within mixed-status households (referring to family members who have different immigration statuses, e.g., a U.S.-born child of immigrant parents).[96] Photos 1–3 illustrate residences commonly found within colonias.

Organization of the Book

Chapter 1 provides a historical overview of collaborative immigration enforcement initiatives between local police and federal immigration officials (USBP) in order to contextualize the intersection between race, policing, and immigration enforcement. This historical overview illustrates that local police participation in federal immigration enforcement on the U.S.-Mexico border has a long-standing history that continues to this day. After discussing the historical overview of local police collaboration with the USBP in the borderlands, I provide an overview of local police and the USBP that relates specifically to Texas border security initiatives (dubbed "operations"). Finally, this chapter provides further insight into a national local police-federal immigration grant, Operation Stonegarden (OPSG), which is still in effect today.

Chapter 2 explores the racialization process and contextualizes the practice of racialization through a chronological recollection of my experiences with the racialization process throughout my life as both a civilian and a police officer. The chapter begins by providing an example of my recollection of the practice of racialization, which occurred when I was in high school. This section highlights how racialized terminology is normalized and notes that even I was subject to racialized terminology at the hands of my peers. The chapter then focuses on my socialization as a police recruit in the police academy with regard to the practice of racialization and the policing profession. Next, I discuss how I navigated my differing researcher role and police officer role in the study as a result of my socialization as a sociology graduate student and police officer.

Chapter 3 begins by detailing the surge of unaccompanied minors and families from Central America who crossed through the borderlands beginning in the summer of 2014 to provide insight into their migration experience. I witnessed firsthand the "humanitarian crisis" experienced in the RGV while working as a police officer ("boots on the ground"), and I illustrate my interactions with unaccompanied Central American minors and families. Through these conversations, I provide explanations for why these unaccompanied minors and families make the dangerous journey from their country of origin to the United States.

The chapter then describes the harrowing journey undocumented immigrants take into the United States through the borderlands only to have their immigration journey far too often end with capture. Several calls for service I responded to as a police officer involved undocumented immigrants located inside stash houses. These calls for service provided me with the ability to interact with undocumented immigrants and obtain their perspective on the migration experience into the United States. Undocumented immigrants shared with me the difficulties they experienced as they traversed the borderlands, often being constantly victimized at the hands of their immigrant smugglers, or *coyotes*. This chapter seeks to humanize the migration experience of undocumented immigrants and asylum seekers by sharing their stories. Thus, in chapter 3 I examine the victimization experience of undocumented immigrants as it unfolds during their migratory journey into the United States.

Chapter 4 explores the criminalization process of undocumented immigrants at the South Texas–Mexico border by the police. Based on my conversations with colleagues, I describe how Mexican American police officers criminalize Latino

(Mexican, Central American, and South American) undocumented immigrants by interpreting them as criminal-prone individuals. The chapter then illustrates the manner in which police officers collaborate with USBP to apprehend, detain, and deport undocumented immigrants, thus illustrating how the phenomenon of crimmigration occurs along the South Texas–Mexico border. In these illustrations, I provide examples from calls for service involving my participation with USBP agents in the apprehension and detention of undocumented immigrants at stash houses. This chapter provides much-needed institutional insight into the flow of shared information from local police to federal immigration officials regarding racialized immigration enforcement practices. Further, this chapter reveals the manner in which local police officers become enforcers of the racial contract in the borderlands and how these practices reflect racist nativism.

Chapter 5 examines the racialization process from a police officer perspective and provides a theoretical explanation for such practices. In particular, I examine the thesis that the racialization of undocumented Latino-origin immigrants through dehumanizing and objectifying terminology only reinforces the image of undocumented immigrants as subhuman foreign invaders. The chapter illuminates the various ways undocumented Latino immigrants are racialized by Latino police officers, in particular, Mexican American police officers. I provide several incidents that illustrate the manner in which police officers utilize racialized terminology when referring to Latino immigrants. As such, some Mexican Americans internalize the white racially framed narrative of Latino-origin undocumented immigrants and thus become advocates of the anti-Latino immigrant subframe.

Chapter 6 provides insight into the use of deportation threats as a method to resolve disputes among civilians in the RGV. As a former police officer in the borderlands, I witnessed firsthand the manner in which civilians wanted to have their fellow coracial/coethnic immigrant counterparts deported by federal immigration officials as a means of problem-solving. Individuals called the police with the hope that local police would refer them and/or the situation to USBP. This chapter presents calls for service that I responded to as a former police officer and illustrates how civilians within the borderlands utilize deportation threats as a means of maintaining coercive control over each other, thus illustrating how racist nativism occurs in a majority-minority community and how some Latinos become advocates of the anti-Latino immigrant subframe and enforcers of the racial contract.

The conclusion summarizes the data presented in the book and provides a discussion on the findings revealed from my research. This chapter illustrates how *Enforcing Order on the Border* moves beyond the Black/white binary to extend the body of race research by exploring intraracial/intraethnic conflict at the South Texas–Mexico border between Latinos. In particular, the conclusion discusses how race and nativism are central features of a majority-minority community in the borderlands that pits Latinos against each other. Whether through the use of deportation threats, the racialization of Latino immigrants, or the Constitution-free policing method, the intraracial/intraethnic conflict illustrated in the book serves to ensure the maintenance of white supremacy.

The appendix, "Reflexivity," illustrates my reflexivity regarding the research study and provides further insight into the study. Within the appendix, I describe why I chose to conduct the research study and the theoretical frameworks that I used to guide the study. In addition, I discuss my positionality as an academic and police officer and how I navigated both roles, which ultimately influenced the research study. Lastly, I also reflect on the method I used for the research study. Consequently, the appendix provides an overview by illustrating how the afore-mentioned aspects of the research study framed the research and its outcomes.

CHAPTER 1

Racialized Policing in the
U.S.-Mexico Borderlands

One aspect of this book examines how individuals on the South Texas–Mexico border, both civilians and police officers, inflict racialized mistreatment on Latino immigrants as a result of their chosen terms of reference when referring to immigrants. Specifically, this book illustrates how some Latinos on the South Texas–Mexico border adopt the dominant white racial frame narrative when referring to Latino undocumented immigrants by referring to immigrants as "illegal aliens," "illegals," "wetbacks" (*mojados*), and "mojankers."[1] In addition, this book also examines the collaboration between local police and USBP agents in regard to immigration enforcement practices.

This chapter provides an overview of the social construction of racialized terminology that is synonymous with immigrants—"illegal aliens." The chapter then provides a historical overview of nativism discourse that has affected racial and ethnic immigrant groups. The chapter next provides a historical overview of local police and USBP collaboration to demonstrate the history of such collaboration initiatives. Next, the chapter provides further insight into policing practices in Texas regarding immigration enforcement by illustrating several police and immigration-related initiatives that have occurred in Texas. The chapter then delves into a discussion of a nationwide immigration-related grant that requires local police collaboration in immigration enforcement. Finally, the chapter provides an overview of the policing profession that illustrates the complexities associated with the policing profession. Moreover, in order to understand the use of

racialized terms of reference for immigrants illustrated in this book, it is important to contextualize the emergence of the term "illegal alien," since it is the most
widely used among anti-immigrant proponents.

The Social Construction of Illegal Aliens

The racialization of immigrants as "wetbacks" was crystallized by the creation of
the USBP in 1924.[2] Before the creation of the USBP, undocumented immigrants did
not have a racialized term that referred to those individuals engaged in the clandestine act of immigrating into the United States. The only racialized term closely
associated with Mexican-origin individuals in particular, prior to 1924, was the
term "greaser," which was derived from the Anti-Vagrancy Act of 1855.[3] The purpose of the act was to penalize vagabonds and vagrants, referred to as greasers, that
is, Mexican-origin individuals. However, the Alien and Sedition Acts of 1798 were
the first official documents to demarcate non-U.S. citizens with the racialized term
"aliens" rather than the less incendiary "undocumented immigrants."[4] Moreover,
with the creation of the USBP, the primary focus became to apprehend and deport
undocumented immigrants.[5] Thus, the term "wetback" acquired a new meaning;
namely, it became a status or stigma by which the undocumented immigrant was
known.[6] The freedom of interaction the undocumented immigrant had before the
creation of the USBP was significantly reduced by this new label of "wetback."

As sociologist Jorge Bustamante noted, "He [an undocumented immigrant]
now had to walk, to speak, and to bear any treatment with the fear of being caught
by or 'turned in' to the Border Patrol."[7] The usage of "wetback" continued well
into the 1950s but gave way in the 1980s to the term "illegal alien." Since then, "illegal alien" has been used as the popular term of reference involving the racialization of undocumented Latino immigrants.

In particular, the term "illegal alien" helps rationalize the harsh treatment of
individuals from other countries.[8] Moreover, the definition of "illegal aliens" as
"a group distinct and apart from citizens facilitates in guaranteeing that undocumented immigrants are only short-term, conditional, and temporary members of
the United States."[9] The derogatory term "illegal alien" implies criminality, thereby
suggesting that individuals who fall within this category deserve just punishment
rather than legal protection within the criminal justice system. Furthermore, "illegal alien" has emerged as a media-sensationalized term of racial difference that
serves as a racialized description of Latinos in general, regardless of immigration
status.[10]

This kind of terminology is common within the current debate in the Southwest, if not the entire nation, regarding undocumented immigration.[11] Even

though "illegal alien" appears to be race neutral, the term popularly refers to un-documented Latino immigrants—in particular, Mexican immigrants—and facili-tates stereotypes of Mexicans as criminals.[12] Moreover, the racialization of Latino immigrants as "illegal aliens," which often aids their negative portrayal as crimi-nals, does not necessarily mean that they have committed a crime against some-one. Instead, "when undocumented migrants are criminalized under the sign of the 'illegal alien,' theirs is an 'illegality' that does not involve a crime against any-one; rather . . . [it] stands only for a transgression against the sovereign author-ity of the nation-state."[13] For example, undocumented immigrant farmworkers are not even afforded the opportunity to be referred to as undocumented workers. In fact, most immigrants who occupy low-wage-sector jobs, as farmworkers do, are not categorized as undocumented workers but are instead criminalized as "illegal aliens."

It is this stereotype of Latino-immigrant criminality that contributes to the anti-immigrant rhetoric that particularly affects Latino immigrants. For example, as seen in past anti-immigrant enforcement efforts (e.g., Operation Hold the Line, Operation Blockade, and California's Proposition 187), fears of criminality and undocumented immigration focused solely on Mexicans by emphasizing that the United States must secure its border with Mexico.[14] Therefore, as a result of their immigration status, undocumented Latino immigrants will always be in the pub-lic eye.

Emerging scholarship has examined the basis by which terms such as "wet-back" and "illegal alien" are applied (e.g., level of assimilation, economic and ac-ademic success, or phenotypic characteristics) and how these terms are used for control purposes in order to distinguish group boundaries and create internal hierarchies.[15] Consequently, one aspect of this book analyzes the basis on which these aforementioned racialized terms are ascribed among coracials/coethnics in the majority-minority Latino community of the RGV in Texas. Aside from utili-zation of racist terminology, nativistic discourse has contributed to the targeting of the immigrant community, as noted in several historical initiatives focused pri-marily on differing racial/ethnic groups.

Nativism Discourse

The concept of nativism may be defined as a potential relationship and standpoint between self-identified natives and perceived foreigners.[16] Inhabitants mark the boundaries of natives and their claims in relation to foreigners through processes such as anti-immigrant media campaigns.[17] When addressing the issue of nativ-ism, critical race theorists illustrate the historical process of nativism and how it has affected people of color at different points in time.[18] In addition to addressing the issue of nativism, critical race theorists have specifically focused on similar topics, such as the U.S.-Mexico border region and immigration issues.[19]

Furthermore, nativistic antipathy toward undocumented immigrants has occurred periodically in U.S. history for various reasons. Irish immigrants in the 1800s were targets of anti-immigrant animosity based on religion and political concerns.[20] Near the end of the nineteenth century, nativistic hostility focused on Chinese immigrants, with the controversial Chinese Exclusion Act of 1882.[21] In addition, during the 1940s, animosity was directed at Japanese immigrants and Japanese-origin citizens, culminating in their internment during World War II.[22]

Following World War II, nativistic animosity shifted toward Mexican immigrants with the infamous draconian immigration deportation program of the 1950s, dubbed Operation Wetback.[23] Since then, Latino undocumented immigrants, Mexican immigrants in particular, have been the targets of anti-immigrant sentiment campaigns. At the end of the twentieth century, three different anti-immigrant sentiments marked nativistic hostility: fear of linguistic difference, discomfort with multiculturalism, and drain of public resources by undocumented immigrants. These became the prominent anti-immigrant sentiments directed at undocumented immigrants.[24] Fear that undocumented immigrants would refuse to learn English caused nationwide proposals of English-only movements during the 1990s. In addition, during this time period, Mexican immigrants continued to be the focus of nativistic sentiment, as evidenced by the U.S. government's Illegal Immigration Reform and Immigrant Responsibility Act of 1996 (IIRIRA). IIRIRA allowed state and local police departments to perform immigration law enforcement functions based on Section 287(g) of the act. In 2010 now former Arizona governor Jane Brewer exacerbated police-community relations in that state by signing the country's first and most controversial anti-immigrant police enforcement act: Arizona Senate Bill 1070, the Support Our Law Enforcement and Safe Neighborhoods Act.[25] Other state governors in states such as Georgia and Alabama soon followed Brewer's anti-immigrant onslaught by proposing similar bills in their respective states.[26]

On May 7, 2017, Texas governor Greg Abbott signed controversial Texas Senate Bill 4 into law; the law essentially banned sanctuary city policies even amid fears and concerns that police would engage in race-based immigration enforcement practices as a result of such a ban.[27] Senate Bill 4 was introduced and ultimately passed into law based on nativistic anti-immigrant attitudes that declared that local law enforcement agencies needed to comply with ICE-detainer requests in order to curtail undocumented immigration in Texas.

The primary targets of these draconian state senate bills have overwhelmingly been Latino immigrants. In addition, some of the popular misperceptions of immigrants currently held today by nativists include the following: (1) most or a large proportion of immigrants to the United States come here illegally; (2) public benefit programs are generally available to and widely used by undocumented immigrants; (3) immigrants pose a criminal threat; and (4) the generous U.S. social welfare system serves as a magnet that attracts undocumented immigrants.[28] Aside from these varying nativistic initiatives targeting different racial/ethnic immigrants throughout U.S. history, something that has been constant is the systemically racist collaboration between local police and federal immigration authorities. Namely, Latino immigrants (also U.S.-born Latinos) have been and continue to be the primary targets of racialized policing initiatives such as local police assistance and participation in federal immigration practices.

Local Police and USBP Partnerships

As previously mentioned, the long history of local police collaboration with federal immigration authorities in regard to immigration enforcement dates back to the late 1920s, as evidenced by the Mexican repatriation campaign (1929–39).[29] This apprehension and deportation campaign was built on two simple factors that caused immigrants to leave the United States. First, there were public announcements made to announce the deportations, and second, arrests were made to illustrate that the U.S. immigration officials were carrying through with their deportation campaigns. The apprehension of immigrants served as a psychological gesture aimed at the Mexican community that established an environment of hostility and fear.[30] The deportation sweeps occurred in cities across the United States (e.g., New York, Boston, Chicago, Detroit, Kansas City, and Oklahoma City), and all Mexicans, whether documented or undocumented, looked similar to immigration officials. Consequently, "in street sweeps throughout the nation's major cities, people who 'looked Mexican' found themselves at risk of being picked up and taken into custody."[31] Since Southern California apparently contained most of the Latino-origin undocumented immigrant population in the country, it became the main target area of deportation raids. Local police departments were criticized by the civilian population for being active participants with the USBP in carrying out immigration raids. That is, as noted by Abraham Hoffman, "[Los Angeles County] Sheriff Traeger's deputies in particular were criticized for rounding up Mexicans in large groups and taking them to jail without checking whether anyone in the group had a passport."[32]

Moreover, the most infamous raid during this period was the La Placita raid, in which four hundred Mexicans were detained within the grounds of La Placita Park for over an hour. The Los Angeles Police Department (LAPD) and USBP agents surrounded the park to ensure that no one left the park. This raid was unlike others in that it was conducted in broad daylight at a public venue. Although the interrogation process only lasted a little over an hour, the message was clear to the Mexican community: the U.S. government wanted to get rid of the Mexicans.[33] As a result of the deportation campaign, hundreds of residents were deported on a daily basis. Specifically in relation to the geographical setting of this book, during 1929 "more than 17,600 Mexicans were deported from the Rio Grande Valley, alone."[34] Thus, the deportation campaign laid the groundwork for the repatriation movement of the Mexican community and contributed significantly to the mass exodus of Mexicans from the United States back to Mexico. Most notably, the repatriation campaign set the foundation for local police participation in immigration enforcement with the USBP in the Southwest.

Two and a half decades later, during Operation Wetback of 1954, local police collaborated with USBP to enforce federal immigration law while working in conjunction with each other. During that summer, Operation Wetback commenced in California and Arizona, and, similar to the Mexican repatriation campaign of the 1930s, the primary goal of the USBP initiative was apprehending, detaining, and deporting Mexican-origin individuals.[35] Operation Wetback was a short-lived immigration enforcement initiative that also targeted Mexican-origin individuals residing in New Mexico, Texas, and midwestern cities such as Chicago. When the operation began in California, local police departments were more than willing to assist the USBP with their efforts to deport Mexican-origin individuals. Then LAPD chief William H. Parker and then Los Angeles County sheriff Eugene W. Biscailuz each assigned sixteen officers to assist the USBP with their apprehension efforts during the initiative.

In addition, Chief Parker and Sheriff Biscailuz issued alerts to all the stations in their respective departments advising officers to arrest and detain all undocumented immigrants on criminal charges of vagrancy until USBP arrived at the stations to take custody of the immigrants.[36] Between June 17 and July 1, 1954, the concentrated area of enforcement was the Los Angeles metro area, and after July 1, approximately 60 percent of the USBP agents who worked the LA metro area were divided into groups of four and assigned to work with other neighboring police departments in Southern California for a period of two weeks.[37] Similar to the LAPD and the Los Angeles County Sheriff's Department, other local police departments in Southern California were more than willing to go out of their way to assist the USBP with apprehension efforts of their main targets: Mexican-origin individuals.

For example, the Azusa police department notified the USBP that a local movie theater showed Mexican movies on Wednesday nights, and they primarily were attended by undocumented Mexican immigrants. The Azusa police department further notified the USBP that they had made prior arrangements with management to stop the movie midway, turn on the lights, and have USBP check the immigration status of the patrons, all while Azusa police department officers blocked all the exits to ensure that no one would be allowed to leave until the immigration status of the patrons was verified. Even though this plan never came to fruition, it is demonstrative of how willing local police departments in Southern California were to assist USBP with their efforts in apprehending and detaining Mexican-origin individuals during Operation Wetback. Consequently, the USBP supervisor who oversaw the LA area enforcement of Operation Wetback notified his managers that local police departments "within the area had been very cooperative and had 'rendered assistance far in excess of what could be expected.'"[38] It is estimated that the racialized Operation Wetback led to the apprehension of roughly 1.1 million Mexican-origin individuals—in particular, approximately 42,000 individuals in the RGV of Texas.

During the late 1990s, local police in Chandler, Arizona, collaborated with the USBP in a five-day immigration enforcement initiative dubbed the Chandler Roundup.[39] Similar to the aforementioned local police-USBP immigration enforcement initiatives (the Mexican repatriation campaign and Operation Wetback), the Chandler Roundup revealed that the USBP and local police profiled individuals based solely on racial attributes. The initiative was rationalized based on the perception that (1) the city of Chandler served as a major undocumented immigration transportation hub; (2) undocumented immigrants contributed to an increase in crime; and (3) local developers wanted to revitalize the downtown area, which was populated primarily by low-income Mexican Americans and undocumented Mexican immigrants. The Chandler police department described their joint initiative with the USBP as doing their part to contribute to what they referred to as Operation Restoration. Indeed, "restore" is exactly what they did in the downtown and surrounding areas of Chandler. As Mary Romero and Marwah Serag argued, the focus of the Chandler police on apprehending and detaining Mexican-origin individuals was "consistent with the Police Department's claim that the Chandler Roundup was their contribution to Restoration because the five-day raid reclaimed the area as only safe for whites to drive, walk, and shop."[40]

Findings from the five-day joint operation reveal that undocumented immigrants were arrested in residential areas, in front of convenience stores, in mobile home parks, and while driving in the early hours of the morning.[41] Moreover, during the five-day joint initiative, about 432 undocumented Mexican immigrants were apprehended and arrested by the USBP and the Chandler Police Department. Besides apprehending and arresting undocumented Mexican immigrants, the USBP and Chandler Police Department also stopped and questioned Mexican Americans and other Latino-origin permanent residents during the five-day operation. Some Chandler police officers went so far as to raid a local trailer park and detain and apprehend an undocumented immigrant on the premises and then transfer the immigrant to USBP custody.[42]

Furthermore, official investigations of the joint initiative found no evidence that stops and searches were based on probable cause. Based on her analysis of the Chandler Roundup, Mary Romero argues that racialized immigration stops establish and reinforce second-class citizenship while also limiting certain rights and opportunities. She further argues that in communities of color, racialized policing practices result "in identifying urban space racially, in classifying immigrants as deserving and undeserving by nationalities, and [serve] to drive a wedge dividing Latino neighborhoods on the basis of citizenship status."[43]

Policing Immigration the Texas Way

Operation Linebacker began in September 2005 after the Texas Border Sheriff's Coalition announced a plan designed to enhance border security along the Texas-Mexico border. Consequently, the program sought to increase police presence on the border through the use of increased manpower and surveillance technology.[44] Then Texas governor Rick Perry guaranteed $9.7 million in state funds acquired through federal grants for Operation Linebacker. This operation consisted of several activities, such as increased police presence and random checkpoints in alleged high-crime areas, use of state-funded cameras along the Rio Grande, and deployment of additional state resources to local police departments located on the border. The impetus for this operation was to increase public safety on the 1,241-mile Texas-Mexico border.[45]

Consistent with the previous police-USBP collaborations discussed earlier, this initiative revealed that local police officers were engaged in immigration enforcement rather than criminal enforcement. Namely, local residents argued that deputies from the El Paso County Sheriff's Office handed over individuals to the custody of USBP after instituting randomized vehicle checkpoints. Reports also surfaced that deputy sheriffs were also inquiring about the immigration status of individuals they came in contact with as part of this operation. By November 2006 self-reports from the participating sixteen county sheriff's offices demonstrated that deputy sheriffs working as part of Operation Linebacker were in essence de facto immigration officials because they detained undocumented immigrants seven times more often than they arrested criminals.[46] During this operation, local police departments on the Texas-Mexico border failed to make a substantive contribution to public safety because they were focused on immigration violations instead of criminal violations.

Several years later, local police departments on the Texas-Mexico border continued to function as de facto immigration officials by participating in state-funded prevention through deterrence initiatives implemented by the governor of Texas. In the summer of 2014 the RGV experienced an influx of unaccompanied minors and mothers from Central America who were seeking asylum in the United States. The institutional response from Texas to address this issue was a militarized multiagency initiative spearheaded by the Texas Department of Public Safety (DPS) and dubbed Operation Strong Safety (OSS).[47] OSS was a state and local law enforcement version of previous USBP "prevention through deterrence" strategies that were implemented in El Paso, Texas, in 1993 to prevent undocumented immigration.[48] As such, Texas DPS troopers, National Guard troops, and local police officers conducted "line watches" by parking along the Rio Grande for a prolonged period of time to deter unaccompanied minors and mothers from Central America from crossing into the United States.

The results from OSS reveal that it was ineffective in deterring Central American mothers and unaccompanied minors from crossing the Rio Grande, even though then governor Perry claimed that the impetus to authorize OSS was to deter criminal activity (e.g., drug smuggling). OSS also illustrated that state and local police agencies serve as de facto immigration officials by policing the U.S.-Mexico border through their emulation of previous USBP prevention-through-deterrence strategies such as Operation Hold the Line in El Paso. In point of fact, the vast majority of individuals officers encountered during OSS were Central American asylum seekers and not criminals who posed a threat to national security. Moreover, utilizing the DPS or local police agencies as de facto immigration officials did not end with OSS.

On March 4, 2021, Governor Abbott initiated a militarized collaboration between DPS and National Guard soldiers dubbed Operation Lone Star (OLS), which sought to prevent human and drug smuggling across the South Texas–Mexico border; in other words, it sought to bolster federal immigration enforcement. In his press release when announcing the implementation of OLS, Governor Abbott stated, "The crisis at our southern border continues to escalate because of Biden Administration policies that refuse to secure the border and invite illegal immigration. . . . Texas supports legal immigration but will not be an accomplice to the open border policies that cause, rather than prevent, a humanitarian crisis in our state and endanger the lives of Texans. We will surge the resources and law enforcement personnel needed to confront this crisis."[49] However, it was clear that OLS was implemented to address the large influx of Central American asylum seekers who crossed the Rio Grande through South Texas to obtain asylum in the United States. That is, Governor Abbott devised a new approach to deter undocumented immigration into the United States that had never been seen before. He ordered the DPS to arrest all immigrants, many of whom were Central American asylum seekers, who crossed into the United States and charge them with the state criminal charge of criminal trespass.[50]

Notably, on April 1, 2021, Governor Abbott held a press release touting the continued success of OLS by revealing that as of that day, DPS had made 598 criminal arrests and, most alarmingly, over 16,000 referrals of undocumented immigrants to the USBP. Governor Abbott stated in his press release, "I want to thank the men and women of the Texas Department of Public Safety, the National Guard, and U.S. Border Patrol for putting their lives on the line every day to secure the border, arrest dangerous criminals, and protect the victims of trafficking and smuggling."[51] In Abbott's update of statistics regarding OLS, the results clearly revealed that the primary targets of OLS were undocumented immigrants, and as such, OLS was falling short of addressing criminal (as opposed to immigrant) activity along the Texas-Mexico border.

Several months later, in August 2021, Governor Abbott provided another update regarding OLS that furnished arrest statistics up until that point. By late August, DPS personnel had arrested roughly 4,600 individuals for the crimes of criminal trespass and criminal mischief.[52] Moreover, the total number of immigrants apprehended by DPS and transferred to USBP custody since the inception of OLS in March had grown exponentially to 61,900.[53] Proponents of OLS argued that it was necessary to assist USBP with their immigration enforcement efforts because DPS was primarily apprehending undocumented immigrants who avoided USBP detection and not asylum seekers who were turning themselves in to USBP. One critic of OLS, however, argued, "Whenever you ask untrained law enforcement officers to engage in immigration enforcement efforts, they are going to revert to racial profiling [and] that's exactly what an initiative like this invites."[54]

The following month, the Texas-Mexico border experienced a large influx of Haitian asylum seekers who had crossed the Rio Grande through Del Rio, Texas, in an attempt to obtain asylum in the United States. The surge made national headlines. As part of OLS, Governor Abbott ordered the DPS to deploy additional assets and manpower from other regions in Texas to the Del Rio border area in an attempt to regain control of the Texas-Mexico border. Governor Abbott even took a play out of the playbook of former El Paso Sector USBP chief Silvestre Reyes, the initiator of Operation Hold the Line in 1993, by having the DPS perform line watches along the Rio Grande.

Nearly 150 marked DPS vehicles lined up side by side as they faced the Rio Grande, creating a steel barrier and sending a message to Haitian asylum seekers that the DPS was going to deter them from crossing into the United States.[55] USBP agents welcomed the assistance of DPS officers along the Rio Grande. The president of the USBP Del Rio Sector Union stated, "DPS has thankfully come out here and helped us out dramatically. We literally could not control this or have even some semblance of control without DPS, National Guard, all the other local stakeholders that are out here."[56] The local DPS spokesman reciprocated by stating that the DPS was there to assist USBP with enforcement actions as long as they were needed in the Del Rio area.

On October 14, 2021, Governor Abbott announced that additional funds from grants were going to be made available to support the enforcement efforts of OLS. More than $36.4 million in grants for the prosecution of individuals ($22.3 million) and assistance to counties along the border to enhance interagency border security actions supporting OLS ($14 million) were going to be made available by Governor Abbott to address Texas-Mexico border security issues.[57] As was made evident by OSS in the summer months of 2014 during the influx of unaccompanied minors and mothers from Central America, state funds are best utilized if allocated to the local communities that incur most of the costs associated with assisting asylum seekers.[58] OLS, similar to other state-funded police-USBP initiatives (e.g., Operation Linebacker and OSS), illustrates how local and state police agencies in Texas are utilized as de facto immigration officials who collaborate with the USBP in apprehending and detaining undocumented immigrants who cross the Texas-Mexico border. OLS is still in operation—with no plans of stopping—since Governor Abbott has advocated for the Texas legislature to continue funding this ineffective migrant deterrent initiative.

Policing Immigration the U.S. Way: Operation Stonegarden

A clear distinction exists between federal law enforcement agencies such as the USBP, state law enforcement agencies, and local law enforcement agencies in regard to the scope of their duties and responsibilities. The primary mission of the USBP is to detect and prevent the entry of undocumented immigrants and illicit drugs into the United States. The duties of the USBP fall beyond the scope of state and local police departments. However, local police departments occasionally enforce federal immigration law whether consciously or unconsciously when responding to routine calls for service involving undocumented immigrants.[59] Such is the case with the DMCSO's participation in OPSG. The DMCSO is an active participant in this federally funded grant program under the authority of the Department of Homeland Security (DHS). OPSG is one of three interconnected grant programs that constitute the Homeland Security Grant Program.[60]

The purpose of OPSG is to increase cooperation and coordination among federal, state, local, tribal, and territorial law enforcement agencies, with the goal of securing the United States' northern, southern, and water borders. USBP is the lead agency for operations under OPSG; therefore, participants in this grant program must support the mission of USBP in order to continue receiving funding. The Federal Emergency Management Agency (FEMA) is responsible for distributing OPSG funds to law enforcement agencies. OPSG funds may be used for personnel-related costs such as overtime pay for officers and the purchase of police vehicles. Even so, most of the money allocated from this grant program is spent on securing the U.S.-Mexico border.

OPSG is a border security initiative launched by former DHS secretary Tom Ridge. It consists of a series of pilot programs that seek closer coordination between local, state, and federal law enforcement agencies.[61] The pilot programs were heralded as a success in 2005, and then DHS secretary Michael Chertoff decided to expand OPSG into a standalone program. In 2009 then DHS secretary Janet Napolitano not only doubled OPSG's budget but also modified the eligibility requirements and restructured the program by requiring participating agencies to cooperate with local USBP sector stations. This changed the dynamic of OPSG, since "the Border Patrol has exerted strict participation requirements for local agencies that are designed by the Border Patrol to support the Border Patrol's mission and deployment strategy."[62] Therefore, participating law enforcement agencies are aware that their participation in OPSG necessitates collaboration with USBP in order to receive funding.

According to DHS statistics, OPSG total funding has increased significantly over the years, from $55 million in 2016 to $90 million in 2021.[63] In 2019 the combined counties of the RGV were awarded a total of $11,225,857 for their participation in OPSG.[64] This funding is not surprising, though, especially since the RGV USBP sector is the busiest of all USBP sectors and relies on its state and local police department counterparts in the RGV to assist with enforcement efforts. Moreover, as previously mentioned, tribal law enforcement agencies also receive OPSG funding for their collaboration with the USBP. Consequently, during the 2019 fiscal year, the Kickapoo Tribal Police Department (Texas Kickapoo Indian Reservation) received $700,000 for their participation in OPSG.

In regard to OPSG participation, it is worth noting that not all eligible local police departments participate, even though such participation can provide much-needed monetary assistance for a department. Since 2017 at least three counties, three cities, and one indigenous tribal police department have opted out of participating in OPSG—none were from Texas. For example, the Sheriff's Office in Jefferson County, Washington, decided to opt out of OPSG. Sheriff Joe Nole stated that the reason for opting out of OPSG was because "it seemed like dirty money. . . . It felt like we were being paid money to assist Border Patrol."[65] In late January 2020 the Tucson Police Department in Arizona decided to opt out of OPSG because of ethical dilemmas associated with participating in OPSG. Then Tucson Police Department chief Chris Mangus noted that the department could not continue participating in OPSG because the program's performance metrics and desired results (meaning its immigrant apprehension rates) were contrary to the department's mission and the expectations of the community it serves.[66]

When the Tucson Police Department was still an active participant in OPSG, Chief Mangus made a request to the DHS to use 20 percent of the $600,000 in funding to support community organizations in Tucson that were assisting with the humanitarian crisis. When the request was denied by DHS, that was the breaking point for Mangus, and he decided that the department was going to opt out of OPSG.[67] In February 2020 the Pima County Board of Supervisors (Arizona) also opted out of participating in OPSG due to the DHS's rejection of the board's request to use a portion of the OPSG funds for humanitarian aid. Pima County officials made a request to use a portion of their 2019 OPSG funds to assist a local community organization (Casa Alitas Migrant Shelter) that incurred costs associated with providing humanitarian aid. The DHS denied the request because the request provided "no border security operational benefit."[68]

Most local U.S.-Mexico borderland law enforcement agencies are appreciative of their participation in OPSG and have even received accolades from the USBP for their partnership. A case in point is the Sunland Park Police Department in New Mexico. In mid-September 2021 the department received the USBP Second Quarter Stonegarden Partner Award for their continued collaboration with the USBP in OPSG. Sunland Park police chief Javier Guerra said, "We have a great relationship with Border Patrol. We help each other with public safety in Sunland Park. They have their priority: enforcing immigration laws. Our job is answering 911 calls. . . . [Sometimes] it turns out those calls are immigrant cases, so we'll just call them to come and take charge."[69] Indeed, most contact with undocumented immigrants arises out of routine calls for service made to the department via 911. However, one notable exception is a 2007 incident involving New Mexico's Otero County Sheriff's Office, which was sued by the American Civil Liberties Union for utilizing overzealous policing tactics while active participants of OPSG.[70] During the summer of 2007, Otero County Sheriff's Office deputies conducted a series of immigration-related raids in Chaparral, New Mexico, in an attempt to apprehend and detain undocumented immigrants. The deputies harassed, interrogated, and searched the homes of residents in Chaparral, many of whom had been born in the United States, in search of undocumented immigrants. The deputies apprehended and detained several individuals who were then deported by the USBP.

Aside from the 2007 Otero County incident, most contact by local police authorities with undocumented immigrants arises during 911 calls for service. Such was my experience working for the DMCSO. A majority of my contact with undocumented immigrants resulted from these 911 calls for service to which I was dispatched.

The Complexities of Police Work

A general discussion of police work provides further insight into the policing profession. Perceptions regarding the police vary, and many people have unclear images of the function of police officers and their role in society. Put simply, "To some, a police officer is a 'fucking pig,' a mindless brute working for a morally bankrupt institution. To others, a police officer is a courageous public servant, a defender of life and property, regulating city life along democratic lines."[71] However, most people believe that police officers represent the social institution of social control; namely, they are enforcers of laws.

Civilians tend to have a distorted crime-fighter image of the police based on the media's portrayal of police work. This portrayal of the police gives rise to impracticable expectations of police: members of the public assume that police officers solve crimes.[72] Contrary to popular belief, only a very small amount of the work conducted by the police entails major crime. Approximately 80 percent of police work involves calls for service that have nothing to do with crime.[73] Specifically, a police officer's daily work routine consists of monotonous and mundane activities, such as answering calls for service, enforcing traffic violations, and making minor arrests for offenses such as public intoxication. Police officers basically spend a significant amount of time waiting for something to happen, conducting routine patrol until dispatched to a call for service.[74]

Police officers designate as important only those tasks that involve criminal apprehensions, whereas officers complete noncriminal enforcement tasks with indifference as part of everyday work routine activity.[75] In essence, "most police work is neither social service nor law enforcement, but order maintenance—the settlement of conflicts by means other than formal law enforcement."[76] The majority of a police officer's workday involves order maintenance functions, such as serving as a mediator between individuals who have either a domestic or a civil dispute.

Maintaining order and resolving grievances among individuals continue to be the primary functions of the police. In sum, "seeing crime as the be all and end all of the police mission is to dispatch them to pursue a quixotic impossible dream."[77]

The Status of the Police Officer

One of several divisions within a police department is the patrol division. Officers assigned to the patrol division hold a position at the bottom of the police organization; they are commonly referred to as rank-and-file officers or patrol officers. Patrol officers are the face of the department, since they are responsible for a majority of the interactions with community members, namely, responses to calls for service and arrests. Given the nature of a patrol officer's normal duties, the fact that policing is not an appealing profession to most individuals is no surprise, especially since the police are primarily responsible for performing society's "dirty work."[78]

David Bayley states that three factors contribute to the unappealing nature of police work. First, policing is a physically demanding profession because there are certain instances in which police officers are forced to use physical force (hands-on contact) while responding to calls for service. Police officers come in contact with people who are dirty, foul smelling, and at times covered with vomit or blood. Aside from physical contact, the twenty-four-hour shift worked by police officers takes a toll on their bodies. Second, police officers are cognizant that they run the risk of being killed in the line of duty, and they are willing to pay the ultimate sacrifice as part of their policing duties. Third, as stated above, police officers deal with the unglamorous aspect of society—society's dirty work.[79] The police interact on a daily basis with certain individuals who are viewed as problematic. For example, sometimes police officers come in contact with people who have a wide array of issues, including drug use, psychological imbalances, and abusive tendencies, to name just a few.

If the abovementioned factors cause the policing profession to be unappealing, who then is willing to become a police officer? Most police officers come from a low socioeconomic background, which makes the profession of policing an attractive means of achieving upward social economic mobility.[80] Unfortunately, for the most part, police recruits normally lack the skills or education that can make them marketable in other fields. Only a small number of police officers possess a postsecondary education. Policing expert Anthony Bouza notes that this lack of an advanced education in the police can be traced back to class differences: "The job peculiarly belongs to the upper segment of the lower class, who generally don't send their children to college. Cops come from hard-working blue-collar families."[81] It is also worth noting that racial inequality is another contributing factor to the lack of postsecondary education for police officers, especially for Black and Latino officers. During the 1960s and 1970s, several police departments were sued to ease their minimum education requirements (e.g., bachelor's degrees) because they discriminated against potential Black and Latino applicants.[82]

Even though the salaries of some police officers can be similar to the salaries of some white-collar professionals, policing remains primarily a blue-collar occupation. In any case, it should come as no surprise that certain individuals (people of low socioeconomic status) view the policing profession as a means of upward social economic mobility irrespective of the danger and the aforementioned unappealing aspects that are normally associated with the police occupation. I remember that I had wanted to be a police officer since I was about seven years old.[83] I viewed policing as a means of upward social economic mobility due to the pay, the job security, the health benefits, and the pension benefits.

The same holds true for some federal law enforcement agents. Recent scholarship regarding Latino-origin ICE agents' motivation for electing to work for a law enforcement agency that has systematically targeted the racial community to which they belong reveals that economic self-interest (upward social and economic mobility) serves as the primary motivating factor for choosing to work for ICE.[84]

Police Culture: Social Isolation and Solidarity

Having contextualized the social conditions that make the occupation of policing appealing to certain individuals, I now turn the discussion to the two aspects of policing that generate a distinct police subculture: isolation and solidarity.

It is commonplace now that within the scholarship on police culture and behavior, the patrol officer is the primary source that researchers examine.[85] As previously mentioned, patrol officers are the face of the police department, since they are responsible for a majority of contact with civilians. The socialization process of police officers begins at the police academy, where new recruits are familiarized with the occupational environment. The socialization process continues once the officers begin patrol work and are assigned to a field training officer. Socialization within the police academy represents a more formal method of teaching police recruits the inner workings of the occupation. In contrast, field training is the typical informal method of socialization for police officers after their graduation from the police academy. In essence, "the former reflects most of the 'what to do and expect' teaching, while the latter is more of the 'here's how things operate in the real world' teaching."[86]

Once newly hired police officers begin working on the streets, they soon realize that their role is to control irritable and defiant individuals who despise their presence. Instead of being appreciated for their work, police officers encounter hostility. The need to maintain order and their own authority governs every aspect of their occupation. This scenario gives rise to feelings of misunderstanding; police officers internalize an "us versus them" mentality, since they feel society does not understand them. This way of thinking that develops between the police and civilians helps to forge a strong bond between police officers.[87] In addition, it increases the dependence they have on each other for assistance and safety. Jerome Skolnick and John Van Maanen have reiterated this point by noting that the danger innate in policing is part of the central force that pulls police officers together and contributes to their role as strangers to citizens.[88]

Skolnick further asserts that a police officer's occupational environment consists of their relationship to society and includes the two elements of danger and authority.[89] The element of danger makes the police officer attentive to potential violence and lawbreaking. In contrast, authority reinforces the element of danger in police officers by isolating them as a result of requiring them to enforce laws. Danger and authority "are mutually dependent in the occupation of policing, which leads police officers to come up with rules, rhetoric, and rites to deal with those tensions."[90] The element of danger that is associated with the occupation of policing alienates police officers from both criminal-prone individuals and law-abiding citizens.[91]

Social isolation and occupational solidarity are the price paid by police officers as a result of their occupational culture. Internal solidarity results not only from isolation but also from the interdependence police officers form with each other as a result of the danger associated with the profession.[92] Thus, solidarity within the police seems to be stronger than solidarity within other occupations, such as industrial fishing, that are far more dangerous than policing. Another disturbing discovery for police officers is that they need to suppress their feelings in order to perform the job well. Police officers develop this emotional rigidity so that they can cope with the various issues they are confronted with, such as seeing dead people, encountering injured adults and children, and dealing with society's ill will, among other things. Police officers cannot let their feelings get the best of them; therefore, they must distance themselves from all emotions.

This book examines the relationship between police officers and the civilians they come in contact with during routine police activities. For example, most of the interactions between local police officers and undocumented immigrants happen during calls for service to stash houses. During these calls for service police officers get a firsthand look into the inhumane treatment of undocumented immigrants.

In order to carry on with their work routine, officers must cut off their emotions from the horror stories of hardship told by immigrants. Thus, police work entails "emotion work." As noted by Arlie Russell Hochschild, "Emotion work refers more broadly to the act of evoking or shaping, as well as suppressing, feeling in oneself."[93] Police officers need to desensitize themselves from all the inhumane treatment suffered by immigrants as a result of being held in stash houses. Chapters 3 and 4 provide further insight into the lived experiences of undocumented immigrants while being held in stash houses after crossing into the United States. Far too often I witnessed the harsh living conditions of undocumented immigrants inside stash houses and listened to their stories of hardship and victimization.

In sum, with regard to police culture, "the world of the police, shaped by isolation and dependence on each other for safety, might be likened to a latter-day Atlantis because of the mystery in which police operations are shrouded and the public's ignorance about the internal realities of the police world."[94] The succeeding chapters take an inside look into the relationship between racism, immigration, and the police profession on the South Texas–Mexico border that I experienced while I was a police officer responding to routine calls for service.

CHAPTER 2

Racialization and Socialization in the Borderlands

Autoethnography is a method of qualitative research writing in which the researcher illustrates their own experiences as a result of being an active participant in the research study. Specifically, autoethnography blurs the distinction between the researcher and the researched, and the researcher utilizes the principles of both autobiography and ethnography to perform and write autoethnography.[1] Along with being a researcher in this study, I was an active participant because I was a police officer directly connected to the people I was researching. Consequently, I situated my dual roles of researcher and researched (police officer) through the qualitative research-writing method of autoethnography, which is both a process and a product.[2] In addition, because one aspect of this book focuses on racialization among Latinos in the borderlands, I contextualize this practice through a chronological recollection of my experiences with the racialization process throughout my life in order to lay the foundation for this and other chapters of this book.

Racialization in High School: The Mojos

One of my memories from high school demonstrates the racialization process. The non-English-speaking high school students were enrolled in English as a second language (ESL) classes. Students enrolled in ESL classes generally associated with each other because they had the same classes and usually kept to themselves. The ESL students at my high school were commonly referred to as *mojos* because they did not speak English, and if they did, they spoke it with a heavy accent.[3]

No one ever put much thought into the idea that the ESL students were being racialized as mojos, a term whose origin is unfamiliar to me. It was just assumed that if a student was in an ESL class, they were simply regarded as a mojo. My high school was no different from any other, because students were categorized into separate groups, such as jocks, cheerleaders, nerds, goths, band geeks, gangsters, preps, emos, and so on. However, my high school experience differed in the sense that at my high school, students were racialized as mojos based on several characteristics (e.g., language, music preference, style of dress, sport of choice, etc.).

Though ESL students bore the brunt of racialized terms such as mojo, students who spoke Spanish, listened to Spanish music, dressed in a certain way, and played soccer were also deemed worthy of being racialized as mojos. My first language is Spanish, so I would occasionally speak Spanish to some of my friends, who also happened to be my football teammates. I played football and baseball in high school but was not caught up in the stereotypical jock label typically associated with student athletes.

Occasionally, however, when I spoke Spanish, some of my teammates would make comments such as, "Oh, stop it, you mojo." One common ritual among my teammates was that prior to a game, we normally listened to music to either relax us or pump us up. Most of my teammates listened to rap music or rock music as we waited in the locker room. I, on the other hand, would always listen to Spanish music and was sometimes the butt of jokes among my teammates. I was not ashamed of my musical preference, but what bothered me was that some of my teammates would call me mojo for simply listening to Spanish music instead of English music as part of our pregame rituals. I would listen to what my teammates referred to as "grandpa music"—Carlos y José, Ramón Ayala y Sus Bravos del Norte, Los Cachorros de Juan Villareal, Los Cadetes de Linares, and others—but even though my musical preference was not as cool as theirs, their racialization was unwarranted.

Aside from speaking Spanish and having a particular musical preference, the way a person dressed also made them susceptible to being racialized as a mojo. What one wore to school said a lot about a person. Therefore, it was very important for some of my high school classmates who were trying to fit in to dress in name-brand clothes so they could feel good about themselves. A few students, though, did not care about dressing in name-brand clothes and instead dressed cowboy style. Those students went to school dressed in jeans and cowboy boots made from ostrich skin, crocodile skin, or some other exotic skin.

There was a distinction between two groups of students who dressed cowboy style. What differentiated these two groups was the type of boots they wore—the boot material and the color of the boots. Students who wore boots made of exotic skin (e.g., ostrich or crocodile) usually wore boots dyed with bright colors, such as yellow or orange. On the other hand, students who wore regular leather boots wore boots that were either black or brown. The students who wore boots made of exotic skin were racialized as mojos, whereas students who wore regular cowboy boots were not ridiculed; they simply dressed "kicker" style.[4]

Besides dress style, the sport one played in high school facilitated the racialization process. The athletes in my high school who played soccer were known as mojos. It did not matter if one were a male or a female soccer player; if they played soccer, they were a mojo. That was the general understanding among student athletes who played other sports. To the best of my knowledge, soccer was only popular among primarily Spanish-speaking students in my high school and not among the rest of the student population. Therefore, not surprisingly, student athletes who played soccer at my high school were students who primarily spoke Spanish and dressed cowboy style with bright-colored exotic-skin boots.

Another recollection I have of the racialization process during my high school years was when I was a senior and was reminded by my friend Humberto that I once was a mojo like the ESL students. He and I were walking through a hallway when all of a sudden he told me, "Remember when you began school? You were a mojo that didn't speak English. You're not a mojo like them [pointing to the ESL class we were walking past] anymore." As previously mentioned, I was born in Illinois but raised in the RGV. When my family moved to Texas and enrolled me in elementary school, I did not speak a word of English. Spanish was the primary language spoken in my household.

Humberto was in my first-grade class, and he remembered that I was the only student in the class who did not speak English. My mother went against the wishes of the school administrators and enrolled me in a general education class rather than the ESL class they suggested. Humberto remained my friend all the way through high school. He was the only one who remembered that I did not speak a word of English when I was enrolled in elementary school after moving from Illinois. According to Humberto, I was no longer a mojo because I showed mastery of the English language. Previous scholarship regarding intraethnic relations among Mexican-origin individuals in a California school setting found that some Mexican American high school students disparaged their coethnic Mexican immigrant counterparts enrolled in English language development classes by racializing them as *chunties*.[5]

My experience as an adolescent being racialized as a mojo by my peers, whether classmates or teammates, is symbolic of how white children first learn (and continue to learn as adults) through everyday socialization practices and through daily interactions with others major aspects of the dominant white racial frame.[6] In particular, "at an early age, white (and other) children learn the white frame in everyday interactions in networks of relatives, friends, and peers. The elements of this dominant frame are acquired by children at home, at school, at play, and from the media."[7] Thus, similar to how white children learn the dominant white frame and how to act out of it by witnessing the actions of their parents or peers, my teammates and classmates more than likely learned the aspects of the dominant white frame in a similar manner: through a process of communication and interaction with family members and peers. Consequently, my peers became promoting and advocating agents of the anti-Latino immigrant subframe of the dominant white racial frame by racializing me as a mojo without realizing that they were operating out of the dominant white frame to engage in racist practices.[8]

Police Socialization

THE POLICE ACADEMY

After I obtained my bachelor of science degree in criminal justice in the spring of 2005, I began working at the Le Grand Police Department in the late fall of 2005. As a recent college graduate in my early twenties, I was ready to embark on a policing career but first needed to obtain my official training at the police academy. As is customary in the policing profession, one must attend the police academy before beginning fieldwork as a police officer. Consequently, I attended the Le Grand Police Academy as a police recruit for five months and became familiarized with the criminal and traffic laws of Texas, among other police-related functions.

One of the several state-mandated courses I received as part of my police academy training, which I distinctly remember because it relates to this book, was the eight-hour cultural diversity course given to the academy class. Every police officer in Texas must complete a mandatory eight-hour course on cultural diversity as part of their overall 728 hours of police academy training. The course's purpose is to make police officers racially and culturally sensitive when encountering civilians from different racial/ethnic backgrounds. Because the Le Grand Police Department is located on the South Texas–Mexico border, which is comprised primarily of Mexican-origin individuals, our cultural diversity instruction focused specifically on Latino civilians.

The cultural diversity course at the police academy was given by a Mexican

American studies professor from a local university named Dr. Mascóte. He was chosen by the police chief to teach this course based on his academic research expertise. Dr. Mascóte taught the course from a racial conflict perspective and was viewed as a radical by the police academy training staff. For example, when talking about racial identity politics, Dr. Mascóte told us he felt as if he was trapped between two borders. He explained to the class that he could not understand why a person needed to prove their citizenship twice when traveling north into the interior of the state from South Texas. Dr. Mascóte was referring to the U.S.-Mexico border and the USBP checkpoints that are located several miles north of the U.S.-Mexico border: the Falfurrias, Texas, Border Patrol Station and the Javier Vega Jr. Border Patrol Checkpoint.[9] These checkpoints are on two major routes of egress from the RGV. Therefore, for example, persons wanting to travel to San Antonio from the RGV will be inspected at a USBP checkpoint and will be asked their immigration status.[10]

Dr. Mascóte told the police academy class that even though he was a U.S. citizen, he did not feel like one, because he needed to prove his immigration status when traveling north from the RGV: "Why do we need to prove our citizenship status again when traveling out of the Valley? Is it because we're Mexican descent? It's assumed that once we're on this side [points down with his right index finger] of the border, there is no need to be asked if we are citizens!"

While on lunch break in the lunchroom of the police academy, Cicero, one of my fellow recruits, asked a police academy instructor, Officer Dimantero, why Dr. Mascóte was in charge of teaching the course. Cicero was bothered by Dr. Mascóte's comment about being trapped between two borders because he felt Dr. Mascóte was trying to indoctrinate us with his race and citizenship status issues. Officer Dimantero told him that Dr. Mascóte was specifically chosen by the police chief due to his educational expertise on the subject. Officer Dimantero then said that the police academy staff believed Dr. Mascóte was a radical trying to brainwash the police recruits with his "race crap." Officer Dimantero then said, "Who cares how he feels about two borders?" He further added that the USBP checkpoints were needed in order to secure the border from "criminal aliens" who came from Mexico.

Aside from the socialization on cultural diversity we received within the police department, the academy instructors were the first to introduce us to the informal police organizational training regarding police-community relations. As organizational theorist John Van Maanen noted, "[Police] socialization refers to the process by which a person learns the values, norms, and required behaviors which permit him to participate as a member of the organization."[11] The police academy instructors made it clear that we would not be liked or even appreciated by civilians. They warned us that even though this was bound to happen, we needed to expect it, because we would be "agents of social control."

One instructor provided us with an analogy we could use to cope with this issue: "For you to last in this profession, you need to put your heart in the freezer when you get to work, take it back out when you get home." From the onset, the socialization at the department regarding police-community relations indicated that we were bound to encounter hostility from civilians during our everyday work routine; therefore, we needed to be apathetic during those encounters in order to succeed in the policing profession. Police socialization is strong in that it molds recruits into the expectations that come with being a member of that social institution. That is, as noted by Bouza, "The police department is really a subculture with powerful rules. It shapes everyone. It takes fine young women and men, mostly working class, and shapes them to its needs."[12]

In addition, the high-stress paramilitary academy structure is also problematic, because police recruits are trained to have a warrior mindset, yet after successfully graduating from the academy, recruits are expected to go out and work in the communities by serving as social workers. Thus, a paradox exists between the warrior mindset instilled in police recruits at the police academy and the public's expectations once recruits start working in the community as police officers and public servants.[13]

EVERYDAY POLICE PRACTICES: CALLS FOR SERVICE

Despite the numerous calls for service dealing with undocumented immigrants that I experienced while I was employed at the Le Grand Police Department, only two stand out in my memory. One day while on routine patrol, I heard over my patrol radio an Officer Gordado advise the dispatcher that he was going to stop two suspicious male pedestrians for questioning: "I'm going to check these males to see what they're up to."

After several minutes passed, he provided the dispatcher with the names of the two males and asked her to conduct a warrant check on them to determine if they were wanted.[14] The dispatcher told him that neither man had a warrant or a driver's license. Shortly thereafter, Officer Gordado told the dispatcher, "OK, go ahead and send me BP to my location for these two illegals."[15] I never found out why the two males attracted Officer Gordado's attention, especially since they were walking along a major thoroughfare of Le Grand in broad daylight.

It was stated within the policy and procedures handbook of the police department that we could not ask questions related to immigration status when we encountered individuals during our daily routine work activities. Obviously, Officer Gordado violated the department's policy and procedures, but, oddly enough, no one questioned or sanctioned him for requesting that the two males be deported by the USBP. Why? That is the way things worked in the department. The officer's action was part of the socialization process among the police when they encountered immigrants out on the street and part of institutionalized practices that became normalized and acceptable behavior. Consequently, if an officer encountered immigrants, they could ask the USBP to deport them at their discretion, since the situation was seen as a federal immigration issue, even though the officer(s) more than likely violated departmental policy by asking questions about immigration status in order to reach that conclusion.[16] This situation occurred other times as well, but I do not remember the exact details of such incidents.

My second socialization recollection at the Le Grand Police Department when I encountered undocumented immigrants was when Officer Lablico and I responded to a call for service at an apartment complex. We were advised by the dispatcher that the department had received a phone call from a concerned citizen who witnessed several people coming in and out of an apartment.[17] The concerned citizen wanted a police officer to check the apartment, because the citizen believed it was being used to stash immigrants. Consequently, we were dispatched to the location on a "suspicious circumstance" call for service.

Officer Lablico arrived first at the apartment complex because I was several blocks away from the location. Shortly before I arrived, I heard him transmit on the police radio and say, "Le Grand, I have several runners. I need more units!" Immediately thereafter, several officers notified the dispatcher that they were also responding to the scene to assist. As soon as I arrived at the apartment complex, Officer Lablico told me that several individuals had run away from the location. I walked up to him as he stood by the entrance door of the apartment. As I stood next to Officer Lablico by the door, I observed roughly ten to fifteen individuals sitting down inside the unfurnished apartment.

I did not stay by the door too long, because Officer Lablico told me that the individuals who had run away had a head start on me already; therefore, I needed to get on with my pursuit to catch them. I informed him that I would drive around the neighborhood and check the surrounding area for the immigrants. As soon as I walked back to my patrol car, Officer Ragero drove up to me and asked me in a harried tone, "Where'd they go?!" I told him I had no clue where they went. He said he would check the area and left the parking lot at a high rate of speed. I then got inside my patrol car and drove away from the apartment complex in search of the immigrants.

I must note that even though I was driving through the neighborhood and surrounding areas in search of the immigrants, I was not actively seeking to find them because of my own personal morality issues regarding searching for immigrants when that objective was beyond the scope and legal parameters of my policing duties.[18] By now, Officer Lablico had confirmed that the individuals who ran from the apartment complex were undocumented immigrants.[19] In addition, all of the police officers involved in this call for service were aware that the USBP was already on their way to the apartment complex to take custody of the undocumented immigrants.

As I drove back to the apartment complex (approximately twenty minutes had elapsed by this point), I heard Officer Hartez notify the dispatcher that he had two "illegals" in custody who were found hiding in a nearby alley of the apartment complex. Upon my return to the apartment complex, I observed several immigrants sitting down cross-legged with their backs to the driver's side of a USBP fifteen-passenger van. Some sat motionless with their heads facing down to the ground, while others cried as they all waited to be placed inside the USBP van. The immigrants had their hands tied behind their backs with zip ties.

Some of the officers (two additional police officers had responded) involved in this call for service, including myself, were standing next to the USBP van as one of the two USBP agents on scene along with Officer Lablico briefed our patrol supervisor inside the apartment of the incident. As we waited in the parking lot, Officer Hartez arrived with the two undocumented immigrants he had detained. He then exited his vehicle and told me to wait by his patrol car with the immigrants while he briefed the supervisor.

I walked to Officer Hartez's patrol car and stood next to the left rear passenger door while he briefed our supervisor. The rear passenger windows of the patrol car were rolled halfway down. As I stood next to the door, it was obvious the immigrants were distraught, because they were crying as they sat handcuffed in the rear of the vehicle. One of the males then pleaded with me in Spanish, "Let us go, please, sir! I beg you. We only came to work to support our families in Mexico, who depend on us!" The other male made a similar plea as tears rolled down both men's cheeks.

I felt empathy for both individuals, even though, as I previously mentioned, I was not supposed to let the circumstances of the call for service affect me emotionally. Besides empathy, I felt a great deal of hopelessness, since there was nothing I could do to help them. After pleading for several minutes, they stopped and then conversed with me. It was at this point that I felt the only thing I could do to give them solace was to let them know that even though they had been caught during this crossing attempt, they should not be deterred and should continue trying to cross into the United States until they were successful. I shared my own personal life experiences with them about my parents being Mexican immigrants and how that and my own previous work experiences working alongside undocumented immigrants had shaped the way I view the immigration issue. After several minutes, agents removed the men's handcuffs and replaced them with zip ties, and they were escorted into the USBP van along with the other immigrants.

The previous two vignettes illustrate how officers with the Le Grand Police Department operated as de facto immigration enforcement officials by collaborating with USBP agents to apprehend and detain undocumented immigrants. This collaboration is facilitated because of the department's geographical setting in the U.S.-Mexico borderlands and the USBP's authority to operate within one hundred miles of any U.S. external boundary. The previous two vignettes and collaborative racialized efforts between local police and the USBP in the borderlands (discussed further in chapters 3 and 4) constitute a distinct method of policing that I refer to as "Constitution-free policing." Police departments whose law enforcement jurisdiction lies within the one-hundred-mile zone are able to serve as de facto immigration officials by collaborating with the USBP when encountering immigrants as part of their everyday work routine. Thus, as evidenced by the incident involving the Maverick County Sheriff's Office deputy in the introductory chapter, Constitution-free policing, as a policing tactic, is still utilized by local police departments on the U.S.-Mexico border.

The Fourth Amendment of the U.S. Constitution protects individuals from random and arbitrary stops and searches; however, these basic constitutional principles do not apply fully within the one-hundred-mile zone.[20] Police departments in the RGV do not have to worry about having official immigration enforcement agreements such as 287(g) because their police jurisdiction falls within the one-hundred-mile zone. That is, if an officer comes in contact with an undocumented immigrant, all the officer needs to do is have USBP respond to the officer's location to have the immigrant deported, as evidenced by the two previous vignettes. In contrast, police officers who work in the interior of the United States (beyond the one-hundred-mile zone) normally have some form of official immigration enforcement agreement in the form of Section 287(g), among others, with federal immigration authorities (e.g., ICE) in order to enforce immigration law.[21] In short, my concept of Constitution-free policing applies to the Fourth Amendment, as evidenced by local and state policing practices in the U.S.-Mexico borderlands.

Racialization: Academia versus Everyday Practices

As part of my academic graduate school training at Texas A&M University, I became exposed to the concept of racialization and became familiar with its process. However, my racialization exposure through academia differed to some extent from what I actually experienced in practice as a Mexican American residing on the U.S.-Mexico border.

Latinos have been racialized during different historical periods to serve the interest of maintaining a white hegemonic dominant racial structure.[22] Evidence that this is the case can be seen in several events in U.S.-Mexican history, such as the Mexican repatriation, Operation Wetback, "prevention through deterrence" strategies on the U.S.-Mexico border, and California's Proposition 187 (the Save Our State initiative), among others.[23] Latinos have been and continue to be racialized as perpetual foreigners because that characterization helps reinforce the white racial, social, and economic hierarchy in the United States. Legal scholar Natsu Taylor Saito argues that this racialization serves two purposes, "first . . . placing them [Latinos] as a buffer zone between whites and blacks and also . . . constructing them [Latinos] as outsiders against whom real 'Americans' can unite in times of crisis."[24] In addition, if a person is identified as white or Black, that person is presumed to be legally a U.S. citizen and socially a real American.[25] In contrast, Latinos are not afforded that ability due to being racialized as perpetual foreigners, even if they were born in the United States.

As this chapter illustrates, Latinos are not immune from racializing each other as foreigners based on certain attributes, a process that serves to maintain the white racial hierarchy in the United States. Whether at high school with my teammates and classmates or while I was a police officer, I observed Latinos reinforcing the white hegemonic racial structure because of intraracial/intraethnic racialization practices. In contrast to the experiences of Latinos who have been racialized only during different historical periods, my experience with racialization in practice has been constant throughout my entire life, because as a Mexican American residing on the U.S.-Mexico border I have continually borne witness to it.

Living on the U.S.-Mexico border presents Mexican Americans with a different set of mirrors that reflect different identities. Being a U.S.-Mexico border resident ensures that the mirror that initially reflected their identity (i.e., being Mexican) still stands before them. For example, sociologist Pablo Vila asserts that Mexican Americans who reside on the U.S.-Mexico border are always struggling with the recognition of their identity as a racial and ethnic group. Mexico, the country defining Mexican American ethnicity, is still present and visible from the U.S.-Mexico border. Thus, for Mexican Americans living on the U.S. side of the U.S.-Mexico border, the origin of their difference (Mexico) is always there and consequently serves as a constant reminder of their ethnic identity.[26] Moreover, recent scholarship in the RGV found that some Mexican Americans identify as "white" on U.S. census forms as a way to distance themselves from their coethnic Mexican immigrant counterparts.[27] Other scholarship notes that the stigma of being undocumented, which is often associated with markers of *Latinidad*, may cause U.S.-born Latinos to dissociate themselves from that stigma.[28]

Academic scholarship focuses on racialization as a practice in which Latinos are racialized in order to maintain the white racial hierarchy. My experience with racialization in practice as a Latino residing on the U.S.-Mexico border illustrates that my peers in high school and my coworkers at the police department racialized their coracials/coethnics as foreigners to distance themselves racially/ethnically. My peers and coworkers accomplished this process by racializing certain individuals as either mojos or illegals. In doing so, they tried to demonstrate that they were Americans because they did not speak English with an accent, did not dress as mojos, did not primarily listen to Spanish music, and did not hesitate to turn over other Latinos to the USBP. Ultimately, my peers in school and my coworkers were trying to associate themselves with whiteness by racializing their coracials/coethnics as foreigners, since there is a general tendency to equate Americanness with whiteness.

Competing Worldviews

RACIALIZATION OF IMMIGRANTS: EVERYDAY PRACTICES AT THE SHERIFF'S OFFICE

Several DMCSO patrol deputies carried out racialized immigrant practices daily. These practices were accomplished either at the police department during roll call or out in the street during calls for service. While I was at the police department, several officers racialized immigrants by calling them "illegals" or "illegal aliens." This common practice can be illustrated by examples of what transpired in roll call on two separate occasions.

One day while conducting roll call, Lieutenant Lorenzo described an incident from the day before during which we, the DMCSO, assisted the USBP with a call for service dealing with a stash house. The sheriff's office had received a phone call about suspicious activity coming from a residence. When the deputies responded to the house, they found thirty-five male and female immigrants inside. The immigrants had been inside the two-bedroom house for about a week. Lieutenant Lorenzo then told us about the conditions of the residence: "Guys, you should've seen how this house was. There was no running water and no electricity inside. . . . The illegals had been there for several days and were all crammed in the two-bedroom house." He then reminded us that we needed to be vigilant in the areas we patrolled because there might be several stash houses within those neighborhoods (colonias): "Don't just drive by real fast through the neighborhoods without checking for any suspicious activity like potential stash houses."

Lieutenant Lorenzo referred to immigrants as "illegals" whenever he mentioned them. Several days later while conducting roll call again, he reiterated to us that we needed to be alert in the neighborhoods we patrolled due to the number of potential stash houses in rural Del Monte County: "Yesterday we had another call in which we found a lot of illegals. We received a call from a concerned citizen about suspicious activity going on in a mobile home on Hueneme Street." Lieutenant Lorenzo stated that the deputies who responded to this call encountered "thirty-plus illegals" who were from Mexico and Central America. He then reiterated to us that we needed to "watch out for suspicious activity" (potential stash houses) while on patrol, since in his view, there were several stash houses in the county.

Lieutenant Lorenzo's preferred term of reference for immigrants was "illegals." He rarely referred to immigrants as immigrants, and, as seen in the two vignettes, he used the term "illegals" as if there were no negative connotations behind its use. Aside from racializing immigrants, he stressed to the officers that they needed to "watch out for suspicious activity" in the colonias. This warning, in turn, sent the underlying message that officers should enforce federal immigration law by locating possible stash houses so that the USBP could be notified in order to deport the immigrants. Of course, Lieutenant Lorenzo was probably stressing this point to us in good faith in order to have us remove these people from the deplorable, dangerous conditions to which they were exposed inside stash houses.[29] Regardless, among several police officers, the preferred terms of reference for immigrants at the sheriff's office were "illegals," "IAS" (illegal aliens), "UAS" (undocumented aliens), and "mojankers." Immigrants were seldom called "immigrants" at the police department.

CONFLICTING WORLDVIEWS

Out on the street, the everyday practice involving the racialization of immigrants was best illustrated by calls for service. Even though the DMCSO did not participate in immigration enforcement programs such as 287(g) and Secure Communities, it was understood that if an officer encountered an undocumented immigrant during a call for service, that officer should notify the USBP.[30] This behavior was expected because of the socialization process within the department. As noted earlier, if an officer came in contact with an undocumented immigrant, the officer could have the immigrant deported at the officer's discretion. It was the norm to notify USBP to respond to an officer's location if the officer was dealing with a call regarding an immigration issue—an encounter with an undocumented immigrant.

Notifying the USBP to deport an immigrant is expected behavior when police work on the U.S.-Mexico border. The close proximity to the border ensures strong odds that a police officer will come in contact with an undocumented immigrant. These constant encounters with immigrants serve as socializing factors that lead officers to believe it is OK to enforce federal immigration law. When officers come in contact with an immigrant, and if upon further questioning (which most of the time is done illegally; officers do not have the authority to ask immigration-related questions) it is determined that the immigrant is undocumented within the United States, the general trend is to notify the USBP (usually done by the dispatcher) to come take custody of the immigrant(s). Officers are socialized to notify the USBP to take custody of immigrants, since violations are federal immigration law issues and not state criminal law issues. Recent scholarship in El Paso County, Texas, found that first-generation Latino immigrants and second-generation Latinos are more likely to be questioned by law enforcement officials about their citizenship status than third-generation and later Latinos.[31] Such practices can be detrimental to police-community relations in regard to police legitimacy.[32] Thus, notifying the USBP is expected behavior among police officers because it is continuously carried out during calls for service. This process is yet another example of how Constitution-free policing, as a method of policing in the borderlands, occurs periodically on the South Texas–Mexico border.

Oddly enough, police discretion, which grants officers flexibility in daily work decision-making activities, such as how they handle a certain call, is also an aspect of policing. For example, if an officer pulls over someone for a traffic violation, the officer can choose to give the motorist either a ticket or a warning. Officers also have discretion regarding arresting individuals. Just because a crime has occurred does not guarantee that an arrest will be made. For example, if an officer responds to an assault call for service involving a husband and wife, the officer can choose either to make an arrest or to have the aggressor leave the scene to avoid further problems.[33] Thus, if an officer makes an arrest, the call for service will be classified as an assault report; however, if the officer chooses not to make an arrest, the call for service will be classified as a domestic disturbance (an argument among the individuals involved).[34] Consequently, officers have discretion when either pulling over a motorist or responding to a call for service.

However, discretion does not exist when an officer encounters undocumented immigrants during a call for service, because officers have been led to believe that such a call is outside the norm. Officers have little autonomy when responding to calls for service that involve federal immigration law issues and are expected to notify immigration enforcement authorities to resolve the issue, since it is an immigration issue. The following real-life example illustrates the intense pressure placed on police officers to notify the USBP when officers encounter undocumented immigrants.

One day while working the evening shift, Deputy Espolon and I were dispatched to an unknown 911 call for service.[35] I was told by dispatch that they had received about ten 911 calls; though dispatch did not have an exact location, they had narrowed it down to close proximity based on tracking the calls. We were dispatched to a rural area of the county that had four mobile homes adjacent to each other. Upon arrival, I contacted a female who lived in one of the mobile homes. I asked her if anything suspicious had happened at the location. She said that everything was fine, and when I asked her about the owners of the other three mobile homes, she said that two were vacant and that the owner of the other mobile home was at work. I checked the other mobile home and could not contact anyone at the residence. I then walked over to the other two mobile homes, which appeared as if they were unoccupied. Tall weeds and tall grass surrounded the two vacant-looking mobile homes. As I approached one of the mobile homes on the west side (the east side was the front entrance), I saw a male exit the mobile home through a window on the north side and then run away southward into an open field. I figured something suspicious was going on at the location and walked to the other side to tell Deputy Espolon what I had just witnessed.

He told me, "Yeah, I think it's a stash house!" He knocked on the front door of the mobile home, but no one answered the door. After knocking, he peeked inside the mobile home through the southside bedroom window. As I stood guard on the north side of the mobile home, Deputy Espolon screamed at me, "Hey, hey, Gamino! Yeah, it's a stash house! I can see several mojankers inside!" A man eventually opened the door and allowed us inside.

While I was inside, I noticed several other people sitting down on the floor of the dilapidated mobile home. I also noticed that the mobile home had no furniture and that there were two 120-quart ice chests in the kitchen area. All the individuals inside notified us that they were undocumented immigrants from Latin America (Mexico, El Salvador, Ecuador, and Nicaragua).[36] I then asked them if anyone had called 911, and they all said no. I also asked them if anyone had been assaulted or was a victim of any type of crime. Again, they replied no.

As part of the normal socialized and expected routine, I told Deputy Espolon that I was going to let dispatch know that there were several immigrants inside the stash house so that dispatch could notify the USBP to come to our location. He stayed inside the mobile home with the immigrants while I walked back to my patrol car to use the car radio (my portable radio was not transmitting properly). I notified dispatch, "Status 10-4, it's just a stash house. Go ahead and notify BP."

Dispatch replied that they were going to advise the USBP to respond to my location, but they needed to know how many immigrants were at the location so that USBP agents could know what type of vehicle to take to the scene.[37] I radioed Deputy Espolon and asked him to get an exact number of the immigrants in-side the mobile home. He notified me that there were four women and ten men. I then told dispatch the number of immigrants inside the mobile home, and they advised me that USBP agents were on the way to the location, but dispatch did not provide an estimated time of arrival.[38] After notifying dispatch of the number of immigrants, I walked back to the mobile home (about ten to fifteen minutes had elapsed since my arrival), but then I thought, Damn, what have I done? There was no need for me to request BP. They were all fine, and if BP comes out here, they're going to get deported. I walked back inside the mobile home and told Deputy Espolon that USBP had been notified but had not provided an estimated time of arrival.

As I waited inside the mobile home, I began thinking of how to cancel USBP from coming to the scene, all while I was conversing with the immigrants about their journey and their destination. Luckily for me, the dispatcher called me while I was trying to figure out how to solve my dilemma and asked if I had seen anyone running from the location, because the dispatcher was still receiving the 911 phone calls, except according to their map, the calls were being made from a location sev-eral streets west of our current location. I notified the dispatcher that I had seen an individual running from the location as I arrived at the scene and that I would call my supervisor to make him aware of the situation.

After ending the phone call, I told Deputy Espolon that we should leave, since the 911 calls were still being received at the police department and not being made from anyone at our location. He replied apprehensively, "Uh, uh, I don't know, Gamino. I'd call Sarge if I was you before taking off from here." I quickly realized that this was my opportunity to deter USBP agents from coming to the location.

I walked outside and called Sergeant Aviar, my patrol shift supervisor, and in-formed him of the details of the call for service. I let him know that I was going to have the dispatcher tell the USBP to disregard the request to come to the location because everything was fine with the immigrants, and no one had called 911 from the mobile home. He told me that Deputy Espolon and I could leave the location to find the 911 caller, but before we left we needed to "let dispatch know that the mojankers are still going to be at the mobile home so they [USBP] can go and get them later on if they want."

I told him that I would go ahead and do that. However, my intention all along was to find a way to keep USBP agents from being dispatched to my location. After talking with Sergeant Aviar, I walked back inside the mobile home and told Dep-uty Espolon that Sergeant Aviar said we could leave so that we could locate the 911 caller. The immigrants appeared nervous as I talked with Deputy Espolon and just kept looking down at the floor. I then told the immigrants in Spanish, "Look, we do not work for Immigration; therefore, you are free to go if you want." They said they had been there for about three days and that the human smuggler would bring them food only once a day. They were not allowed to go outside because they had been told by their human smuggler that if they were seen outside, the USBP was going to be notified so that they could get deported.

I told them that we were not immigration officials and that I was going to notify the dispatcher to cancel the USBP. I then said it was up to them if they wanted to stay there but that more than likely the location was "burned" because the USBP had been informed that the location had immigrants.[39] The immigrants sighed with relief when I explained to them that they could leave the mobile home (not that they had been detained to begin with).

At this point, one male stood up, walked up to me, interlocked his hands in front of his chest, and stated in Spanish, "Thank you, sir, thank you, sir, thank you very much!" He patted me on my back, and I told him there was no need to thank me. He said, "You don't know how happy I am. I just come here to the United States to work to provide for my family. I'm not here to do anything bad."

Another male stated ecstatically in Spanish, "Thank you, sir. Thank you, sir! May God bless you!" I told him there was no need to thank me because I understood their plight and hoped they reached their final destination. Everyone inside continued thanking me and expressed how thankful they were that they would not get deported.

Another male told me in Spanish, "Thank you, sir, for not deporting us!" I then said in Spanish, "May God bless you on your journey, and may you arrive well at your destination." I told the immigrants that we were going to leave but that there was no guarantee the USBP was not going to come to the location, so if they decided to stay at the mobile home, it was at their own risk.

Deputy Espolon just stood there next to me as I talked with the immigrants and said nothing. When we walked back to our patrol cars, all he said regarding the situation was, "Poor people." I am sure he was indifferent toward the undocumented immigrants and did not say much because he clearly knew my stance on the situation. As I drove away from the mobile home, I advised the dispatcher to have the USBP disregard the request to come to the call.

The dispatcher seemed surprised at my request and stated, "Umm, 10-9, 17 Adam 62? Just verifying, you're requesting to have BP disregard?"[40] I notified the dispatcher that I did not need USBP anymore at my location. The dispatcher said they were going to call USBP to have them cancel. Deputy Espolon and I searched the other area that the dispatcher had said the 911 calls were coming from. We searched the area for several minutes and could not find anything. Deputy Espolon and I then drove away from the location. As I left, Sergeant Ontario asked me via radio, "17 Adam 62, what's your 20?"[41] I told him I had barely left the location, and he advised me to wait where I was until he arrived.

Shortly thereafter, Sergeant Ontario arrived at the location, and while he was inside his patrol car, he asked in an excited tone, "Hey, Gamino, uh, so where's the stash house?" (it was farther east from there) and "Why did you cancel Border Patrol?" I explained that I had done so because the immigrants in the stash house had not been injured or victimized. He responded, "Well, you shouldn't have canceled Border Patrol!" I then advised him that I had already notified Sergeant Aviar that I was going to cancel USBP. I told him that while I was at the location, we were still receiving an unknown 911 phone call from a nearby location, so obviously those immigrants we were talking to at the mobile home did not have anything to do with the unknown 911 call. He then told me that if I had already notified Sergeant Aviar about canceling USBP, that it was fine. However, he said that he found it odd that I canceled USBP if the mobile home was a stash house, knowing that USBP is responsible for those types of calls for service.

I told Sergeant Ontario that I knew immigration enforcement was USBP's responsibility but that the reason for us responding to the location was regarding a 911 call that none of the immigrants we encountered had made; therefore, we needed to leave the location to locate the 911 caller. He said fiercely, "Just for future reference, don't cancel Border Patrol!" Sergeant Ontario then called the dispatcher and asked them to notify USBP to respond back to the mobile home (stash house). He told the dispatcher that we would not be at the location but that the immigrants were still at the mobile home. The dispatcher advised him that they were going to notify USBP to respond again to the mobile home.

That vignette illustrates the intense social pressure placed on patrol officers when responding to calls for service that involve undocumented immigrants. When I discovered that this call for service dealt with undocumented immigrants, my initial response was to have the USBP respond to my location, since it was a federal immigration law issue. As evidenced by my initial reaction to have USBP agents dispatched to my location, I and my fellow officers were socialized into having USBP respond to our call as a method of resolving a call for service involving undocumented immigrants.

Another thing worth noting from this vignette is the dispatcher's surprised reaction to my request to have USBP canceled. I had to reiterate to the dispatcher that, indeed, I did not want USBP to be dispatched to my call for service. However, Sergeant Ontario later overrode my cancellation and still had USBP respond to the call for service, even though I had already notified and gotten approval from Sergeant Aviar to cancel USBP. As mentioned earlier, there is no official written agreement between the USBP and the DMCSO indicating that the sheriff's office has the authority to enforce federal immigration law. The tacit enforcement is just another aspect of the socialization process and institutional practice within the sheriff's office. Officers are socialized into thinking that they need to notify the USBP to come to the officers' call for service whenever it entails undocumented immigrants, and officers are also expected to notify the USBP since a call could involve federal immigration law.

I too was susceptible to this socialization process, as evidenced by the above illustration. It was obviously not the first time I had responded to a call for service involving undocumented immigrants at a stash house. However, in all honesty, I distinctly remember that I automatically notified the dispatcher to call the USBP because it was just another one of many stash house calls for service that I encountered, and I was trying to close out the call and move on to the next item on the laundry list of calls for service that I had to respond to that day. As soon as I realized what I had done, I knew that I quickly needed to find a way to cancel the USBP. However, Deputy Espolon's insistence that I call Sergeant Aviar to inform him that I wanted to cancel the USBP, the dispatcher's insistence that I confirm that I wanted to cancel the USBP, and Sergeant Ontario's request to have the USBP sent to the mobile home even after I canceled my request demonstrates the lack of autonomy an officer has when handling a call for service that involves undocumented immigrants. From dispatchers to patrol officers (even supervisors), police are socialized into thinking they need to request the USBP at all calls for service that deal with undocumented immigrants. Aside from socialization, the frequent collaboration among federal, state, and local law enforcement agencies reinforces the expected institutional practice of calling the USBP to resolve incidents related to federal immigration law, such as undocumented immigrants being held at a stash house. Thus, this process of asking USBP to resolve calls for service in the borderlands that are related to federal immigration law exemplifies one component of what I argue is a distinct method of policing on the U.S.-Mexico border: Constitution-free policing.

SOCIALIZATION THROUGHOUT THE YEARS

As a Latino who has lived most of my life on the U.S.-Mexico border, I was socialized to believe that there was nothing wrong with racializing coracials/coethnics as foreigners. My recollections as an adolescent and my examples as a police officer in the DMCSO have taught me that immigrants are racialized based on certain characteristics.

While I attended high school, students racialized each other based on certain features, such as attire, the way one spoke, music genre preference, and sport of preference. My socialization with the racialization process continued as I began my career as a police officer. Some of the police officers in the Le Grand Police Department racialized immigrants through using racialized terminology, as evidenced by the term "illegals." Nonetheless, racialization was not limited to the terminology used, for it also entailed racialized police practices based on immigration status, that is, Constitution-free policing.

As noted in the two service call examples, officers enforced federal immigration law by having undocumented immigrants deported. The immigrants did not have any constitutional protection in the form of the Fourth Amendment and were ultimately deported. Constitution-free policing ensures that police on the U.S.-Mexico border can have anyone deported at their discretion by relying on assistance from the USBP because of the one-hundred-mile geographical immigration enforcement authority of USBP. This racialized police practice was part of my socialization as a police officer in South Texas while I worked for both the Le Grand Police Department and the DMCSO. It has also been accepted as a legitimate and unquestioned institutional practice. Moreover, throughout the years, I was socialized into thinking that it was fine for immigrants to be racialized as illegals, illegal aliens, mojos, or mojankers, even by fellow coracials/coethnics. As a police officer, I was also socialized into thinking that the terminology used to racialize immigrants is acceptable and even into accepting racialized institutional police practices, such as having an immigrant detained and deported based on an undocumented immigration status.

BATTLE OF THE HABITUS: THE DIVIDED SELF

Because I was a full participant in this research, I had to navigate my roles as both an academic and a police officer respectfully. This process is best contextualized through Pierre Bourdieu's theoretical concept of habitus, which he defines as "a system of lasting, transposable dispositions which, integrating past experiences, functions at every moment as a matrix of perceptions, appreciations, and actions."[42] Everything I experienced as a sociology graduate student, such as my academic training, influenced the creation of my academic habitus; similarly, my socialization and experiences as a police officer throughout the years influenced the creation of my police officer habitus.

Bourdieu further noted, "The habitus could be considered as a subjective but not individual system of internalized structures, schemes of perception, conception, and action common to all members of the same group or class."[43] Essentially, according to Jay MacLeod, the habitus comprises "the attitudes, beliefs, and experiences of those inhabiting one's social world."[44] One issue I had to cope with while I worked as a police officer dealt with everyday police practices involving immigrants. Issues such as racialized terminology used to refer to immigrants and racialized police practices during calls for service set the stage for the battle of my habitus.

MacLeod has also noted, "The habitus engenders attitudes and conduct that enable objective social structures to succeed in reproducing themselves."[45] The social structure within both police departments I worked for facilitated the racialization process with regard to undocumented immigrants by using racialized terminology and racialized police practices. This process filters down to a police officer such as myself situated in my habitus because of my socialization within the department. In response to the objective structure, as evidenced by the vignette in which I canceled USBP from answering my call, USBP was still dispatched to my location, which ultimately reinforced the racialized institutional police practice of immigration enforcement in the borderlands. I argue that such practice represents a distinct method of policing on the U.S.-Mexico border: Constitution-free policing.

Because of racialized terminology used in the police department and racialized police practices, I was in a constant battle with my academic habitus and police officer habitus, and thus I constituted a divided self. MacLeod argues, "[The] habitus functions as a regulator between individuals and their external world, between human agency and social structure."[46] Even though I was a police officer like my colleagues, my academic habitus enabled me to remember my researcher role.

As previously stated, little dissent existed among police officers in both police departments when referring to immigrants in general. Immigrants were frequently referred to with racialized terminology. In addition to using racialized terminology, police officers at both departments were socialized into thinking that it was necessary and acceptable to have USBP respond to calls for service at the officers' discretion. Obviously, my familiarity with the racialization process differed from when I was a Le Grand police officer to when I was a deputy for the DMCSO. I had formal graduate academic training when I worked as a deputy because of my graduate student status with Texas A&M University.

Besides the difference in my educational background when I worked at both police departments, both departments differ in regard to the communities they serve. The Le Grand Police Department serves the local residents of an urbanized area, whereas the sheriff's office serves residents of Del Monte County, which is mostly rural. Le Grand lies within Del Monte County. Most individuals who reside in rural Del Monte County are mixed-status families. Thus, as a deputy sheriff for Del Monte County, I encountered immigrants more often than when I was a police officer for Le Grand. Immigrants were also more frequently discussed when I worked for DMCSO than when I worked for Le Grand PD because a large portion of the local immigrant community resides in rural Del Monte County; that is, most immigrants served by the DMCSO resided in colonias. In addition, as a deputy sheriff, I encountered far more calls for service involving stash houses than when I worked as a police officer for Le Grand.

As a police officer, I experienced constant conflict between my academic habitus and police officer habitus due to the socialized structure within the police department to conform to racialized terminology and racialized institutional police practices. My academic habitus was in constant battle with my police officer habitus throughout my research and even after because it kept me from conforming to the social structure within the department, thus creating a divided self.[47] My police officer habitus enabled me to carry out my daily work routines as a police officer, but my academic habitus intervened when my daily work routines involved the immigrant population. Even though my academic habitus allowed me to critically analyze and, to a certain extent, resist racialized institutional police practices, I was often a participant in racialized police practices concerning immigration enforcement, as will be evidenced in chapters 3 and 4. Nonetheless, I navigated the conflicting perspectives between my police officer habitus and academic habitus by relying on my own social history of being a Mexican American raised in the borderlands.

PERSONAL HABITUS: RESISTANCE TO THE STRUCTURE

Both my academic habitus and my police officer habitus played important parts in influencing the way I coped with the racialization process. As an academic, I have become familiar with this concept and its function. As a police officer, I have learned how this concept is carried out in a daily work routine through either conversations or calls for service. However, besides these two competing habitus, the overarching and superseding habitus that has influenced my comprehension of racialization practices—specifically, my open-mindedness toward immigrants—is my personal working-class habitus. This habitus results from my own personal experiences through socialization at home and my prior work experience in labor-intensive jobs. Both of my parents were Mexican immigrants, and thus at a young age I was socialized to have a positive image of immigrants, including undocumented immigrants. I learned from my family members about the discrimination they endured as immigrants in the United States.

My personal working-class habitus regarding undocumented immigrants is also influenced by my experiences working in labor-intensive jobs. As a teenager, I spent one summer working as a farmworker in the cornfields of Illinois, detasseling corn.[48] Because of this experience, I gained greater appreciation and respect for individuals who work daily as farmworkers across the United States. Several years later, when I turned eighteen and could legally work in a factory, I continued my labor-intensive employment by working in a local vegetable canning factory in Illinois. I worked at this factory for several years during my summer breaks while I attended college. Several of my coworkers at this facility were immigrants from Mexico. I worked six days a week (sometimes seven days) for twelve hours daily by working the second shift (7:00 p.m. to 7:00 a.m.). As hard as it was and as much as I dreaded going to work every day, I can honestly say that job was a true blessing in disguise. The life lessons I learned from that employment experience shaped me into the person I am today.

During those long workdays, I had lengthy conversations with my coworkers and learned about the hardships of their migration journey and their reasons for coming to the United States. Several immigrants I worked with always stressed that I should take advantage of being a U.S.-born citizen. They told me not to take my U.S. citizenship for granted and to become a productive member of society. As a result of working alongside immigrants, I realized that their stories were similar to my family members' stories, and their journey to the United States was for self-improvement.

Based on my personal experiences with my parents' immigration status and my labor-intensive work experience alongside immigrants, I was socialized to believe that immigrants are hardworking individuals whose primary purpose in coming to the United States is to live a productive and prosperous life. Therefore, these experiences impacted my working-class habitus, which in turn influenced my acceptance of immigrants. In sum, similar to my academic habitus, my personal habitus helped me resist the use of racialized terminology and to question and resist whenever I could racialized practices as a police officer, even though I was a member of that social structure.

CHAPTER 3

Immigrant
Vulnerabilities in
the Borderlands

This chapter sheds light on those individuals most severely impacted by the enforcement of the racial contract in the U.S.-Mexico borderlands: undocumented Latino immigrants. My conversations with these immigrants revealed the motivating factors that bring them to the United States and the hardships they experienced in their migration to the United States. This chapter provides insights I have gained from some of the many conversations I had with apprehended, detained, and undocumented Latino-origin immigrants who realized, as we interacted during the call for service, that their journey into the United States was at an end. These conversations illustrate the immigrants' victimization, whether by psychological, physical, or sexual abuse. The following section of the chapter addresses my encounters with Central American mothers and unaccompanied children who crossed into the RGV during what was known as a humanitarian crisis.[1]

The Central American Humanitarian Crisis of 2014

One Wednesday morning while on routine patrol, I was dispatched to a suspicious circumstances call for service regarding a female who was lying beside a major thoroughfare of the county. As I drove the road, I did not detect anything abnormal at first, but upon further inspection, I observed under a tree about ten yards from the roadway a female lying on her right side, holding a sports drink in a thirty-two-ounce plastic bottle. I parked on the side of the road and spoke with the female, who was visibly pregnant. I asked the female, Ester, if she needed medical attention, but she declined. Ester told me that she was a twenty-one-year-old immigrant from Honduras who had crossed the Rio Grande on Sunday with a large group of immigrants. After they crossed, she and the group were then taken to an unknown location (a stash house) until they were able to escape. Ester said that the human smugglers at the location were violent with everyone inside.

Ester said everyone at the stash house was treated badly by the caretakers of the stash house but that she was spared bad treatment due to her pregnancy. Although she was not mistreated, she still feared for her safety because of the caretakers' abusive practices. She then said in Spanish, "The coyotes slapped the females who did not want to have sex with them. The men were punched and kicked by the coyotes for no reason." I then asked her if she knew the location of the stash house where she had been held, to which she replied no.

Ester told me that on Sunday night, she and some of the immigrants were able to escape from the stash house as the coyotes slept. They walked all day Monday through a desolate area without any particular destination in mind. The only thing certain was that they were going to continue walking northward with the hope that they would eventually get help from someone. As they walked on Monday evening, she injured her right ankle and was left behind by the group. They told her that it was best for her just to stay in the area and seek help from a motorist. Ester told me that even though she was injured and separated from her group, she felt it was necessary for her to continue walking as long as she could. When her injury became more debilitating, she decided to walk closer to the road so she could be helped by a motorist. Ester then said that she had not eaten anything in the past two days, but several minutes before our encounter, a male stopped by the side of the road and gave her some food and drink. The male also told her that he was going to call the police so she could get help.

Ester told me that she did not want medical attention and wanted to go back home. I advised the dispatcher to have USBP respond to my location to take custody of Ester. I then helped Ester get up from the ground and had her wait inside the back of my patrol car until USBP arrived to take custody of her. As we waited, we talked for a bit about her migration experience and her destination. Ester told me she had paid $3,500 to be brought to the United States from Honduras, and her destination was New York. She wanted to be reunited with her father and sisters in New York since she had not seen them in several years. She also planned to work in New York and send money back home to Honduras to help her other family members financially. She then said, "Things are bad in Honduras, and there is no hope for a good future."

Ester told me that she wished people in the United States would change their perspective about immigrants, because North Americans had no understanding of the hardships Central Americans were fleeing from in hopes of a better future in the United States: "If only you all would put yourselves in our shoes [for] one day, you would know that we are fleeing to the United States for a better life. . . . No one would like to leave their home country, but when you have no other option, what are you to do?" (paraphrased from field notes).

Ester and I continued our conversation while we waited for the USBP agents to arrive. After several minutes, two uniformed USBP agents arrived and took custody of Ester. They notified me that they were going to take her to the hospital to treat her injuries and check her health before processing her at the USBP station. I talked with them for a while longer and then left. I never saw Ester again, the same experience I had with every other undocumented immigrant I encountered during my routine work activities who were taken into USBP custody. However, through my conversations with immigration officials during this particular time period when the RGV experienced an influx of Central American mothers and unaccompanied children, I learned that some of the immigrants were eventually reunited with relatives currently residing in the United States.

The following vignette details my interaction with an unaccompanied minor from Central America. One drizzly Sunday morning as I conducted my routine patrol, I was flagged down by an adolescent male standing on the roadway. I drove up to the teen, who notified me that he was an immigrant from El Salvador who had crossed into the United States on Friday evening and wanted help. I told the teen, Alfonso, in Spanish that I was not an immigration official and that it was completely his decision whether to turn himself in to immigration authorities. He told me that he was tired and just wanted to go back home. He said in Spanish, "I'm tired, sir. I just want to go back home to El Salvador to be with my family." I told Alfonso that I was going to have USBP respond to the location to take custody of him. I then placed Alfonso in my patrol car and advised the dispatch center to have USBP agents respond to my location. Shortly thereafter, I asked Alfonso if he had eaten. He replied no.

I drove to a nearby gas station and notified the dispatcher of my new location so that USBP could be directed there instead. I exited my patrol car and opened the rear door, and together we walked inside the gas station. Alfonso's pants from the knees down were wet and muddy, including his shoes, and he looked very timid and shy as we walked inside the store. We drew some bemused stares from the patrons outside the store, and once we were inside, the stares continued as we made our way through the store. I told Alfonso to get something to drink. As he stared at the refrigerator with the beverages, he asked if he could get whatever drink he wanted. I replied, "Of course. Get any drink you want."

Alfonso replied, "I'm going to get Sprite. I love Sprite." We both smiled at his comment. We then walked to the warm meal counter, where the cooks were making breakfast tacos. We stood in line, and I again noticed that the customers in line, along with the others milling around in the store, gave us perplexed looks while Alfonso and I chatted. Once it was our turn to order, I told Alfonso to choose whatever he wanted to eat from the various dishes on display. He peeked through the glass window at the dishes and asked the cook questions about the different foods. He ultimately chose a barbacoa taco and two chorizo and egg tacos. After purchasing the food, we walked outside, and Alfonso got back in the rear seat of my patrol car.

While we waited for USBP agents to arrive at the location, we talked about his migration experience, and Alfonso ate his food. He seemed fairly calm, given the circumstances. Alfonso told me that his destination was South Carolina because he had an uncle who lived and worked there. He told me that he was the oldest of three boys and wanted to come to the United States to help his family make ends meet. A coyote wanted to charge his family $3,000 to transport Alfonso into the United States, but they did not have the total amount, so he decided to venture out to the United States on his own. He said, "My family didn't have all of the money, so I decided to come out on my own. I didn't want my family to die of hunger. . . . It is very dangerous over there [El Salvador], and that is also another reason why I wanted to come to the United States." Alfonso came with a group of individuals from his hometown without relying on a coyote. He also told me that several women were sexually assaulted on the journey into the United States, and the men were physically assaulted: "Some of the women were raped along the way. I feel bad for them, because that is something they went through just to cross over here. . . . I also saw some of the men along the way get beat up. The men were kicked during our journey over here."

Alfonso told me that even though he was not sure whether he was going to be deported back to El Salvador, he was going to make another attempt to get into the United States.[2] He said there was no hope for him if he stayed in El Salvador, since his family did not have money to pay for college after he graduated from high school. We continued talking about his plans for the future, and he mentioned that he wanted to work in construction here in the United States because he heard that it was a well-paid profession. He told me that his ultimate goal was to purchase a brand-new home for his parents in El Salvador.

After several minutes of conversation, a USBP agent pulled up next to us at the gas station to take custody of Alfonso, who asked me what he should do with the taco that he had not eaten. I advised him to take it with him so he could eat it later. I ushered him out of the rear of the patrol car and told him to wait by the passenger door. I spoke with the USBP agent, who informed me that he was there to take custody of Alfonso.

The USBP agent instructed Alfonso to stand by the USBP vehicle so the agent could search him. As Alfonso walked toward the USBP agent while holding the plastic bag with his taco and plastic bottle of Sprite, the USBP agent grabbed the bag and threw it onto the trunk of my patrol car, then ordered Alfonso in Spanish, "Hands up! Turn around and spread your legs!" He then searched Alfonso and placed him in the rear of the USBP vehicle. I asked the USBP agent if Alfonso could take the food with him, but the USBP agent refused to allow it because he said Alfonso would be fed later after being processed. After the USBP agent and I exchanged information with each other, both of us left.[3]

Stash Houses: Insight into the Migration Experience

This section covers my conversations with some immigrants I encountered at stash house calls for service. One morning while on routine patrol, I was dispatched to back up Deputy Salomón, who had responded to a call for service at a stash house where about thirty immigrants were being held against their will. Lieutenant Obrero also responded and had dispatch call USBP to see if they were going to respond to the location, since there were no available OPSG units available to respond.[4] Before we entered the property, Lieutenant Obrero was notified that USBP—along with an ICE agent—intended to respond. Deputy Salomón made a big production of cinching up his police duty belt and stated, "Might as well start tightening up this belt. I'm getting ready to run."

I asked him why he was preparing to run if the call was in reference to a stash house, to which he replied, "Well, it's a stash house with illegals. If the illegals start running, I'm going to start running after them." I, however, responded that if the immigrants ran from the location, I was not going to run after them. We all got back into our patrol cars and drove down the long, dirt-road driveway of the property. Not far onto the property, I observed a mobile home and a small vehicle parked beside it. I stood by the rear of the mobile home as Deputy Salomón and Lieutenant Obrero stood by the front door. Deputy Salomón then stated in Spanish, "Police! Police! Open the door!" As soon as Deputy Salomón announced our presence, I heard a lot of footsteps inside rushing about in a hurried manner as if the individuals inside were darting from one room to the next.

I also heard the individuals inside talking with each other as Deputy Salomón continued commanding someone to open the front door. All of a sudden, someone opened the window of a rear bedroom, and three men exited the window and ran from the location. I just stood there as the three men ran from the location. Shortly thereafter, another man peeked out of the window and observed me standing behind the mobile home. The man did not jump out of the window; instead, he remained inside the mobile home, along with all the other individuals.

Deputy Salomón screamed in Spanish, "Don't move! Don't move!" I walked to the front door and entered the mobile home as Deputy Salomón and Lieutenant Obrero questioned the people in the living room. The entire mobile home was unfurnished, and thirty to forty immigrants were either sitting in the living room or walking around inside the mobile home. I walked to the rear of the house and spoke with a Mexican immigrant named Alberto. I advised him to tell everyone else to gather their belongings, because USBP was on the way. Alberto asked me what was going to happen to all of them, so I notified him that USBP was going to take custody of them.

A woman named Ingrid standing nearby began crying intensely because she overheard me telling Alberto that they were more than likely going to be deported. Ingrid then hugged a woman standing near her, and both continued to cry uncontrollably. Alberto and I then began conversing with each other. He told me that his destination was Alabama because he was going to join his brother, who lived and worked at a meatpacking facility in that state. He also told me that he paid a coyote $2,500 to help him cross the border into the United States.

As I talked with Alberto, Ingrid again confirmed with me that they were going to be deported. Ingrid placed her face in her hands, shook her head from side to side, and said in Spanish, "No! No! I don't want to go back! There is nothing for me over there!" (She was referring to El Salvador.) I tried my best to console Ingrid as I spoke with her. She told me that although she felt like running away from the location, she had no other choice but to stay at the mobile home. The coyote was not currently at the mobile home, so she had no guide to lead her north into the interior of the United States. Ingrid had paid a coyote $4,000 to cross into the United States, and her destination was Houston, because she had family members living there. After Ingrid finished speaking with me, she walked away and hugged another woman who was also visibly upset about the situation and crying.

I spoke with another immigrant, a man named Hector, from El Salvador who asked if I could let them go. I told him that as much as I wished that they were free to go, my colleague (Deputy Salomón as the primary officer) and my supervisor (Lieutenant Obrero) would more than likely not allow them to leave the mobile home. I conveyed to those immigrants standing around me that I empathized with them and understood their plight. I tried my best to brighten the circumstances, given that everyone was sad and dejected. I told them that even though they had been unsuccessful in this attempt, they were at least alive and could try again at a later time. I shared that several days prior to my interaction with them, I responded to a call for service in which a male immigrant had drowned trying to swim across the Rio Grande. I knew my words rang hollow to some, but my hope was to try and lift their spirits by reminding them that at least they had not perished on their migration journey to the United States, even though they were going to be deported by the USBP.

Hector told me that they were not criminals and shared with me his migration experience. Hector broke down in tears and, while brushing them from his cheek, said in Spanish, "We're not criminals. I'm not here to hurt anyone." He then told me that the reason for him coming to the United States was to provide for his family back home, since he was the oldest of his siblings and the sole provider for them. His mom was also terminally ill, and her illness served as another motivating factor, since he wanted to work in the United States to pay for his mother's medical treatment.

Another immigrant nearby, Ezekiel, asked how we, the police, had found the location. I told Ezekiel that someone had called from the mobile home indicating that they were being held against their will. Ezekiel told me that he highly doubted someone from their location had called the police. I replied that as odd as it might seem to him, the only reason we responded to the location was because someone had called from there asking for our assistance.[5]

After I had talked with the immigrants for several minutes, uniformed USBP agents arrived at the location, as did a white bus. Lieutenant Obrero then had Deputy Salomón and me escort the immigrants out of the mobile home and into the front yard. The immigrants were told to sit on the ground and remove their shoelaces while the USBP agents questioned them. While the immigrants were being questioned, Deputy Salomón grabbed a bandana with a U.S. flag pattern from his back pocket and wiped the glistening sweat from his face as we stood in front of the immigrants who were being processed by the USBP agents. He stated, "Fuck, it's so damn hot out here, Gamino." I did not respond. Instead, since I was Deputy Salomón's backup officer, I left the scene while the immigrants were being processed.

At another stash house call for service, the suspected human smuggler was located at the stash house. Here is a description of what transpired at that call.

One October morning around 4:00 a.m., while I was working the graveyard shift, Deputy Dorantes and I were dispatched to a call for service that involved someone being held against their will. The sheriff's office had received a phone call from an unknown individual indicating he was an undocumented immigrant from Guatemala who had escaped from a stash house and needed help. Sergeant Aquino also responded to the call to assist us in the search for the 911 caller. We drove around the neighborhood for several minutes until we were waved down by the 911 caller. I made contact with the man, Renan, who was breathing heavily and sweating as he spoke with me.

Renan stated that he and other immigrants had been housed inside a storage shed for a couple of days. He said that several minutes prior to our encounter, the coyotes were going to take them from the location, and as they were being placed inside the vehicle, he ran away from the property to go seek help. Renan stated that as he ran away, the coyotes threatened that they were going to harm him if he did not stop running. He ignored their threats and continued running in search of help. I then asked him if he knew where the property was located, to which he replied in the affirmative. I placed Renan in my patrol car and had him direct me to the location of the stash house. Once we arrived at the location, Deputy Dorantes and Sergeant Aquino walked onto the property to make contact with the owner.

I stood by my patrol car as Deputy Dorantes and Sergeant Aquino walked onto the property, which included a mobile home and a large wooden shed located in the rear. While Deputy Dorantes and Sergeant Aquino made contact with the property owner, I spoke with Renan about his migration experience. Renan told me that they were only fed twice a day while at the shed, but that was not the worst part of their experience. He said that at the previous location they were held, the female immigrants suffered more than the men while being held there. He stated in Spanish, "In the morning they give us slices of white sandwich bread to eat, and at night they feed us sandwiches. . . . That's not the worst part of being in there [in the shed]. At the other location we were before coming here, the coyotes raped the women." I then asked him if he had any general idea of the previous location he was at, to which he replied that he did not know but was sure it was nowhere close to our current location. He then said, "When they [the coyotes] brought us here, they drove for a while before getting here and had us blindfolded." Renan stated that at their previous location, the women would be taken out of the stash house for several minutes, sexually assaulted by the coyotes, and then returned to the stash house.

Renan felt hopeless because he, along with the other male immigrants, was not able to prevent the women from getting raped. Renan said, "Each time they [the coyotes] walked in and took a woman out, we knew she was going to get raped." Renan stated that luckily during the time period they had been held at this most recent shed, no woman was raped.

I asked him if he could remember anything in particular about the previous stash house at which they were held, and he said that they were not allowed to go outside; thus he could not help with my inquiry. As I spoke with Renan, two uniformed USBP agents arrived at the location, and I told them that Deputy Dorantes and Sergeant Aquino were speaking with the property owner.

Several minutes later, Deputy Dorantes exited the house and told me that the other immigrants had been located. He said that they found the other "illegals" inside the shed, even though initially the property owner did not want to give them consent to search the shed. Once the USBP agents spoke to the property owner, he then complied with the request to have his property searched. I asked Deputy Dorantes if the property owner gave them a hard time, and Dorantes said, "Yeah. He didn't want to let us search, because last time his house was searched, they found several kilos of coke [cocaine] y se enchorizarron al vato [and they screwed over the guy]." I later asked him how the immigrants were doing, and he replied, "Están agüitados [They're sad], but they were just sitting down when we found them. . . . There's only about ten of them."

I repeated to Deputy Dorantes what Renan had said about the women being raped at the previous location, and he notified me that he would check into that further. After a short while, he returned to the property to obtain information from the immigrants. Renan and I spoke further, and after several minutes, Sergeant Aquino told me to escort Renan to the USBP van. As the USBP agents were placing the immigrants inside the van, Deputy Dorantes, Sergeant Aquino, and I spoke about the incident. Deputy Dorantes told me that the immigrants had notified him that they were not victimized while they were at the location but that some of the women had been raped at the previous location. I told Sergeant Aquino that we, the sheriff's office, should further investigate the issue. He replied, "It's their damn fault this happens to them. No one told them to come from their country over here. . . . Besides, they don't know where the previous stash house is located."[6] Visibly frustrated, I simply shook my head in disapproval; if my supervisor did not want to investigate the issue further, nothing else would be done. Such situations are usually seen as a federal immigration issue, since the sexual assault occurred within a stash house involving undocumented immigrants; therefore, the onus is placed on USBP and/or ICE to investigate the sexual assault further.

Sergeant Aquino then said, "The good thing is that the BP agents are going to look into this guy [the property owner] and the location further." They were going to forward the information about the property owner and the location to the USBP intel agents so they could investigate the human smuggling aspect further. Human smuggling is considered a state crime, but as is often the case, these incidents are always deferred to federal counterparts (i.e., the USBP and ICE), since the crime involved undocumented immigrants while they were held in a stash house.[7]

Random Encounters

One muggy summer evening while I was on routine patrol with Deputy Ravina, we were dispatched to a residence in a desolate rural area of the county. A woman named Sandra had called the sheriff's office to report that seven undocumented immigrants had entered her property asking for assistance. When we arrived at the residence, I observed several individuals sitting down in the front yard of Sandra's property. I spoke with a woman named Monica, who stated that prior to arriving at Sandra's house, they were at a stash house at an unknown location. Monica told me that she and the six other undocumented immigrants were placed inside a van and told by the coyote that they were going to be taken to a different stash house. The coyote had an AK-47 rifle and ordered them to lie on their stomachs in the van and not look up until after they had left the stash house. After several minutes of traveling, the coyote suddenly stopped the van and ordered them to get out. They complied with his demands and exited the van. Once they exited the van, they realized that they had been dropped off on a dirt road. The coyote drove away from the area, and they walked to an illuminated roadway in hopes that someone would eventually drive by and see them. Several vehicles drove by as they walked on the roadway, but none stopped to assist them. They ultimately walked to Sandra's house because it was the first house they came to on the street.

Monica divulged that she was not afraid of being caught by immigration authorities because at least the immigrants no longer had to deal with the violent conditions of the stash house. Sergeant Aviar arrived at the location while Deputy Ravina and I were speaking with the undocumented immigrants. Sergeant Aviar notified us that he had the dispatcher call the USBP to respond to the location to take custody of the undocumented immigrants. Monica told me that her destination was New Jersey and that some of the others were also headed northeast. Sandra provided water bottles, bags of potato chips, and hot dogs to the undocumented immigrants as we waited and continued questioning them.

I then spoke with Luis, who stated that they had been at the stash house for about a month; he described the stash house conditions to me. He told me in Spanish, "Some of us are from El Salvador, and others are from Guatemala, Honduras, and Mexico. . . . They would only feed us twice a day. In the morning we would eat a biscuit, and at night we ate a slice of pizza and drank a Coke." I asked him if they had been assaulted while at the stash house, and he informed me that they were not, but they were threatened on a daily basis. He told me that the coyotes threatened to hurt them if they tried to escape from the house. He then said, "We were all scared, because all of the coyotes always had AK-47s with them. . . . There was about thirty of us and about seven coyotes." Luis also told me that two of the coyotes would stay at the house during the night, while the other five would leave and return the next day.

Luis's destination was Washington, D.C., because he intended to join some of his family members who worked in restaurants in the Washington, D.C., area. The motivating factors that compelled him to leave El Salvador were violence and poverty. He said the MS-13 gang practically controlled everything in El Salvador, and he did not want to be one of their many victims. He then told me, "They recruit you, and if you refuse to join their gang, they will kill you."

As I spoke with Luis, a teenage boy named Juan joined our conversation and elaborated on his reasons for coming to the United States. Juan said he had a friend who worked as a delivery boy in El Salvador, but the friend was killed by the MS-13 gang for not paying a quota. Juan told me that his friend had a daily route, and as part of his daily routine, he had to pay the MS-13 gang a quota to travel through his delivery route. Juan said that the day his friend did not pay the MS-13 gang the daily quota, his friend was shot in broad daylight. Once Juan's parents found out what happened to his friend, they decided he should leave El Salvador and come to the United States to have more hope for his future. Juan's destination was Maryland.

Unfamiliar with law enforcement in El Salvador, I asked Luis about the police. Luis replied, "The country is controlled by the Maras [MS-13], and that's why we're all afraid of them. . . . If you live in El Salvador, you know who controls the streets."

After Juan shared his experience in El Salvador with me, an older Latina, Yingrid, spoke to me about her motive for leaving El Salvador. She told me that she owned a clothing store and that business was OK, but she had to close her business when she could no longer continue paying the quota to MS-13. Yingrid told me that the MS-13 gang increased their weekly quota to fifty dollars, and when she told them she could not afford that amount, they threatened to burn down her business. She averaged twenty to thirty dollars a week, so there was no possible way she could pay the quota. At the request of her daughter, Yingrid closed the store and decided to come to the United States to seek employment with her sister in

Los Angeles. I asked them how much they paid to cross into the United States; prices ranged between $3,000 and $6,000.[8]

Luis then said, "Imagine, Officer, there was about thirty of us at that house. Just do the math. At a minimum, the coyotes made about $90,000 off of us." When addressing the costs associated with crossing into the United States, each one confessed that it would be difficult to return to the United States, since they had already paid a lot of money for this unsuccessful attempt. They were disheartened because their families had paid so much money for them to cross into the United States, and the coyotes abandoned them on a rural road without fulfilling their promise of transporting the immigrants to their destinations.

I asked them if they knew the whereabouts of the other immigrants who were with them in the stash house. Juan stated that the other immigrants were also transported in vans and dropped off on the dirt road. He said that after everyone was dropped off, they split into separate groups and went their own way.

As I talked with them, OPSG deputies arrived at the location and questioned them about the other immigrants. After speaking with the immigrants, the OPSG deputies left the location in an attempt to find the other immigrant groups. As the OPSG deputies left, two detectives with the sheriff's office arrived at the location to speak with the immigrants. The detectives questioned the immigrants about their victimization while in the United States. Some of them told one of the detectives, Detective Briones, that their money and cell phones had been stolen while they were in the stash house. Detective Briones questioned them about the location of the stash house, but neither of the immigrants who had their property stolen were able to provide geographical information regarding the location of the stash house. Frustrated, Detective Briones told me, "Fuck, Gamino. That's the shitty thing about these incidents. Most of the time when they steal from these illegals, they [the immigrants] are never able to provide us with an exact location of the stash house. . . . They don't know where they're at."

I then asked what that meant for the investigation. That is, I wondered aloud if these types of investigations often went unsolved. Detective Briones told me that essentially these incidents are challenging to solve since it is difficult to determine the exact location of the crime scene. Undocumented immigrants are unfamiliar with the geographical area. Detective Briones continued talking to me about the complexities of trying to solve these types of cases until, several minutes later, two uniformed USBP agents arrived at the location in a fifteen-passenger van and questioned the immigrants. Deputy Ravina and I left the location once the immigrants were placed in the van.

Another illustration of the emotional toll of the migration experience for immigrants can be demonstrated by another incident that occurred during my police tenure. One cool evening while on routine patrol, I was dispatched to a closed gas station because someone had called the sheriff's office to report that there were seven males standing by the street who looked suspicious. When I arrived at the location, I spoke with the men, who advised me that they were undocumented immigrants and needed help. The men told me that for the past two weeks they had been detained at an abandoned mobile home with other undocumented immigrants, but then that day they had been taken from the home and dropped off by the coyote in a rural area. I asked them if they needed medical attention, and each replied no. They told me they had walked for several hours until they arrived at the gas station parking lot.

Sergeant Aviar arrived at the location as I spoke with the men and notified me that he had told the dispatcher to call USBP to respond to our location. One of the men told me that while they were at the stash house, the coyotes demanded more money from them. Once they received the money from their family members, the coyotes said that they would continue to take them northward into the United States. There were three immigrant women at the stash house as well, but they were left behind when the men were placed in the bed of a pickup. The coyote dropped the men off at an unknown location and left the area after commanding them to get out of the pickup.

The men were from Central America and Mexico. We spoke with each other as we waited for the USBP agents to arrive. José, who was from El Salvador, and Edwin, from Mexico, were the most talkative members of the group. Even though the mood was somber, José tried to make a joke out of the disheartening situation. He said in Spanish, "We saw you drive by the area and waved at you, but I guess you didn't see us. The one time we want to run into you all, it doesn't happen." We smiled at his comment. A food truck was parked nearby, and I asked them if they had eaten. Edwin stated that earlier in the day, they were fed a mayonnaise sandwich, but that for the past three days, they had not eaten anything. I pulled out my wallet and noticed that I did not have cash; I only had my debit card. I asked Sergeant Aviar to ask the food truck workers if they accepted debit cards. He replied, "Don't worry, Gamino. I have cash. I'll buy them some food." Sergeant Aviar told me that he was going to have the OPSG deputies respond to our call and then walked to the food truck to purchase food for the immigrants.

Near the gas station was a closed fruit stand that had several boxes of fruit outside its closed front door. The immigrants asked me if they could get some fruit from the discarded boxes, and I gave them the OK. They immediately walked over to the boxes and started quickly searching through the boxes of fruit to see what they could find to eat. I also walked over to see what the boxes contained, and I noticed that the boxes were filled with rotten oranges. It was no coincidence that those boxes had been discarded—they contained rotten fruit. Each immigrant quickly grabbed a rotten orange from the box, peeled it, and consumed it without caring that it was rotten. As they ate the oranges, I could not help but feel overwhelmed with empathy for what I was observing. If only people could witness what I was observing, they might have some compassion and empathy for undocumented immigrants. They did not care that the oranges contained visible green mold. The sheer desperation of not eating for several days was enough for the men to overlook the fact that they were consuming rotten food.

While they ate their oranges, we talked about their migration experience and their lives back home. Of the seven, five were fathers who left their families behind in their home countries. José told me that his house had burned down in El Salvador, and he envisioned himself working for five to ten years in the United States until he earned enough money to build another home in El Salvador. José told me that the violence in El Salvador was another motivating factor for him to come to the United States. He stated that the MS-13 gang made people live in constant fear and that he could not rely on local police for protection.

Sergeant Aviar notified me that the food was ready, and we all walked back to my patrol car. He then placed the bags of food on top of the hood, and we told each of the men to grab a bag. Each bag contained a hamburger, fries, and a soft drink. The men all grabbed a bag and ate their food as we continued talking with each other while waiting for USBP and OPSG deputies to arrive at the location. Sergeant Aviar walked back to his patrol car and waited inside because he wanted to review police reports.

After the men finished eating, I asked them what their vision was of the United States. Braulio's (a Salvadoran) eyes began to water when speaking of the United States. He said that he wanted to come to the United States to provide for his family. Suddenly, as he spoke, he walked away from us and squatted down behind my patrol car. The sound of his mournful weeping filled the air.

While looking at Braulio, Edwin stated in Spanish, "It's very tough coming to the North [El Norte]. Even when we crossed. A lot of times you feel down, but I try to keep our spirits up. . . . We have to think positive. From the outside, I show them I have a positive attitude, but from the inside, I'm dying of all the sadness" (paraphrased from field notes).

Edwin then said that aside from the hardship of their migration, what mattered most was that they were alive to see another day. I told him that I agreed and shared with them the stories of calls for service that I experienced in which undocumented immigrants perished on their journey to the United States.

Some told me that this was their first attempt to cross into the United States. One of the men told me that his family paid $8,000 to cross from El Salvador and be taken to Baltimore, and others said they paid anywhere between $2,500 and $7,000 for their crossing attempt.[9]

Deputy Ventura, who was working OPSG that day, eventually arrived at the location. Sergeant Aviar told him that he had also notified USBP to respond to the location, but he wanted Deputy Ventura to wait until USBP finished so he could claim the apprehension statistics. After speaking with Deputy Ventura, Sergeant Aviar left the location to resume his patrol duties while I prepared the immigrants for what to expect when USBP arrived at the location. I told them that depending on the USBP agent's demeanor, they more than likely were going to be transported by a rude and unsympathetic USBP agent. After we waited for several more minutes, the USBP agents finally arrived. Deputy Ventura and I spoke with one of the USBP agents about the immigrants and how they had been abandoned on the road by the coyote.

The USBP agent asked the men how they were doing and if they had eaten anything. At first, I thought he was actually concerned about their well-being, but as he continued talking with them, I realized that he was being condescending with them. He asked them in Spanish, "Have you all eaten?"

They replied, "No. Not until today."

He smirked, "OK. What do you say, guys? You guys ready to go eat?" (He clapped his hands with glee.) "We'll feed you tonight and then run into you again in a couple of days."

I asked the USBP agent what he meant by the comment about seeing them again in a couple of days. He replied, "It's like a revolving door, Deputy. We'll have to deal with these aliens again in a couple of days." The USBP agent asked me if any more immigrants were part of this group, and I told him there were three women who had been left behind at the unknown stash house location. He then said, "Oh, man. That's not good for them." He explained that he was more than sure the coyotes were going to do something bad to the female immigrants. The USBP agent and his partner then had the men remove their shoelaces from their shoes and began searching them. After a few more minutes, I left the location. The following section details my conversation with colleagues after this call for service and reveals an important theme my department noticed when responding to stash house calls for service.

Connecting the Dots: Human Smugglers and Stash Houses

When I returned to the police station to end my shift, I came across several officers in the roll call room. We spoke about the call I had gone on with Sergeant

Aviar earlier in the shift. Deputy Tapanes told me in a jocular tone, "What's up, Gamino? I heard you fed the mojankers." I told him that while we were at the call for service, it was actually Sergeant Aviar who purchased the food for the undocumented immigrants but that either way, we should provide food for them if we could.

Deputy Tapanes told me that when he encountered undocumented immigrants, he did not provide food for them. He said that he was wary of providing food for immigrants due to liability concerns. If they happened to choke on the food he provided them, he did not want to be held liable for them choking.

Deputy Archuleta also stated that he had liability concerns about providing food for undocumented immigrants he encountered. I told them, "I don't care about liability. I'm more concerned about being judged by the man upstairs. We're not eternal." After I said this, the mood became serious.

Lieutenant Obrero then chimed in, "Sí, Tapanes, tiene razón, Gamino [Yes, Tapanes, Gamino is right]. Es algo bueno que el hizo [It's something good that he did]. Angels come in different forms." The conversation then changed to immigrant victimization at stash houses and the rarity of solving those types of cases.

Sergeant Aviar shared with us a call for service he had with Deputy Salomón in which they were able to locate the coyote while at the stash house. The immigrants were able to identify the coyote. Sergeant Aviar stated, "At this call with [Deputy] Salomón, the mojankers were able to positively ID the smuggler, and I thought we were good to make an arrest." Sergeant Aviar told us that the detective unit also responded to the stash house to investigate the incident further. However, the detectives told him that they were not going to arrest the coyote. Sergeant Aviar then called the captain in charge of the detectives and told him that an arrest needed to be made, since the suspected human smuggler was at the stash house. He told us that the captain ordered him not to do anything regarding the arrest of the coyote and to refer the incident to USBP, since USBP was going to respond anyway to take custody of the undocumented immigrants.

Sergeant Aviar was upset, and the captain told him, "I already told you. It's not going anywhere!" Sergeant Aviar told us that no arrest was made of the coyote for human smuggling. As I previously mentioned when describing the call for service I had with Deputy Dorantes, when immigrants are victimized while inside a stash house, those situations are referred to USBP and/or ICE, since those types of incidents are seen as the responsibility of federal immigration authorities.

After Sergeant Aviar shared that call for service anecdote, Deputy Archuleta shared an incident he had when assisting USBP with a traffic stop. However, his story differed in that it was USBP that did not arrest the coyote. Several months prior, Deputy Archuleta assisted USBP intel agents with a traffic stop involving undocumented immigrants. The USBP intel agents notified Deputy Archuleta that the driver of the truck he pulled over was a coyote who had just transported undocumented immigrants to a stash house. He told us that he noticed that the bed of the pickup truck had several muddy shoe prints but that the driver's pants and boots were not dirty or muddy. He was upset that the USBP agents did not arrest the man. He said that the driver obviously was the coyote but that USBP agent only wanted Deputy Archuleta to identify the driver.

Sergeant Aviar told him not to worry, because eventually that individual would be arrested by USBP, since Deputy Archuleta had identified the driver for the agents by obtaining that individual's identifying information (i.e., name, date of birth, home address, etc.). Deputy Archuleta said that even though he obtained the driver's identifying information, he did not know why the USBP agents did not take custody of the individual, since they knew the person was a coyote. Deputy Archuleta told us that after that incident, he became disillusioned with USBP's ability to arrest coyotes.[10]

Lieutenant Obrero then noted how on several occasions we responded to stash house calls for service based on information provided by individuals who were themselves involved in some way with the human smuggling organization. Generally, when a stash house call for service is reported, the 911 caller provides the same basic information, such as the fact that several individuals are being held against their will at a particular location. The 911 caller is always anonymous, and the only information obtained from the dispatch center is the phone number of the 911 caller. When we are dispatched to these types of calls for service, we are able to see in our patrol car's mobile data terminal the pertinent information related to the call for service (i.e., location, phone number of the 911 caller, brief synopsis of the call, etc.).

Lieutenant Obrero noted that he had found a theme related to stash house calls for service. He said that when some of the calls that involved undocumented immigrants are made to the sheriff's office, the person calling had a phone number with a Houston area code (either 713 or 832). He told us that he believed the people who made these calls to the sheriff's office were the immigrant smugglers (coyotes), because they provided the exact location of the stash houses. Lieutenant Obrero said, "Just pay attention next time you get dispatched to a stash house. . . . The caller is probably going to be someone with a Houston area code." Deputy Archuleta had also noticed the same thing when responding to stash house calls for service: "These fuckers [coyotes] call us to report the illegals so we can deport them. They probably call us after collecting the money from the illegals."

I revealed that I also had noticed that trend with some stash house calls for service. It all made sense, though. The caller who made the phone call was a member of a human trafficking organization transporting undocumented immigrants from the RGV to the interior of the United States—Houston is the most important human smuggling hub in Texas. More than likely, once the coyotes have collected the money from the undocumented immigrants, the coyotes report the stash house to the police in order to have the immigrants deported. Coyotes can repeat this process over and over again. Lieutenant Obrero stated that the unfortunate circumstance of our involvement with immigration enforcement is that we experience firsthand how undocumented immigrants are commodified: "They're just seen as a dollar bill sign. . . . Se los llevan [They're taken] from one stash house to the next, and once the smugglers get paid, nos hablan [they call us] to report the stash house." Lieutenant Obrero further stated that the commodification of undocumented immigrants was an aspect of the migration process that made human smuggling just as lucrative as drug smuggling.[11] He told us that he felt bad for the undocumented immigrants because they pay a lot of money to cross into the United States, and for some, once they're in the United States, coyotes take advantage by reporting the immigrants to law enforcement authorities after collecting their crossing fees.

CHAPTER 4

Latino Immigrant Criminalization in the Borderlands

This chapter focuses on the enforcement of the racial contract through racialized immigration enforcement practices.[1] The chapter reveals the ambiguity of patrol shift supervisors regarding police participation in immigration enforcement. Some patrol supervisors do not want officers to be involved in immigration enforcement because of logistic and liability concerns, whereas others explicitly approve of assisting immigration enforcement practices. This chapter also reveals what occurs when officers assist USBP agents with immigration enforcement during calls for service and traffic stops when officers have been assigned to regular patrol shifts or when they are working the border security overtime detail: OPSG. The following description of a conversation I had with a colleague reveals the nuances of policing on the U.S.-Mexico border.

One afternoon while I was conversing with Deputy Esqueda about policing, our conversation shifted to the topic of assisting the USBP with traffic stops. Deputy Esqueda said that unlike police officers in other areas of the United States (e.g., Houston, Chicago, and Atlanta), police officers on the U.S.-Mexico border need to be cautious when pulling someone over because of the possibility that the motorist might be a cartel member. He said that due to our collaboration with USBP regarding traffic stops, police departments in the borderlands are at higher risk of coming in contact with a cartel member than police officers who work in the interior of the United States. I told him that traffic stops are inherently dangerous regardless due to the uncertainty of such situations. He then pivoted to discussing stash houses as another dynamic of our collaboration with the USBP: "We also assist BP with the stash houses, and most of the time, we don't know who the fuck we're dealing with. . . . You got a bunch of different nationalities with these illegals, like Hondurans, Salvadorans, Brazilians, and so on."

Our conversation reveals the nuances of policing in the borderlands because unlike police officers who work in the interior of the United States, officers on the U.S.-Mexico border are confronted with various federal immigration issues. That is, police officers in the borderlands encounter calls for service that deal with stash houses and involve traffic stops that at times may lead to a pursuit involving undocumented immigrants. This chapter provides further insight into these region-specific situations and reveals how my proposed concept, Constitution-free policing, operates as a distinct method of policing in the borderlands. The following section of the chapter exposes the importance placed on immigration enforcement during roll call by patrol shift supervisors and discusses the various issues involved when police officers assist USBP agents with immigration enforcement.

Roll Call: To Enforce or Not to Enforce

One Wednesday morning while I was working the morning shift, Sergeant Galarraga and Sergeant Valbuena were conducting roll call, and the subject of immigration enforcement was raised. Sergeant Valbuena mentioned that we should not spend a lot of time assisting USBP agents during the calls for service that involved them. He said that if we were called to assist USBP regarding undocumented immigrants, we should only spend at most fifteen minutes at that particular call so that we could make ourselves available for other calls for service. Sergeant Galarraga then discussed the issue of vehicle pursuits. He reminded us that if we were involved in a pursuit, we needed to make sure that a crime had occurred in order for us to be allowed to continue pursuing the fleeing vehicle. Sergeant Galarraga said, "A lot of times, guys, we have these pursuits that deal with illegals, so just be careful out there. . . . Use your wise judgment, because we don't want to have innocent motorists injured for a pursuit dealing with illegals."

Once Sergeant Galarraga finished, Sergeant Valbuena commented further about the pursuits. He stated that we needed to be careful when involved in pursuits, since most of the time, those individuals fleeing from police do not care about the consequences: "These motherfuckers have no regard for anybody else on the roadway. . . . They just literally don't give a fuck!" He then switched to a discussion about assisting USBP with stash house calls. He said that whenever we were dispatched to a call for service involving an immigrant stash house, we needed to call our supervisors and notify them of the particulars, such as the number of immigrants at the house and/or if there were children at the residence, as well as to determine how long we were to wait at the stash house until USBP agents arrived. He pointed out, "Obviously, if there's little children involved or if there's thirty or fifty illegals, well, of course, you can't just take off."

Both sergeants discussed the logistics of assisting USBP with immigration enforcement. Sergeant Valbuena stressed the importance of not taking too long at a call for service that dealt with a stash house, because it was very time-consuming and consequently pulled away resources from the patrol shift if the responding officer was working that shift. Sergeant Galarraga stressed the importance of making the distinction in vehicle pursuits between pursuits that involved immigration enforcement and pursuits that involved crimes. However, no consensus among shift supervisors existed regarding immigration enforcement, whether it happened at stash houses or during traffic stops, which created ambiguity among patrol officers. The general concern among all supervisors regarding immigration enforcement dealt only with logistic or liability issues. Although officers in essence were de facto immigration officials and ultimately enforcers of the racial contract as a result of our racist nativistic institutional practices,[2] the following vignette demonstrates that patrol shift supervisors did not want us to enforce immigration law because of logistic and liability concerns.

One Sunday evening while he was conducting roll call, Lieutenant Obrero reminded us of what to do when responding to a call for service involving undocumented immigrants at stash houses: "Whenever you guys go to these stash houses donde tienen mojaditos [where they have wetbacks], if you arrive and they [the immigrants] take off running, let them run. You shouldn't be running after the mojaditos, because they haven't done anything wrong." He continued the roll call session and expressed his frustration with some deputies who did not make a clear distinction between our policing duties and immigration enforcement. He said in a frustrated tone, "Chingado [Damn it], a lot of you guys get there and see these mojaditos running, y allí van [and there you go], you guys want to take off running after them. That's Border Patrol's job. . . . If they want to run, pues que corran [then let them run]."

Lieutenant Obrero continued giving instructions on what to do regarding stash house calls for service. He noted that we were just there to assist USBP by providing the dispatcher with the number of undocumented immigrants, and we should wait at the stash house until USBP arrived, since we needed to clear the call to make ourselves available for other calls for service.[3]

After Lieutenant Obrero finished, Sergeant Galarraga shifted the discussion to the topic of the liability involved when we were assisting the USBP with traffic stops. It was widely known within the department that the USBP relied heavily on local police to conduct traffic stops on the USBP's behalf, even though, as previously mentioned, USBP has the authority to conduct traffic stops due to their one-hundred-mile inland immigration jurisdiction within the United States.

Sergeant Galarraga said that we needed to be careful when we were assisting the USBP with traffic stops, because if something wrong occurred, the liability would rest with the sheriff's office. He said that the USBP depended on us to pull people over for them, but if the driver refused to stop, resulting in us pursuing the vehicle, and if the vehicle crashed during the pursuit, the liability would fall solely on the sheriff's office, since we initiated the pursuit, not the USBP. He then said that he was aware that we frequently collaborated with the USBP, but we needed to establish a valid reason for conducting a traffic stop when assisting the USBP. Usually, officers rely on the simplest form of probable cause (nonmoving violations) when assisting the USBP with traffic stops. Sergeant Galarraga stated, "If you have PC [probable cause] to pull [the vehicle] over, then pull it over. If you don't have PC, then don't go making up some BS [bullshit] PC just to pull over the vehicle because BP wants you to pull it over."

Lieutenant Obrero interjected and told us that he was aware that we were to assist USBP when we were asked for assistance but that the liability of crashing while involved in a pursuit when assisting USBP with a traffic stop would eventually be placed on the sheriff's office: "It's going to all fall back on us, because we're the ones that initiated the pursuit, even though we were assisting Border Patrol with the mojaditos." He also said that the general public would put the blame on the sheriff's office and not the USBP, since we were the law enforcement agency involved in the pursuit and not USBP. Clearly, both shift supervisors were concerned with liability issues regarding immigration enforcement.

Vehicle pursuits when assisting the USBP with a traffic stop was a recurring topic periodically discussed during roll call because sometimes patrol deputies were involved in accidents.[4] Sergeant Galarraga wanted officers to have probable cause when assisting USBP with a traffic stop, because if an accident occurred, it would be easier to justify the traffic stop with probable cause than to pull the vehicle over solely at the request of USBP, even though the traffic stop was a pretext for immigration enforcement. In addition, Lieutenant Obrero knew that if we were involved in a traffic accident while assisting USBP with a traffic stop, the liability was going to rest only on the sheriff's office. Again, these patrol shift supervisors were not concerned with us being enforcers of the racial contract and participating in racist nativistic institutional practices except for the fact that these practices involved logistic and liability concerns.[5] The following section illustrates how the process of assisting USBP with immigration enforcement was carried out during routine patrol activities: Constitution-free policing. Moreover, the following vignette reveals that some patrol shift supervisors differed in their view regarding immigration enforcement for the same incident.

Routine Patrol: Immigration Enforcement in Practice

One fall Wednesday morning while I was on routine patrol, I heard via the police radio that Deputy Gírona had been dispatched to assist the Arandas Police Department with an incident related to a stash house. The Arandas Police Department had requested the assistance of our sheriff's office because the stash house in question was located outside the city limits of Arandas and thus outside the department's jurisdictional boundary. The Arandas Police Department notified our dispatch center that they had received an anonymous phone call indicating that two armed men were at a certain location (a stash house) holding people against their will. Several minutes later, Deputy Gírona notified the dispatcher via police radio that he was involved in a foot pursuit with two men who matched the description provided. Sergeant Escarra then commented over police radio that he was also responding to the location. Shortly thereafter, I heard Deputy Gírona on the police radio request USBP to his location.

Later on during the workday, I met up with Deputy Gírona to talk about how the workday was going. While we were parked next to each other, I asked him about the stash house call he had received earlier in the shift. Deputy Gírona said that when he arrived at the house, he saw the two men who matched the description of the suspects and pursued them as they ran away from the house. While he was chasing them, he could not tell if they had guns, and eventually he lost sight of them after they jumped a wooden fence. He told me that he then went back to the house and confirmed that it was indeed a stash house: "I noticed it was a stash house because all the people inside told me they were illegal aliens. . . . There was about fifteen illegal aliens inside who were just sitting down inside the house." Deputy Gírona told me that officers from the Arandas Police Department had also responded to the location because they wanted to verify if the stash house was within their jurisdictional boundary in order to take control of the scene. He told me that the Arandas officers left the location after they confirmed with their dispatch center that the house was outside their jurisdictional boundary.

I asked him who else was with him at the call, and he replied, "[Deputy] Anzurez was also there" to help look for the two men who ran away from the house. Deputy Gírona said Sergeant Escarra also showed up while he and Deputy Anzurez were waiting at the stash house with the undocumented immigrants. Deputy Gírona said Sergeant Escarra scolded him because the location of the stash house was indeed within the city limits of Arandas. According to Deputy Gírona, Sergeant Escarra told him that the neighborhood where the stash house was located had recently been annexed by the city of Arandas; thus the Arandas Police Department should have taken the report for the call for service. Deputy Gírona said that Sergeant Escarra was upset because the Arandas Police Department, not Deputy Gírona, should have taken jurisdictional authority over the call.

Deputy Gírona told me that prior to meeting up with me, he met up with our other shift supervisor, Sergeant Falcón, to submit some reports from previous calls for service. He said that when he submitted the reports to Sergeant Falcón, he was told that he should not have stayed at the stash house, since it was a federal immigration issue. He said that Sergeant Falcón told him he should not have taken responsibility for the call, since it involved undocumented immigrants, and the USBP is the law enforcement agency responsible for immigration enforcement. More importantly, because we were short-staffed that day, Deputy Gírona needed to make himself available for other calls for service. He told me he did not understand why our shift supervisors for that particular workday informed him that he should not have taken the call: "I don't get it, bro. Sergeant Escarra was pissed because I took that report which Arandas [Police Department] should've taken, and then Sergeant Falcón told me that I shouldn't have stayed at the call." Deputy Gírona told me that regardless of them telling him he should not have taken the report, he rationalized taking the report because the incident needed to be documented: "I feel like, 'What's the big deal?' . . . I mean, yeah, maybe BP will take a while to arrive, but I was going to take a report anyways because we always take reports that deal with stash houses."

Both supervisors differed with respect to how they believed Deputy Gírona should have addressed this call for service. Sergeant Escarra's concern related to jurisdictional boundaries, whereas Sergeant Falcón clearly knew that immigration enforcement was the responsibility of the USBP. Neither supervisor cared that Deputy Gírona had participated in a racialized immigration enforcement practice, since that was an accepted institutionalized practice. As previously noted in this chapter, local police often assist the USBP with immigration enforcement in the form of raiding stash houses and performing traffic stops—Constitution-free policing practices. Next, I present an example that illustrates how the process of assisting USBP with immigration enforcement through traffic stops is conducted during routine patrol activities.

One Thursday summer afternoon, I was parked on the side of a business plaza parking lot working on my reports when I observed a Latino male walking toward my police car. As the unknown male approached my patrol car, I figured that it was more than likely a civilian who wanted to take advantage of the op-portunity to file a police report.[6] My windows were already rolled down, and I was writing my reports from previous calls for service. As the male approached, I thought, Damn it, what the hell does this guy want? I'm going to have to write another report! I distinctly remember that this workday was really busy because I had two other pending criminal reports besides the criminal report I was cur-rently working on. As the man walked toward my driver's-side door, he lifted the right side of his shirt with his right hand, and I observed a badge on his belt above the right front pocket of his blue jeans. He was wearing a T-shirt of an NFL team, blue jeans, black tennis shoes, and a gray cap. The man greeted me, identified himself as Agent Tornillo, and explained that he worked for the USBP intel group.

Agent Tornillo advised me that he and his coworkers (other members of the USBP intel group) were conducting surveillance on a potential stash house that was located several blocks south of my location. He then told me that they needed me to pull over a vehicle they suspected was being driven by the supposed human smuggler in charge of the stash house.

My response to Agent Tornillo incorporated a small white lie: "Let me call my supervisor really quick to let him know so I can see what he tells me, because we're shorthanded on patrol today." Agent Tornillo told me to make sure I made the phone call quick, since there was a possibility that the suspect would leave the stash house soon. I then rolled up the window of my patrol car and called my shift supervisor that day, Sergeant Aviar. As I rolled up the window, Agent Tornillo took several steps back from my driver's-side door, pulled a black portable radio out of his pocket, and used it to communicate with someone. I figured he was communicating with his partners, who were sitting inside an unmarked vehicle parked several parking spaces away from me.

Sergeant Aviar answered his cell phone, and I notified him that the intel USBP agent needed assistance with a traffic stop, but, more importantly, I was backed up three reports and needed to catch up on my paperwork. I figured that he would allow me to continue working on my reports for two reasons: first, be-cause shift supervisors did not like patrol officers to get behind on their reports, since that normally meant that the officer(s) would end up working late and claim overtime pay, and second, the reports I needed to complete were criminal incidents that were going to be investigated later by a detective.[7]

Sergeant Aviar told me to go ahead and assist the USBP agents with the traffic stop, since that was all they needed from me. I could go back to completing my pending reports after concluding the traffic stop for USBP. After hanging up with

Sergeant Aviar, I rolled down the window of my patrol car and told Agent Tornillo that I had been given permission by Sergeant Aviar to assist them with the
traffic stop. He excitedly replied, "Sounds great, partner! Just wait here until I tell
you when to exit the parking lot." He said that his colleagues had the stash house
under surveillance and would alert me as soon as the suspect left the stash house.

After several minutes, Agent Tornillo was notified by his other coworkers
that the male had exited the house they were surveilling and was traveling on the
roadway in a red van. He then told me that the suspect had left the house in a
red van and provided me with the direction of travel. I then exited the business
plaza parking lot, turned right onto El Palmar Street, and drove south in search
of the red van. As I continued south, I observed at a distance a red van also traveling southbound. I sped up to the van and then quickly positioned myself behind it. I followed the van for several blocks as I waited for the driver to commit
a moving traffic violation.[8] Once the driver of the van committed the moving
violation, I pulled the driver over.

When I made the traffic stop, I noticed two unmarked vehicles pull up behind
me. I made contact with the driver, who was a Latino in his early twenties, and
advised him of the reason for the traffic stop (the moving violation). The driver
appeared nervous when I asked for proof of insurance and a driver's license. I then
ordered him to step out of the vehicle and walk toward the side of the road, and he
complied. There were no other individuals inside the van. As I stood on the side
of the road, I told the man that he was going to receive a warning for the traffic violation, and he was going to receive a citation for not having a driver's license or
proof of insurance. As I advised him of what I was going to do, Agent Tornillo and
two other individuals, part of his USBP intel group, walked toward us. I told Agent
Tornillo that I was going to go back to my patrol car to write the traffic citation.

Agent Tornillo told me that they were going to ask the man some questions.
As I stood by the passenger's-side door of my patrol car writing the traffic citation,
I could see Agent Tornillo and his colleagues talking with the driver. Once I finished writing the citation, I walked back to where the driver, Agent Tornillo, and
his colleagues were standing. I notified the driver of the traffic citation and advised him to sign the traffic citation, which he did.

After I issued the driver his copy of the traffic citation, Agent Tornillo told
me that they were going to take him into custody because he had confessed to
them that he was an undocumented immigrant and the caretaker (the human
smuggler) in charge of the stash house the agents were investigating.[9] I then
asked Agent Tornillo what they were going to do with the vehicle, and he replied that they would have the vehicle towed. Agent Tornillo and his two colleagues then shook my hand, and I left the scene. I called Sergeant Aviar as I

left the scene to notify him of what had happened. After talking with Sergeant Aviar, I figured that the agents were going to do as they had advised me, but to my unpleasant surprise, that did not happen.

Several hours later, after responding to other calls for service and still trying to catch up on reports, I received a phone call from the other patrol shift supervisor on duty, Sergeant Escarra. He notified me that he was calling in regard to the call for service that I assisted USBP Agent Tornillo with. He asked me if I had pulled over a red van earlier in the shift, and I replied affirmatively. I told him that I had assisted USBP with a traffic stop. He then told me that the sheriff's office had received several calls from motorists regarding a red van parked on the side of the road with no license plates. Surprised, I responded, "Fuck, Sarge. They told me they were going to tow the van." He said irritably, "Damn it! That's why I hate assisting BP with traffic stops! . . . They always get us into shit and expect us to clean up their shit! Just go back and have the van towed!" (paraphrased from field notes).

I returned to El Palmar Street, and once there, I observed that the interior of the van had been ransacked; the glove box was open, and papers were lying all over the passenger seat and floorboard. I also noticed that both the front and rear license plates of the van had been removed. It is my guess that after taking the male driver into custody, Agent Tornillo and his colleagues decided to remove the license plates from the van instead of towing it, more than likely so that the vehicle would not be drivable.

As the above vignette illustrates, I, like all other police officers in the department, was required to assist USBP agents with a traffic stop because my position as a member of the police compelled my participation in this form of racialized immigration enforcement practice. Sergeant Aviar ordered me to assist USBP agents with the traffic stop because it was a widely accepted and institutionalized practice in the sheriff's office, not to mention other local police departments in the RGV. Sergeant Escarra, on the other hand, was livid with USBP because they did not tow the vehicle as they had promised, which resulted in me having to return to the location and consequently meant pulling away resources from the patrol shift to complete an immigration-related call for service. The above scene is yet another example of how Constitution-free policing functions as a distinct method of policing in the borderlands. Moreover, the following paragraphs depict the Constitution-free policing that occurred when I assisted USBP with a call for service that involved a stash house.

One gloomy, drizzly Sunday morning, I was dispatched to a business parking lot in regard to a stash house call for service; three plainclothes USBP intel agents awaited my arrival. Once I arrived, I observed two plainclothes Latino male USBP agents and one plainclothes Latina female USBP agent. They were all wearing green bulletproof vests with the words "Federal Agent USBP" in yellow lettering on the front and the words "Police U.S. Border Patrol" in yellow lettering on the back. The USBP agents were standing by their unmarked vehicles when I arrived. I spoke with Agent Mazuelos, who told me they were going to conduct a raid at a confirmed stash house and needed our assistance. I then greeted the other male USBP agent, Agent Terceño, and the female USBP agent, Agent Uribe.

Agent Mazuelos asked if there was another deputy en route in response to the call for service, because there was a large number of immigrants at the stash house. I told Agent Mazuelos that another deputy, Najera, had also been dispatched to the location to assist me. As we waited for Deputy Najera to arrive at the business parking lot, I noticed that Agent Mazuelos and his two other colleagues were restless and eager to leave; they kept pacing back and forth next to their vehicles and kept looking at their watches. After several minutes of waiting, Deputy Najera arrived and was briefed about the stash house by Agent Mazuelos. We all left the business parking lot, and Deputy Najera and I followed the USBP intel agents to the stash house.

As we followed the agents into the colonia, I saw the lead vehicle (driven by Agent Mazuelos) make a quick left-hand turn into the front yard of a house. Deputy Najera and I then immediately parked on the street behind Agents Terceño and Uribe as they ran out of their unmarked vehicles and onto the property to assist Agent Mazuelos, who was knocking on the front door of the house. Agent Terceño and Agent Uribe ran to the back of the house. Deputy Najera hastily exited his patrol car and ran to the front door of the house as Agent Mazuelos knocked on the front door. I exited my patrol car and walked onto the property. As I did so, three men abruptly jumped out of a front window and ran in my direction into the street. I continued walking toward the front door of the house as the men whizzed by me. I then turned back and noticed Deputy Najera run after the three men, but when he made his way into the street, he slipped and fell on the rainy pavement. The men continued running away from the house, and after he stood up, Deputy Najera looked at me, raised his open hands, squinted, and shook his head in disapproval, upset because I did not run after the three men. He then said, "Come on, Gamino! What are you waiting for? Let's go!" I waved at him dismissively and replied, "Nah, you run after them if you want. I'm not." Deputy Najera ran after the three men in an attempt to find them while I stood in the front yard.

As I waited in the front yard by the front door, I noticed Agent Mazuelos knocking repeatedly on the front door and screaming in Spanish, "Border Patrol! Border Patrol! Open the door!" After his unsuccessful attempt to get someone to open the front door, Agent Mazuelos then peeked through the front window the three men had leaped out of and screamed at the individuals inside: "I already told you! Open the fucking door! Border Patrol!" The individuals inside told him they could not open the front door because it was locked. He replied, "I don't give a fuck!" As Agent Mazuelos commanded the individuals inside to open the door, I noticed two more plainclothes USBP agents and three uniformed USBP agents, each driving a fifteen-passenger van, arrive at the house.

The three uniformed USBP agents ran to the back of the house while the two plainclothes USBP agents stood by the front door with Agent Mazuelos and me. The USBP agents who went around back were able to make entry through the rear of the house and shouted, "We're in!"

Agent Mazuelos ran to the back as the other agents screamed that they were inside the house. I approached the open front window, and as soon as I stood by it, an unbearably strong odor of urine and trash penetrated my nostrils. I observed several individuals standing and sitting down inside. I also noticed that the house was unfurnished, and a bunch of empty water bottles, empty one-gallon jugs of water, and several filled trash bags were strewn all over the interior of the house.

Agent Mazuelos came back to the front and tried to open the front door as his colleagues questioned the immigrants inside the house. I then took several steps back from the front window and stood in the front yard as another fifteen-passenger USBP van arrived at the house. Agent Mazuelos was not able to open the front door but commented aloud about the conditions: "These damn aliens with their fucking filth!"

As we spoke, some undocumented immigrants were escorted from the rear of the house to the front yard where Agent Mazuelos, other USBP agents, and I were standing. Once the immigrants were in the front yard, Agent Uribe began searching and questioning some female immigrants. As those immigrants were being escorted by the uniformed USBP agents to the front yard, I noticed that they were crying and looked dejected. Agent Uribe questioned and searched the female immigrants, and several uniformed USBP agents questioned and searched the male immigrants. While those immigrants were being searched and questioned in the front yard, they were told to remove the shoelaces from their shoes. Their personal items were placed in clear plastic bags, and they were told to sit on the ground. By now, a large USBP presence had convened in the area. Eight USBP vehicles were parked on the street, several plainclothes (intel) USBP agents walked in and out of the house, and several uniformed USBP agents processed the immigrants. Deputy Najera eventually returned to the house after his unsuccessful attempt to locate the three men who ran away. The plainclothes USBP intel agents were joyful and celebratory about what had unfolded at the stash house.

Agent Mazuelos high-fived Agent Terceño and told him, "Yeah, bro! This was a good hit!" As each smiled at the other, Agent Terceño replied, "Hell, yeah! Knock another one down!" Meanwhile, the immigrants who were being processed in front of them were sobbing and depressed. Several minutes later, Deputy Najera left the call for service and resumed his patrol duties. As Deputy Najera left, I told Agent Mazuelos that I was going to get back into my patrol car to work on some pending reports while the agents finished processing the entire scene.

The scene resembled a factory assembly line, because after the first group of immigrants were processed (questioned and searched), they were placed into fifteen-passenger USBP vans. As those immigrants were placed inside the van, a new group of immigrants was escorted from inside the house to the front yard to be processed. This process continued for several minutes until USBP agents had cleared out the entire stash house. A total of fifty-five immigrants from Mexico and Central America were discovered at this stash house. One oddity I observed during my time at the stash house was a group of teenage boys playing basketball at the house next door on a makeshift basketball rim and backboard. I also noticed that the neighbor across the street from the stash house was mowing his lawn while we conducted our law enforcement activity. The teenage boys and the neighbor seemed unfazed about the law enforcement presence and everything that was happening at the stash house: the teenagers kept playing basketball, and the neighbor continued mowing his lawn. Perhaps they already knew the property was being utilized as a stash house. Either way, they gave the impression that it was business as usual at the colonia.

This anecdote reveals me partaking in racialized immigration enforcement practices as a patrol deputy. I, along with Deputy Najera, were dispatched to assist USBP intel agents at a stash house. If USBP requested assistance, we were expected to respond, since local, state, and federal law enforcement agencies frequently collaborate with each other. During the raid, two patrol deputies were pulled away from their regular duties as local police officers to assist the USBP with immigration enforcement; thus, two officers were removed from regular patrol duties to partake in racialized immigration enforcement practices and serve as enforcers of the racial contract.[10]

Photos 4–8 document the living conditions inside a stash house. The next section describes what transpires when officers work OPSG. As will be seen, the message from supervisors to rank-and-file officers working this overtime detail is that explicit immigration enforcement is expected—Constitution-free policing. That is, officers are required to apprehend and detain undocumented immigrants they encounter.

PHOTO 4. Articles of clothing belonging to a female undocumented immigrant (from left to right: woman's blouse, underwear, bra, pants, and socks).

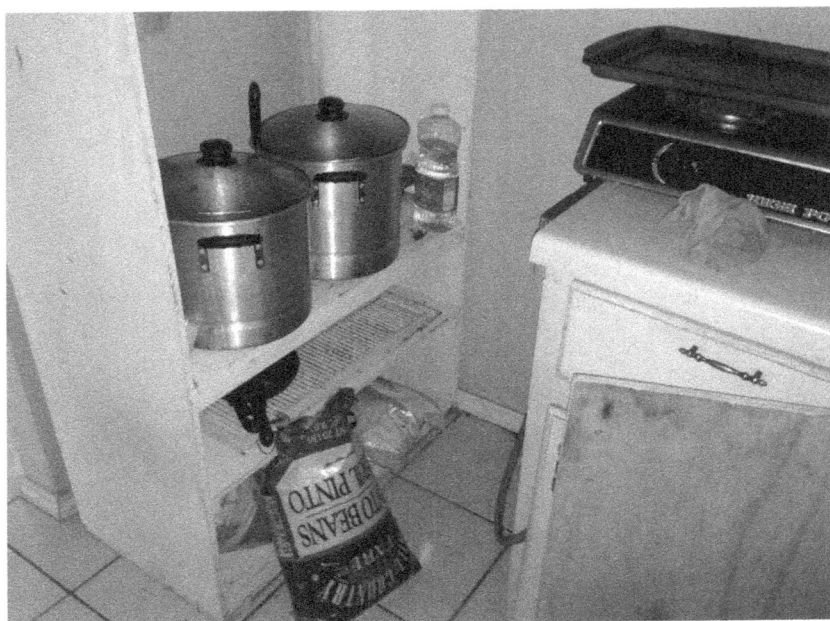

PHOTO 5. Items used to feed undocumented immigrants (two large pots, a ten-pound bag of rice, a twenty-pound bag of pinto beans, and cooking oil).

PHOTO 6. Approximately thirty reusable plastic plates with remnants of a typical meal given to undocumented immigrants (water, soda, rice, and beans).

PHOTO 7. This forty-eight-quart cooler was completely full of eighty-count packages of tortillas.

PHOTO 8. An upturned box spring with women's clothing draped on it.

Operation Stonegarden: Overt
Immigration Enforcement

One Friday evening inside the roll call room, Sergeant Tamayo was conducting roll call for those of us who were working OPSG, which totaled four officers, including Sergeant Tamayo. Sergeant Galarraga, the morning shift supervisor that day, was also present to inform us about a stash house call for service to which the morning shift deputies had responded.

Sergeant Galarraga explained that deputies responding to that call for service apprehended and detained several immigrants. He reminded us that we were not federal immigration officers and therefore should not attempt to apprehend immigrants who flee from stash houses: "Get that through your head. . . . So whenever you go to a call that is dealing with a stash house, and you see these illegals running, don't go running after them." He continued by reminding us that we needed to remember that the USBP is the agency responsible for apprehending and detaining undocumented immigrants: "Just use your radio and provide the clothing descriptions of the illegals to dispatch and the direction they ran to so that BP can know where to look for them." After he finished talking about the stash house call for service from the morning shift, Sergeant Galarraga left the roll call room.

Once Sergeant Galarraga left, Sergeant Tamayo continued with his roll call. After providing us with our assignments for the work shift, he suggested that we needed to be involved in immigration enforcement: "Okay, guys. If there's any calls that deal with illegals, I expect you guys to pick up those calls." He further told us that if someone called the sheriff's office during our shift with information regarding undocumented immigrants and/or stash houses, we needed to respond to those calls. Sergeant Tamayo then said, "We need stats, so pick up those calls."[11] He asked if we had any questions, to which we replied no. Sergeant Tamayo knew that OPSG is a data-driven overtime detail and that the sheriff's office needed to prove to DHS that we were worthy of the multimillion-dollar border security grant. He dismissed what Sergeant Galarraga told us because Sergeant Galarraga was the morning patrol shift supervisor for that day, and regular patrol shift supervisors normally opposed having their patrol deputies involved in immigration enforcement because it caused a strain on already understaffed patrol resources. The following vignette further reveals the explicit nature of immigration enforcement when officers worked OPSG.

One spring afternoon, as Sergeant Cabrales was conducting the OPSG roll call, Sergeant Lisardo walked in and grabbed some paperwork from some file folders that were located in the roll call room. Sergeant Lisardo was one of the patrol shift supervisors on duty that day. He then asked Sergeant Cabrales what area we were going to work for our shift. Sergeant Cabrales replied that we were going to be working all over the county.[12]

Sergeant Lisardo then stated, "If you guys want to catch illegals, just go work the area of Tlaquepaque Road. . . . I know Border Patrol had two pursuits yesterday with illegals over there. So if you all want to catch illegals, just go work that area." Sergeant Cabrales thanked Sergeant Lisardo for that information and told him we would look into it further. He then continued with the briefing. Before releasing us to go out on patrol, Sergeant Cabrales asked if anyone had any questions or comments.

Deputy Jaquez raised his hand and said that he had the personal cell phone number of a USBP agent who had previously provided him with information regarding stash houses. He told the rest of us, "Get his number and write it down so you all can save it. He'll give you a lot of information if you want to catch illegals." He had grabbed his cell phone from his duty belt while making this comment.

All the officers working OPSG that day, except me, took down the number Deputy Jaquez provided for his USBP agent contact. I'm sure my colleagues working OPSG that day figured I also made note of the phone number because I kept writing in my notepad. Sergeant Cabrales then told us that we could go work whatever area of the county we wanted to but to consider the area of Tlaquepaque Road, since Sergeant Lisardo had recommended it. The foregoing scene reveals that immigration enforcement is an expectation when working OPSG. Sergeant Cabrales

had no issues with Sergeant Lisardo sharing particular locations that had seen recent immigrant-related activity or with Deputy Jaquez sharing the contact information of a USBP agent to obtain information about apprehending and detaining undocumented immigrants. As further support of their outlook, the following
conversation I had with a colleague reveals what transpires when local police officers working OPSG collaborate with USBP to enforce immigration.

One summer Sunday at around 3:30 a.m., while I was working the graveyard
shift, I was parked in a rural open field with Deputy Valido having a conversation about what he had experienced two nights prior (Friday) as he worked OPSG.
Deputy Valido was excited to share his experience with me because he said he participated in some "Hollywood shit." He said that on Friday night, while working
OPSG, he was randomly patrolling Colonia El Tapatio when all of a sudden he
came across two USBP vehicles that had their emergency lights on. He drove toward the USBP agents and was able to make contact with one of them. The USBP
agent notified Deputy Valido that they were involved in a vehicle pursuit, but
the driver had fled the scene into a nearby open field along with several undocumented immigrants. Deputy Valido then called his OPSG supervisor, Sergeant Falcón, to ask for permission to assist the USBP agents in the search for the driver of
the vehicle and the undocumented immigrants.

Deputy Valido said that Sergeant Falcón gave him permission to assist USBP
after briefing him on the situation, because they needed stats for that particular
OPSG shift. Deputy Valido told me that he also called Deputy Gírona to assist,
since he was also working OPSG that day. Deputy Valido stated that it was like a
scene from a Hollywood movie, because while he and Deputy Gírona were assisting USBP with the search, the USBP helicopter was flying over them the whole time
spotlighting the area. He stated that the USBP agents entered the open field on one
side while he and Deputy Gírona waited on the opposite side. Deputy Valido said,
"There were two illegals running, a skinny one and a chubby one." Deputy Valido stated that the chubby undocumented immigrant fell as he attempted to run
away from Valido, but Valido ignored him and continued running after the skinny
undocumented immigrant until Valido was able to detain him. One of the USBP
agents and Deputy Gírona eventually detained the chubby immigrant.

Deputy Valido stated, "It was like some Hollywood shit, man! The BP helicopter was hovering over me and spotlighting me as I waited for the BP agents to come
to me." He then told me that the USBP agent who was with Deputy Gírona and
the chubby undocumented immigrant began making threats at the immigrant to
not move or else he was going to get assaulted. Another USBP agent who arrived
to take custody of the skinny undocumented immigrant also made similar threats.
Deputy Valido said, "The BP agent clenched his fists and told the skinny illegal, 'If

only you knew what the fuck I want to do to you!' I don't know, man, I kind of felt bad for the illegals." I asked Deputy Valido if he felt bad for the undocumented immigrants because he had assisted in their apprehension and detention. He replied that although it "was awesome running after the illegals while the BP helicopter flew over," he had mixed feelings, because he had "fun and excitement at the expense of their freedom. . . . The illegals were literally running away for their freedom, bro." Deputy Valido stated that regardless of his feelings about the incident, the overall good thing about assisting USBP with the foot pursuit was that he was able to obtain stats.

Deputy Valido's participation in immigration enforcement while working OPSG reveals the institutionalized pressure that is placed on officers working this overtime detail. Sergeant Falcón notified Deputy Valido that he could assist USBP with immigration enforcement because the sheriff's office "needed stats." Keep in mind that while he was working regular patrol, Sergeant Falcón had notified Deputy Gírona that he should not be involved in immigration enforcement (the stash house call with Arandas Police Department). However, when Sergeant Falcón worked OPSG and served as the OPSG shift supervisor, he was well aware that immigration enforcement was required in order to obtain much-needed statistics about immigrant apprehension rates. The event also reveals the excitement Deputy Valido experienced from working as a de facto immigration official in this incident by partaking in the Constitution-free policing method.

Several weeks after my conversation with Deputy Valido, I was parked next to Deputy Madero, who had been recently transferred onto my shift. Deputy Madero was an ex-USBP agent. While we were parked next to each other and working on reports, I asked him about his experience working for USBP; I hoped that he would be candid about his experience as a USBP agent. Deputy Madero stated that he did not enjoy his employment with USBP because he was always running in the brush and got a lot of tick bites. Because Deputy Valido's observations about what he had witnessed with the USBP agents during the foot pursuit while working OPSG had stoked my curiosity, I asked Deputy Madero, "What about your BP coworkers? Did you at least enjoy working with them?" He answered that he was conflicted because he witnessed several incidents of abuse and mistreatment directed toward undocumented immigrants. He shared some examples of witnessing his colleagues slapping undocumented immigrants after apprehending them: "They would knee them or slap them on their face after questioning them." Deputy Madero further stated that he did not see the point in his colleagues asking for documentation from the undocumented immigrants after apprehending them, since they were obviously entering the United States clandestinely: "Why the hell did they ask them if they had papers to be here? Hello! They're crossing illegally into the U.S. Of course they're not going to have papers." Last, he stated that he felt hopeless when he witnessed his USBP colleagues assault the undocumented immigrants: "I felt bad, because what the hell could I do? It wasn't me who detained them. I was just simply responding as a backup agent." Obviously, my conversation with Deputy Madero regarding abuse by USBP agents cannot be generalized to all USBP agents; however, it is consistent with the scholarship, which notes that USBP abuse is widespread across the entire southwestern United States.[13]

Not all patrol shift supervisors were comfortable with enforcing federal immigration law while responding to a routine call for service involving a potential stash house. The following event reveals how one patrol supervisor resolved this dilemma by having OPSG deputies respond to the call.

One summer afternoon while I was working OPSG, two OPSG deputies, Deputy Encina and Sergeant Toscano, and I were dispatched to assist patrol deputies who had responded to a possible stash house call for service. On arrival, I spoke with Sergeant Camarena, the patrol supervisor, and he notified me that the sheriff's office had received a 911 call from the landlord of the location. The landlord was renting out a mobile home inside the mobile home park, and she said that when she went to collect the monthly rent payment from her tenants, she observed several individuals inside, and she assumed that they were undocumented immigrants. Deputy Encina arrived at the location while I was speaking with Sergeant Camarena and Deputy Losada, the patrol deputy. All four of us were talking with each other about the call as we waited for Sergeant Toscano to arrive. Sergeant Camarena had concerns about responding to this call due to its nature. Departmental policy clearly stated that we were not allowed to ask civilians about their immigration status. The situation concerned Sergeant Camarena because he did not know how to best resolve this call. He said, "Pos chingado [Well, damn], guys, department policy states that we are not to enforce federal immigration laws. . . . I mean, I don't feel comfortable going there and doing Border Patrol's job. . . . That's beyond the scope of our duties, man." Sergeant Camarena continued conveying his apprehension with regard to this call. He talked about the strain it would place on patrol deputies having to respond to these types of calls and said he hated responding to these type of calls for service because they were time-consuming. More importantly, multiple deputies, along with a shift supervisor, would be removed from their normal patrol duties in order to enforce federal immigration law. He remarked, "We don't have time to waste with calls that deal with enforcing federal laws."

Sergeant Camarena continued discussing other apprehensions he had about handling a call that involved immigration enforcement. The sheriff had recently released a memo stating that if someone called the sheriff's office requesting assistance, the sheriff's office needed to respond regardless of the nature of the assistance. In this case, the landlord wanted the sheriff's office to check and verify if the mobile home she was renting was being utilized to hold undocumented immigrants. Sergeant Toscano arrived at our location as we talked with each other about the call. Sergeant Camarena briefed Sergeant Toscano and told him why he needed the assistance of OPSG deputies: he was apprehensive about using his regular patrol deputies to address this potential undocumented immigrant call for service.

All five of us then drove into the mobile home park, and I noticed that every resident entered their mobile home as we approached. The 911 caller, Angela, was waiting for us by her mobile home as we drove into the park. Sergeant Camarena told Angela to wait by the street as we attempted to enter the mobile home. We all surrounded the mobile home as Sergeant Toscano knocked on the front door. An onlooker, seeing all of us surround the mobile home, might have imagined that we were there to conduct a drug raid or perhaps conduct a search warrant for a wanted fugitive, but that was not the case at all; we were simply there because the landlord believed there were undocumented immigrants inside the mobile home. Sergeant Toscano banged on the front door and yelled out, "Sheriff's office! ¡Policía! [Police!] ¡Habran la puerta! [Open the door!]."

Sergeant Toscano continued yelling out commands for someone to open the door. All of a sudden, from inside the mobile home, I heard Deputy Encina and Deputy Losada yell out, "Clear! Clear! Check the restroom!" They had forced entry into the mobile home through the rear without us knowing.

Sergeant Toscano, Sergeant Camarena, and I then entered the mobile home through the front door. As I entered the trailer, I noticed in the living room two large inflatable mattresses with blankets placed over them. I also noticed several pairs of tennis shoes lying on the floor. Neither furniture nor appliances were in the living room. I then walked to the kitchen and noticed a large pot of fideo soup on the stove.[14] It appeared as if the fideo soup had been recently cooked, because I placed my right hand on the pot, and it was still warm. The kitchen area was empty; there was no dinner table or chairs. However, on the floor, I noticed two black, medium-sized backpacks. As the other deputies continued searching the rest of the mobile home, I opened one of the backpacks. It had two small compartments that contained two large rolls of toilet paper. I then unzipped the large compartment and noticed it had food. Inside were several plastic packages of spaghetti and several plastic packages of instant noodles.

As I searched the backpack, Deputy Encina opened the other backpack and stated in Spanish, "Let's see what these fuckers have." After searching the backpack, Deputy Encina threw it back on the floor and stated, "They don't have anything, just some identifying info and healthcare products." He then left, and I picked up the backpack he had searched and began my own search of it. I found several Guatemalan and Honduran identification cards, along with several bars of soap and toothpaste. I also noticed a large Ziploc plastic bag that contained some sort of ground-up brown grain (I later found out it was pinole).[15] I closed the backpack and placed it on the floor. By this time, I had noticed that the other officers were exiting the mobile home, so I did the same.

Once we were outside, Sergeant Camarena told us he was going to talk with Angela to brief her on what we found inside. We all followed him as he walked up to her. All four of us stood near Sergeant Camarena as Angela asked him what we had found. He told her that it was obvious her tenant was using the mobile home as a stash house because there was no furniture inside, and all we found were clothes and backpacks filled with food. He then told her, "These guys [immigrants] probably just left, because there was a hot pot of soup on the stove as we searched the mobile home."

Sergeant Camarena told her there was nothing we could do, since we did not have the authority to enforce federal immigration law. He then pointed at me, Deputy Encina, and Sergeant Toscano and told her that we were called to the location because we were working Stonegarden that day.[16] Angela then waved an open hand at all of us and stated that we always had taken a long time to respond whenever she had called in the past. Sergeant Camarena said that since the call might have involved undocumented immigrants, he needed to wait for us to arrive from the opposite side of the county, since we were working OPSG that day. Angela then asked Sergeant Camarena if she should have called Border Patrol instead of the sheriff's office.

Sergeant Camarena told her that she could have done that, but more than likely Border Patrol would not have responded, because they only respond when the police call them. He informed her that if the police call Border Patrol, they will respond, but if a civilian calls in regard to possible undocumented immigration activity, they will conduct surveillance on the location first. Sergeant Camarena stated, "When we call them, they'll respond out here, but if you call them, they will normally send an unmarked surveillance team to check out the location first." After several minutes spent talking with Angela, we resumed our patrol duties.

As noted in the preceding scene, Sergeant Camarena was apprehensive and uncomfortable having to tend to this stash house call for service because he knew local police should not be involved in immigration enforcement. In addition, he was well aware that department policy indicated that no sheriff's office employees were allowed to ask people we encountered during our routine work activities questions about their immigration status. To circumvent this dilemma, he requested the assistance of OPSG deputies because it was informal knowledge that deputies working OPSG were allowed to partake in immigration enforcement practices. It was widely known in the police department that if a call for service involved immigration enforcement, patrol shift supervisors would periodically require the assistance of OPSG deputies, if they were available, to resolve the call for service in order to free up resources from the patrol shift.

As previously mentioned, USBP relied on local police to assist with conducting traffic stops regarding possible human smuggling violations. The following anecdote reveals how police assist USBP with immigration enforcement even though the task of conducting the traffic stop is not always accomplished. One spring evening while I was working OPSG, the other OPSG units and I responded to a call for service involving a potential stash house. The sheriff's office had received a phone call from USBP indicating that a residence was being used as a stash house. The USBP personnel who placed the call to the sheriff's office notified our dispatchers that there were two trucks at the residence being loaded with undocumented immigrants. The USBP had received information from an anonymous caller and referred that information to us so that we could check out the residence to corroborate the anonymous caller's claim, since the USBP intel unit was understaffed at the moment. The USBP wanted us to conduct a traffic stop on both trucks to verify if the residence in question was indeed a stash house. When I arrived at the two-story brown brick residence, Deputy Casanovas was already parked on the roadway in front of the house. The residence was located within a neighborhood, and the house blended in with the rest of the homes in the subdivision.[17]

Deputy Casanovas advised the dispatcher that no vehicles were currently at the residence and that we would patrol the neighborhood in search of the two trucks. By this time, Sergeant Toscano had arrived at the location and told us he was also going to patrol the neighborhood in search of the two trucks. As we patrolled the neighborhood, Sergeant Toscano came on the radio and requested backup after advising dispatch that he had seen two men run into the house. Shortly thereafter, we drove back to the residence, and two other OPSG units also arrived at the location to assist us. At that point, five OPSG units, including Sergeant Toscano, were involved in this call for service.

Sergeant Toscano ordered us to secure the residence by surrounding the house. I was guarding the southwestern corner of the residence and had a view of the front door. As we stood guard, Deputy Archuleta, who was the patrol deputy assigned to the area, arrived at the residence to provide assistance. Sergeant Toscano and Deputy Archuleta knocked on the front door and shouted,

"Sheriff's office! Open the door!" as the rest of us stood guard at each corner of the house. After several minutes of knocking and screaming commands, Deputy Archuleta, peeking through the front windows of the house, said excitedly, "I see several people inside!" Sergeant Toscano also peeked through the front window and advised dispatch to send USBP to the location, since there were several individuals inside the house.[18]

Deputy Casanovas walked to the front of the house, and since the sun had now set, he and Deputy Archuleta began shining their flashlights into the house. Meanwhile, I walked to the closed garage doors, peeked through a broken window, and observed, in the illumination of my flashlight, several full black trash bags, several one-gallon jugs of water, several empty milk crates, and two large empty produce boxes.

After several minutes, USBP agents arrived at the location with three SUVs and one fifteen-passenger van. Sergeant Toscano briefed the agents about the immigrants he had seen inside the house. Two USBP agents walked to the front door, knocked repeatedly, and shouted in Spanish, "Border Patrol! Open the door!" as a large law enforcement presence—three sheriff's office personnel (including me) and two other USBP agents—stood behind them. After several seconds of screaming for someone to open the front door, a man opened the door, and we all walked inside the house and made our way into different rooms.

Once I was inside, I observed several immigrants sitting cross-legged next to each other in the unfurnished living room. I then walked to the dining room and noticed more immigrants (about ten) sitting on the floor with their heads bowed down. While I was in the dining room, I observed Sergeant Toscano and a USBP agent escort several immigrants down the stairs from the second floor of the residence. All of a sudden, several of the immigrants in the dining room told me that they wanted water because they were thirsty, and I replied that I would go get them some water. I walked to the garage, grabbed the one-gallon water jugs that I had seen earlier, and brought them to the immigrants sitting in the dining room.

The immigrants raised their hands in a desperate motion and screamed in Spanish, "Water! Water! Please!" I tossed the one-gallon jugs of water at the immigrants, which they grabbed excitedly, and I walked back to the garage to get more. I continued doing this until I had handed out all the one-gallon water jugs I could find in the garage. As I handed out the water to the immigrants in the dining room, other sheriff's office deputies and USBP agents continued searching the rest of the residence for all the immigrants. Deputy Casanovas and a USBP agent questioned the immigrants in the living room.

Sergeant Toscano and a USBP agent meanwhile continued escorting more immigrants downstairs. As the immigrants walked down, a USBP agent screamed at them in Spanish in a commanding tone, "Hands on top of your head and don't talk!" I could tell by their despondent facial expressions that some of those who walked down the stairs were scared and dejected. Some of them were crying as they were escorted downstairs.

I then observed a USBP agent kick open the door of the bathroom that was located next to the dining room. Once he had kicked open the door, the USBP agent told the individuals inside in Spanish to get out of the bathroom. The individuals complied with his demands. He then ordered them to sit in the dining room with the other individuals to whom I had provided water. While the immigrants sat on the floor in the dining room drinking the water, I observed and searched several Walmart bags that were next to the kitchen stovetop. The Walmart bags contained several single-serving packets of tuna.

One of the immigrants who was sitting down near me told me that they were hungry because they had not eaten. When I grabbed some tuna packets to hand out to the immigrants, the USBP agent who discovered the immigrants hiding in the bathroom told me, "No! Don't give them that! They'll start fighting with each other as soon as you hand them [the tuna packets] out!" I angrily replied, "Look at them! They're hungry!" Sergeant Toscano quickly interjected, "Just listen to him, Gamino!" I replied, "All right, I'll leave the bags there." The USBP agent later told me, "Don't worry, partner. We're going to feed them in about two hours after they're processed."

I stayed at the house until the USBP agents finished questioning the immigrants. Sergeant Toscano later revealed to us that one of the USBP agents at the scene told him that forty immigrants from Central America and Mexico had been captured at that stash house.

The previous scene depicts another example of how local police in the RGV collaborate with USBP to enforce federal immigration law. The sheriff's office received a phone call from USBP indicating that they needed assistance with a traffic stop to identify the driver and the occupants. Once it was revealed that individuals were hiding inside a residence, the institutional response was to have USBP respond to the location, since it was more than likely another stash house. We OPSG deputies were dispatched to the location to assist USBP with the traffic stop. Even though we did not conduct a traffic stop, we still served as de facto immigration enforcement officials, since we notified USBP that the residence was more than likely being utilized as a stash house. Of note also is the use of racialized language by officers in the situations depicted in this chapter when referring to undocumented immigrants, which is consistent with the anecdotes included in previous chapter, thus making the officers promoting agents of the anti-Latino immigrant subframe.

In addition, the events depicted in this chapter reveal that whether through roll call or calls for service, the racialized institutional practice of immigration enforcement was normalized and viewed as acceptable behavior/action. Not even I could avoid participating in such practices, because I was a member of an institution that does not permit autonomy. Importantly, one central argument that arises from this chapter is that whether consciously or unconsciously, police officers in the RGV ultimately serve as enforcers of the racial contract through participation in racialized immigration enforcement practices (racist nativism), thus revealing a distinct method of policing in the borderlands—Constitution-free policing.

CHAPTER 5

Police Officers' Voices on Immigrant Racialization

As noted in the academic literature, animosity toward certain racial/ethnic immigrant groups has occurred periodically in U.S. history. Irish immigrants in the 1800s were the focus of anti-immigrant sentiment based on nativistic discrimination from Protestant Americans. Moreover, during the late nineteenth century, the focus of anti-immigrant hostility centered on Chinese immigrants, as demonstrated by racialized laws such as the Chinese Exclusion Act of 1882 and the Immigration Act of 1917. Furthermore, individuals of Japanese ancestry faced the wrath of nativistic sentiment during World War II, which resulted in their internment.[1] Currently, the target of anti-immigrant sentiment oscillates between Latino immigrants (Mexicans and Central Americans) and Asian immigrants.

When analyzing racialized terminology such as "wetbacks," "illegal aliens," and "illegals," one must note the impact of race in the creation of the terms. The creation of the USBP in 1924 crystallized the identity of the "wetback" and "illegal alien," since the use of these derogatory terms became the official designation to describe those individuals who bypassed border enforcement controls and found clandestine methods to enter the United States—in particular, undocumented Mexican immigrants.[2] Thus U.S. immigration law produced the "illegal alien" as a political subject, thereby rendering illegality a juridical status in relation to U.S. immigration law.[3] Moreover, legal scholars Kevin R. Johnson and Mae M. Ngai argue that the term "illegal alien" has been associated with minorities of color, specifically, Mexican immigrants, and it is no coincidence that the general public at times still refers to Mexican immigrants as "illegal aliens."[4] According to anthropologist Leo R. Chavez, "Being an unauthorized migrant, an 'illegal,' is a status conferred by the state, and it then becomes written upon the bodies of the migrants themselves because illegality is both produced and experienced."[5]

This chapter provides further insight into illegality and its maintenance among some police officers in the RGV. In particular, this chapter analyzes how the concept of illegality is maintained as a result of everyday racial dialogue. The use of racialized terminology (illegal aliens, illegals, mojados, and mojankers) by Mexican American police officers when referring to undocumented immigrants from Mexico, Central America, and South America illustrates the manner in which they become ardent advocates for the anti-Latino immigrant subframe, thus resulting in the maintenance of white supremacy. The anti-Latino immigrant subframe derives from the dominant white racial frame and is the nativistic view of undocumented Latino immigrants with regard to "racial ideas, terms, images, emotions, and interpretations."[6]

Racialized Dialogue

The use of racialized terminology through racial dialogue reinforces the image of Latino immigrants as permanent outsiders in U.S. society, that is, as the Other. Sociologist Hilario Molina II has reiterated this point: "The racialization of people of color, specifically undocumented immigrants, occurs through racial dialogue, which transforms the manner in which subordinate groups interact with each other as well as with mainstream Americans."[7]

Mexican American police officers racialize their coracial/coethnic immigrant counterparts through racial dialogue. Specifically, the following vignettes exemplify the usage of the terms "illegals," "illegal aliens," "mojados," and "mojankers" by police officers when referring to undocumented Latino immigrants. These racialized terms are based on the anti-immigrant sentiment constructed by natives toward "incorrigible foreigners," that, when used by subordinate groups, only serves to maintain the hegemonic standing of whites in the racial hierarchy by pitting coracials/coethnics against each other.[8]

One late evening, Sergeant Noriego was at a desk in the roll call room checking pending reports. He began talking about the political correctness of using "illegal alien" when describing the immigrant population. At this point, there were five police officers in the room. Sergeant Noriego said, "I don't know why the media is always worried about trying to use correct words when talking about illegals. . . .

Why don't they just call them [immigrants] illegal aliens? . . . I mean, who cares what they're called? Bottom line, they're illegal aliens plain and simple" (paraphrased from field notes). He smirked as he made the comment.

Clearly, Sergeant Noriego disagreed with the way the media talks about using proper terminology when referring to undocumented immigrants. He believed the media put too much emphasis on using politically correct terminology whenever referring to undocumented immigrants. Furthermore, his racialization of undocumented immigrants as illegals and illegal aliens reinforces the common image of immigrants as being nonhuman invaders from outer space.[9] This practice, in turn, can be problematic for the immigrant community because they will be seen as not worthy of protection from the law. Sergeant Noriego was not the only person in the police department who used racialized terminology when referring to undocumented immigrants. Other officers also utilized racialized terms of reference when talking about the immigrant population, as evidenced by what occurred after some of us exited the roll call room.

My fellow officers and I walked outside and continued the discussion of what the proper term to be used should be when referring to immigrants. I told the other officers that I always refer to immigrants as either undocumented or unauthorized immigrants. Deputy Frometa then stated, "Yeah, well, it's like the other day. I heard Paez [a deputy] come on the radio and say, 'Show me out with several UAS [undocumented aliens]' while he was at a stash house. After hearing him say that, I thought, What do you mean, UAS?" Deputy Frometa then stated that whenever he encountered undocumented immigrants, he simply referred to them as "what they are, illegal aliens."

Deputy Valido stated that he also uses the same terminology as Deputy Frometa when referring to immigrants—illegal aliens. We then looked at Deputy Girona and asked him how he refers to undocumented immigrants. He was more nonchalant with his response and stated that he referred to undocumented immigrants as "illegals" because "it's no big deal" how undocumented immigrants are referred to. He further replied, "I don't get into all that political stuff about what is the correct word to call illegals. I just keep it simple."

These officers, similar to Sergeant Noriego, utilized objectifying terminology by referring to immigrants not as immigrants but with demeaning, dehumanizing terms instead. They also shared the same belief as Sergeant Noriego that one should not care about how immigrants are racialized because immigrants should be referred to as what they are—illegal invaders. These officers view immigrants as committing an illegal act that renders their illegality visible, namely, the illegal act of immigrating into the United States through clandestine means. Thus, the officers are in essence naturalizing the use of such dehumanizing terminology.

In addition, these officers were trying to be politically correct by using the acronyms IA and UA when referring to undocumented immigrants. One can make the argument that these officers used acronyms to refer to immigrants because acronyms are shorter than having to pronounce two combined terms. However, if that is the case, officers who use the acronyms IA and UA to describe immigrants can just simply refer to immigrants as "illegals." Instead, there were several supervisors who specifically referred to undocumented immigrants as UAs. The following two incidents that occurred during a roll call illustrate this point.

Lieutenant Ocanto, the previous shift supervisor, was talking about suspect information he had in regard to two vehicles that had been used to transport drugs and immigrants. My squad mates and I were sitting in the roll call room listening to what was being said and taking notes. Lieutenant Ocanto provided us with pertinent information regarding the make and model of two vehicles that were being utilized to transport drugs, along with the roadway travel information (the names of the streets the cars had traveled on). These two vehicles had been involved in two previous separate pursuits with our law enforcement agency. He then said, "They more than likely were transporting delta [drugs] and UAs when they fled from us. . . . So just be cautious with these guys if you come across them, because they more than likely might be transporting UAs and delta traffic."

On a different day during roll call, Sergeant Lisardo was talking to us about an immigrant who was found dead after washing up on the riverbank. The sergeant notified us that a male Latino had died while trying to cross the Rio Grande and looked as if he had been deceased for several weeks. He then said, "As you all know, that area is high for illegal alien smuggling, so we don't know if he is a UA or what, but he probably is. . . . The male had typical alien clothing; he had heavy boots and a long-sleeve shirt. . . . You should've seen him, guys; he was in pretty bad shape. His body smelled real bad and was practically decomposed."

As previously mentioned, the racialization of undocumented immigrants occurs through racial dialogue, which enables the use of racialized terminology to be viewed as the norm. These dehumanizing labels lead to discriminatory actions. In addition, though they did not explicitly say so, these two supervisors were trying to be politically correct by referring to undocumented immigrants as UAS rather than "illegal aliens" or "illegals." A deconstruction of the usage of UA by the aforementioned officers illustrates how its second component (alien) serves as a means to strengthen the objectified image of undocumented immigrants as being something subhuman—extraterrestrials.[10]

By focusing on the undocumented and not the illegal status of undocumented immigrants, these supervisors believed they were using appropriate terminology when referring to immigrants. Moreover, the specific use of UA illustrates that these officers were at best trying to emphasize the undocumented method of entry by immigrants into the United States and at worst emphasizing the dehumanizing component of the word "alien"—foreign invader. By not placing much importance on the illegality aspect of the migration experience, that is, not utilizing the term "illegal," these officers assumed they were being politically correct by racializing undocumented immigrants as UAS.

However, as evidenced in the above vignettes, both supervisors racialized undocumented immigrants as "undocumented aliens" because of the negative connotation of the term's second component—alien. In particular, Sergeant Lisardo, when describing the clothing of the immigrant who had drowned while making an attempt to enter the United States, depicted the immigrant as subhuman. He said, "The male had typical alien clothing." Even though he was associating the term "alien" with "immigrant," his underlying message was that the undocumented immigrant was an Other as a result of wearing clothing typically worn by "aliens." Moreover, the word "alien" conjures up rich imagery—one automatically thinks of space invaders—as a result of popular culture.[11] When many people think of the term "alien," they tend to equate it with terms such as "intruder," "invader," "stranger," and "outsider," just to name a few. Therefore, by using racialized terminology, Sergeant Lisardo implied that the undocumented immigrant was a subhuman foreign invader who unsuccessfully made an attempt to enter the United States and paid the ultimate price—death.

Words are leading agents of the white racial frame because they create certain imagery in the mind and become evident in the physical world through usage of racialized terminology.[12] Similar to the aforementioned officers, there were other officers in the department who expressed anti-Latino immigrant sentiment as a result of racialized terminology. The officers depicted in the next several anecdotes preferred the term "illegals" whenever they referred to undocumented immigrants. Unfortunately, the use of this term by officers is just as discriminatory toward undocumented immigrants as is the term "alien" because it ultimately results in dehumanizing and objectifying immigrants.

One weekday evening while conducting roll call, Lieutenant Samañiego provided us with the prior shift-work activity. He talked about an immigrant who drowned and washed up onshore on the U.S. side of the Rio Grande. Lieutenant Samañiego stated, "And last but not least, they [the previous shift] found a floater earlier in the shift. . . . It was a male illegal who seemed as if he had been there for several hours. . . . Other than that illegal floater, they didn't have anything too significant going on."

Again, words, in particular the term "illegal," function as a method of dehumanizing undocumented immigrants who unfortunately die during their migratory journey to the United States. According to this supervisor, the immigrant was just another "illegal floater" who drowned like the others who wash up on the banks of the Rio Grande on the U.S. side. It is apparent that Lieutenant Samañiego sees immigrants through a white racialized lens as subhuman intruders. This perspective is consistent with the white racial framing of undocumented immigrants who die during their journey into the United States. Specifically, the white racist framing of deceased immigrants implies that undocumented immigrants are merely regarded as illegal floaters rather than drowning victims, which thus dehumanizes immigrants.[13] Consequently, whenever officers refer to a deceased Latino immigrant who drowns as an illegal floater or simply a floater, they are operating out of the white racial framing of undocumented immigrants and become agents who promote the anti-Latino immigrant subframe. Aside from dehumanizing immigrants with such racialized terminology, other officers openly expressed anti-immigrant sentiment whenever they referred to immigrants. However, as shown below, their racialization of undocumented Latino immigrants was based on the racialized emotion of a Mexican reconquest. The following notably alarming vignettes illuminate how some officers held the misperception that the United States was being invaded by immigrants from Mexico.

Envisioning a Mexican Reconquest

On one particular day, I needed to pick up my patrol car. Deputy Quirola gave me a ride to the mechanic shop so that I could get my car and begin my workday. On our way to the shop, we talked about mundane topics; however, as we drove through Basila, he began talking to me about immigration.[14] He said, "Look around. All you see here [Basila] is nothing but illegals. . . . Shit, the valley is full of fucking illegals, bro. No matter where you go, they're fucking everywhere." I then asked him if he believed it was good for us to be involved in immigration enforcement initiatives. He stated that it did not matter because we did not have the time or the resources to be apprehending undocumented immigrants. He then replied, "Like I said, this area is full of illegals, so we can't be wasting our time catching illegals all day. That's what we have BP for."

As we continued driving through the town, Deputy Quirola then switched the conversation to what he interpreted as a Mexican reconquest.[15] He was discussing his discontent with the fact that several businesses utilized Spanish language on their business signs and pointed out a business sign to me as we drove through the street to prove his point. I observed a decaying yellow wooden sign for a gas station that read "Gasolinera el Halcón" (Falcon Gas Station) in red lettering. Other businesses located along the road, varying from restaurants to flower shops to barber shops, also had Spanish-language signs. As we drove along, Deputy Quirola continued venting his frustration and discontent about the businesses having their advertisement signs in Spanish: "You see? Look, everything is in motherfucking Spanish. Pacas de venta [bales for sale]. . . . What kind of fucking shit is that?! . . . These motherfuckers are taking over!"

Deputy Quirola then began making comments about how one cannot differentiate between the United States and Mexico in Basila because it looks as if it is located in Mexico. He suggested that I take a picture of both Basila and Mexico so that I could include them in the book. I looked at him, puzzled, and asked, "Why should I take a picture of both places?" He replied that since Basila looked like Mexico, if my book included pictures from Basila and Mexico, readers would not be able to differentiate between the two, and thus "this way, whoever reads your book, they will be able to see how we've been taken over by Mexico!"

I replied that I would look into that, and then he continued with his discussion about the United States being taken over by Mexico. He felt that the United States was being overtaken by Mexico due to the large concentration of immigrants residing in the rural area of the county and because of the prevalence of the Spanish language spoken in the RGV. He then commented, "That's why I side with the crazy racist bastards, because I'm also frustrated with these fuckers crossing over from Mexico. . . . It's as if we got annexed by Mexico!" Deputy Quirola and I continued our conversation about his frustration with immigration, and he changed the focus to one of our colleagues to further try to prove his point. He said, "I'm not trying to talk shit about Guidero [a deputy], but he's one example. . . . Half the time you can't understand what the hell he is saying 'cuz of his fucking heavy accent. He writes his reports the same way as he talks, all fucked up!" (paraphrased from field notes).

The above vignette sheds light on how some people of color internalize the dominant white racial frame narrative in racialized conversations and perceive Mexican immigrants as posing a threat to the social fabric of the United States. Consistent with controversial political scientist Samuel P. Huntington's view of Mexican immigration, Deputy Quirola believed the RGV was being taken over by Mexicans, which will lead to significant changes, such as language usage.[16] Huntington has argued that due to the large influx of Latino immigrants coming into the United States and the spread of the Spanish language in the United States, the national identity of the United States (i.e., as an Anglo-Protestant culture) is in danger, which will lead to a "Hispanization" of the United States.[17]

Deputy Quirola also shared the common belief that there is a movement toward the Mexican reconquest of the southwestern part of the United States. First, he openly revealed his discontent with the fact that the ethnic demographics of the RGV are changing because this area is being taken over by "illegals." He believed nothing could be done (i.e., local police participation in immigration enforcement) with regard to undocumented immigrants because it would cause a strain on police department resources. As such, he did not oppose such racialized practices for any other reason than logistic purposes. According to him, undocumented immigrants are located throughout the entire RGV, and only USBP agents are capable of dealing with the alleged "immigrant invasion." Second, Deputy Quirola was disturbed by the fact that local businesses in Basila prefer to advertise their establishments using the Spanish language instead of English. Reflecting concerns similarly expressed in the English-only movements of the 1980s and 1990s, Deputy Quirola feared that, due to the widespread use of Spanish by local business owners, the United States is currently being taken over by Mexican-origin immigrants.[18] Finally, his visual image of the RGV—in particular, that Basila is similar to Mexico and that it is difficult to distinguish between both geographical regions—equates the community of Basila with Mexico, even though the community is located several miles north of the Rio Grande. The anti-immigrant sentiment expressed by Deputy Quirola, such as his racialized ideas and emotions regarding Mexican-origin individuals, illuminates the internalization of the white racial frame by some people of color and results in them becoming advocates of the anti-Latino immigrant subframe.

In addition, the above vignette illustrates that not only civilians but also police officers are susceptible to racialized terminology. Deputy Quirola provided me with the example of Deputy Guidero to prove his point that "we've been annexed by Mexico" as a result of Spanish being a dominant language spoken in the RGV. Deputy Guidero was one of the few police officers in the department who spoke with a heavy Spanish accent.

Similar to undocumented immigrants who are subject to being racialized by police officers, Deputy Guidero and other officers were also subjected to racialized practices. For example, his nickname in the department was Fory-Fay because that is the sound he made when pronouncing the number 45.[19] Besides Deputy Guidero, Deputy Domingo was also racialized as a foreigner because he spoke with a heavy Spanish accent. The nickname assigned to him was Dumbingo, and, surprisingly, he took no offense to it and accepted his assigned nickname by fellow officers. According to sociologist Joe Feagin, such white racial framing of individuals includes "deep emotions, visual images, language, and the everyday sounds of spoken language such as accents."[20]

Evidently, Deputy Quirola, along with the rest of the police officers from the sheriff's office, operated out of the age-old white racist framing of people of color in racializing one of their own as a foreigner based on language accent. Notably, just like Deputy Domingo, who accepted his assigned nickname of Dumbingo, Deputy Guidero was also well aware that he was referred to as Fory-Fay by several police officers. Moreover, Deputy Quirola had previously read some of Deputy Guidero's reports, and he judged Deputy Guidero's report-writing ability on the fact that Guidero spoke English with a heavy accent. Deputy Quirola stated, "He writes his reports the same way as he talks, all fucked up!" Thus, according to Deputy Quirola, Deputy Guidero had terrible writing skills because of his inadequate command of the English language. Occasionally, we were able to see each other's written reports because we would hand them over to each other so that they could be submitted to the shift supervisor for that particular workday at the end of the shift. Sometimes when I came across the written reports of my colleagues, I noticed that their writing skills suffered from similar general flaws, such as grammatical and spelling errors.

However, other officers in the department shared a similar view of a Mexican reconquest. As evidenced by the following conversation, some officers were critical of their own and believed foreigners had "invaded" the department. One evening I was having a conversation with Deputy Miramontes about our colleague Deputy Boitez, who had provided wrong information while involved in a call for service. Several hours earlier, Deputy Boitez had responded to a call for service and apparently got lost.

After telling Deputy Miramontes about what happened with Deputy Boitez, he replied, "Pues, sí [Well, yes]. It's like Boitez, Dumbingo, Fory-Fay, all these guys are taking over. Mexico is taking over." I asked him to elaborate, and he replied, "All these guys with accents. They don't even know how to talk English properly. . . . Puro pinche mexicano chingado [pure, fucking Mexican, damn it]." Deputy Miramontes then began talking about another deputy who spoke English with a thick accent, Deputy Anzurez, and then told me about an incident in which Deputy Anzurez had requested backup but had pronounced the street name with an accent. Deputy Miramontes, mimicking Deputy Anzurez's accent, stated, "I heard him over the radio request backup and say, 'Send me a backup unit to Blue Yay [Blue Jay] Street.' After I heard him pronounce Blue Jay with his thick accent I was like, 'Where the hell is Blue Yay?'" Deputy Miramontes further continued expressing his discontent with how Deputy Anzurez pronounced the street with a thick accent: "We're in the fucking U.S.! Speak English! It's not Mexico. The name of the street is Blue Jay, not Blue Yay."

After voicing his discontent with Deputy Anzurez's thick accent, Deputy Miramontes then discussed his feelings about a Mexican invasion: "These guys are taking over. They come from Mexico, and now they've already made it into the system [obtained employment at the police department]." As previously mentioned, the white racial framing of individuals includes the everyday sounds of spoken language, such as accents. Clearly, Deputy Miramontes is a promoting agent of the anti-Latino immigrant subframe who racialized the aforementioned colleagues as foreigners because they spoke English with an accent.

In addition to believing in a supposed Mexican reconquest of the RGV, other officers perceived undocumented immigrants as being a drain on U.S. social services, as evidenced by several conversations. The following examples of my conversations with several officers demonstrate how undocumented immigrants are perceived to be menacing foreigners and a burden on U.S. taxpayers.

A Drain on U.S. Social Services

One Sunday afternoon, I was parked next to Deputy Sayago as I worked on my reports from two previous calls for service (both calls involved undocumented immigrants). We were parked in an open field talking to each other through our driver's-side windows. He said to me, "Oye me, ¿andas muy recio con los illegals o que? [Hey, you're real busy with the illegals or what?]." I asked him, "What are you talking about?" He replied that since both of my previous calls for service dealt with immigration, I must have been actively seeking undocumented immigrants. I told him that it was not my doing and that I simply responded to calls for service that I was dispatched to. Deputy Sayago then asked me what happened on my first call for service, which dealt with an unaccompanied minor Central American male.[21] I explained to Deputy Sayago that the teen had crossed the previous night but that he wanted to go back home to El Salvador because he was separated from his group and was now traveling alone. I told Deputy Sayago that as I waited for USBP to arrive at the location (a gas station), I entered the store with the teenager and bought him some food.

At this point, Deputy Sayago gave a startled jerk and said in a jocular tone, "What? You bought this illegal some food?" I responded that indeed I had purchased food for the teen and did not see anything wrong with that. He exclaimed, "Well, yeah, shit, they come into our country illegally, and then you're still helping them out by giving them food?" I reiterated that I did not see anything wrong with me purchasing food for the teen since he had not eaten since the previous day and he was going to be deported anyway. I figured I would get him some food before USBP arrived at the gas station to take custody of him.

Deputy Sayago said that if he were an immigrant, he would want to get apprehended by a police officer like me, since I would "feed him and treat him right," even though he had committed a crime. After he said this, I looked at him with a confused stare and asked, "No mames [C'mon], what do you mean, crime? What crime did he commit?" He replied that the teen had committed a crime because of his clandestine method of entry into the United States. I then countered and said that the teen was not a criminal, since he was not a murderer, a rapist, a burglar, or a thief; he was an immigrant. I then asked Deputy Sayago to elaborate and explain to me why he associated immigrants with criminality. He replied that immigrants were criminals because they steal from us (U.S. taxpayers). He continued, "We pay for them to have children, to use the hospital, to go to school, to get food stamps, and all that. . . . We're the ones that are supporting them. They're stealing from the U.S. government."

I told him that even with all he was saying, that still did not constitute immigrants as criminals, and he responded by stating that all "illegals" are criminals. I then clarified to Deputy Sayago that "illegal" is not a proper term of reference when referring to immigrants who utilized clandestine methods of entry. I told him that he should instead use the term "undocumented" or "unauthorized," which he took offense to. He replied, "Oh, c'mon, Gamino, you're just with your damn crap. Whatever it is, they're illegals either way. . . . You're just like the left-wing liberal media trying to use different terms for the illegals so that people can feel bad and sorry for them" (paraphrased from field notes).

Deputy Sayago then created a scenario involving the second call for service that I had responded to that day. It dealt with immigration enforcement after fifty-five Mexican and Central American immigrants were found inside a stash house. He asked me, What would sound better in the headlines? "Fifty-five illegal aliens caught or fifty-five immigrants caught?" "Immigrants," I said. He countered by saying that the "left-wing liberal media" and I prefer to change the wording because it sounds much better than using what he believed to be more accurate terminology. He said, "Bottom line, they're here in the country illegally. . . . Illegals. That's what they are."

I then asked Deputy Sayago what he would have done if he were in my situation when responding to the call for service involving the Salvadoran teenager. He stated, "I would've been like, 'Screw you, fucker. It's not my fault you haven't eaten. . . . It's not my obligation to feed you after being in the country illegally.'"

I told Deputy Sayago that I did it out of the kindness of my heart, but above all because the teenager was a human being and deserved to be treated as such. His response did not surprise me. He stated that if he were to ever be an undocumented immigrant, he would want to get apprehended by a police officer like me, and in his opinion, anyone who enters the United States through clandestine means deserves to be associated with the stigmatizing label of "criminal."

This conversation with Deputy Sayago exemplifies all of the typical common nativistic sentiments some individuals have in regard to Latino immigrants. Racial dialogue and racialized emotions are active agents of the white racial framing of the immigrant community. Thus it is evident through his racialization of undocumented immigrants that Deputy Sayago is advocating the anti-Latino immigrant subframe by viewing all Latino immigrants as criminals and a drain on U.S. social services. First, Deputy Sayago viewed undocumented immigrants as subhuman intruders who do not deserve to be treated as human beings. He was appalled at the fact that I had purchased food for the unaccompanied Salvadoran minor and said he would not have done the same. Deputy Sayago felt that immigrants do not deserve to be treated humanely because it is the immigrants' own fault for putting themselves in that situation, and if they go hungry, then so be it.

Second, Deputy Sayago believed that all undocumented immigrants are criminals based on their clandestine migration methods. It does not matter whether the immigrant has committed a criminal violation or not; if he or she used clandestine methods to enter the United States, then Deputy Sayago criminalized the undocumented immigrant based on method of entry into the United States. Aside from criminalizing immigrants, his views of undocumented immigrants are consistent with the Latino threat narrative.[22] That is, anti-immigrant proponents believe that an undocumented immigrant's sole purpose for immigrating to the United States is to benefit from U.S. social welfare programs and, in the case of females, to give birth in order to benefit from social services.

Finally, Deputy Sayago referred to undocumented immigrants by the racialized term "illegals." Consequently, he had internalized the common white racial framing narrative of Latino undocumented immigrants without realizing that he was a promoting agent of the anti-Latino immigrant subframe by using such a dehumanizing term. When we debated with each other over what should be the appropriate term of reference for undocumented immigrants, he was clearly upset with me and believed that I was just like the "left-wing liberal media," which tends to be empathetic toward the plight of the immigrant community. His anti-immigrant sentiment reflects commonly held misperceptions regarding undocumented immigrants: criminality and welfare dependency. Other conversations with my fellow police officers revealed that Deputy Sayago was not the only one who had racialized emotions and believed immigrants are a drain on U.S. social services. The following conversation with Deputy Guidero illustrates this point.

I was partnered with Deputy Guidero one day and was having a random conversation with him as we conducted routine patrol through Colonia Díaz Ordaz. He began talking about his wife, who was a fifth-grade teacher at a nearby elementary school that serves the residents of Díaz Ordaz, which is a predom-

inantly immigrant neighborhood. As we talked about this issue, we drove past
a convenience store that had a large banner on the front wall that read "Food
Stamps Accepted Here." After seeing the sign, Deputy Guidero said that undocumented immigrants were "ripping off" the government in various ways. He
told me that his wife shared stories with him about the parents of her students.
His wife told him that she had seen an increase in parents wanting their children
to be diagnosed with a learning disability, because that would allow the family
to obtain a monthly disability check from the U.S. government. When I asked
Deputy Guidero if his wife normally signed the paperwork that allowed a child
to be classified as having a learning disability, he replied, "No, she doesn't sign
any paperwork, because she knows that the parents are just looking for another
way to rip off the government." Deputy Guidero told me that if parents claim
that their child is suffering from a learning disability, the teacher must sign paperwork to corroborate the parents' story so that they can then take the paperwork to the respective state agency and begin the approval process. If granted
approval, the parents will receive a monthly check from the government for a
certain amount along with the food stamps they are already receiving.[23]

Deputy Guidero later said that he is upset with the federal government for
helping out the immigrant community: "It pisses me off that the government
helps out all of these illegals, and we have to bust our ass for what we have. . . . It's
the government's fault that they are getting ripped off by illegals." I asked him if
he could elaborate. He said that the U.S. government does not accurately verify
the income of welfare assistance applicants to determine the actual need of the
applicant. He further stated, "If the parents claim that their child has some type
of learning disability, that's another government check for the family. . . . It's their
[the government's] fault they're getting ripped off by illegals, since they don't put
an end to this. . . . They just keep helping illegals out" (paraphrased from field
notes).

Deputy Guidero equated the imagery of welfare dependency with undocumented immigrants. The sign that read "Food Stamps Accepted Here" served as
a trigger for Deputy Guidero to bring up the conversation of immigrant welfare
dependency. It was only after he saw this sign that he decided to talk about his
discontent with the U.S. government for helping out undocumented immigrants.
This conversation with Deputy Guidero exemplifies that aside from the stereotypical assumption of welfare dependency (e.g., food stamp assistance), another
assumption is that undocumented immigrants threaten to put additional strain
on U.S. social services as a result of having their children diagnosed with a certain
learning disability.

However, contrary to popular belief, undocumented immigrants cannot receive food stamps easily unless they meet certain requirements. That is, they can receive governmental assistance only on behalf of their U.S.-born children.[24] Moreover, children from birth up to the age of eighteen may receive Supplemental Security Income (ssi) benefits for learning disabilities if they meet certain conditions. In order to qualify, children must have been born in the United States and have a physical or mental condition that hinders their activities, and the condition must have lasted or be expected to last at least one year.[25] In addition, the Social Security Administration considers the household's income and resources as part of its eligibility requirements. If the requirements are met, the Social Security Administration makes monthly ssi payments to children; however, the amount of the payment varies from state to state.

Based on my conversation with Deputy Guidero, it was evident that he assumed that most undocumented immigrants receive food stamp assistance from the government and will seek to further drain U.S. social services by attempting to receive another government assistance check for their children's disability. He was in essence taking a nativistic stance with regard to individuals who need assistance from the government by viewing this issue through the white racialized framing of Latino undocumented immigrants as a group of undeserving/illegitimate "foreign invaders."

As previously illustrated, though, Deputy Guidero was one of the few police officers in the department who was racialized as a foreigner by fellow officers, as evidenced by his nickname, Fory-Fay. Therefore, it is ironic that he took a nativistic stance in regard to the issue of the use of U.S. social services and racialized undocumented immigrants, since he too was racialized as a foreign invader by his fellow coworkers.[26]

Another conversation with a different deputy illustrates how embedded the mindset of racialized dialogue is and how emotions are frayed regarding the perceived use of U.S. governmental benefits by undocumented immigrants. One time I was having a conversation with Deputy Esqueda, and he broached the topic of undocumented immigrants, probably because while we were parked next to each other in a business parking lot, the topic of conversation on Glenn Beck's radio show (he was listening to the radio show as we conversed) was the immigration issue. Deputy Esqueda said that he did not have any issues with undocumented immigrants receiving governmental assistance as long they worked. He further mentioned, "There's some that get food stamps and don't worry about getting a job because they know they'll get governmental assistance. . . . Sometimes it's even a generational thing where these illegals get help each generation." I asked him if he could elaborate, and he replied that if an adolescent youth is raised in a household where his parents receive food stamps, then the child is going to see the accessibility of receiving governmental assistance in the form of food stamps. Therefore, according to him, this would result in a generational dependence on food stamp assistance, because the parent(s) are setting the example for the child to depend on U.S. social services, and when the child eventually becomes a parent themselves, they too will depend on food stamp assistance just like their parents. He commented, "It's basically a cycle: illegals are showing their children how to live off of the government, and the children will do the same thing once they become parents."

Deputy Esqueda had a white racialized framing perspective of undocumented immigrant welfare dependency because he viewed this issue as a prolonged problem akin to that of career criminals. He assumed that undocumented immigrants who receive governmental assistance will be career welfare dependents and that, in addition, welfare dependency will continue with each succeeding generation.

Although unusual, the following conversation with another fellow police officer reveals that at certain times, immigrants were referred to as career offenders. However, the conversation illustrates the manner in which the white racialized framing of undocumented immigrants as being a burden to U.S. taxpayers becomes embedded in the minds of individuals, thus overshadowing their ability to utilize proper terminology whenever they refer to immigrants.

One day I was partnered with Deputy Andrado, and we were conducting routine patrol inside Colonia El Tepehuaje. As we drove through the colonia, we noticed that some people were having a cookout in their front yard. Deputy Andrado stated, "Look at these people; they're barbequing in the middle of the week. . . . Then again, they're probably receiving food stamps, which cause them not to worry about wasting money on food."

I told him that if that was the case, then it was the government that was granting the people the opportunity to have a cookout during the middle of the week. After I made this comment, he glared at me and asked if I was being serious, because it was not the government that made this possible. In his view, it was us, the taxpayers, who "allow[ed] those leechers" to have their barbeques.

Colonia El Tepehuaje, similar to other colonias in the county, is populated primarily by immigrants. Deputy Andrado continued talking about the colonia residents by making comparisons between recently arrived immigrants and past immigrants. He stated that he did not have anything against the immigrants residing in Colonia El Tepehuaje, but they were different from immigrants in the past. I asked him to elaborate, and he said that what he meant by that comment was that immigrants from the past came to the United States to better themselves, as demonstrated by their work ethic, whereas recent immigrants come to drain U.S. social services.[27] He said, "That's why they're [the immigrants] all mostly on food stamps and come here just to give birth to their kids so they can receive benefits."

The discussion then changed to DREAMers.[28] Deputy Andrado had a negative perception of DREAMers as well. He shared with me his discontent with President Obama because he felt President Obama was wrong for proposing a reduction in the G.I. Bill. He asked me if I was aware of this, to which I replied no. He then said, "Now that's messed up; I'd rather pay for a soldier's education than pay for José No Papers's education." I asked him if he could further clarify this point, and he stated that U.S. soldiers deserved having their college education paid for because they had fought for the United States. Regarding DREAMers, he said, "José No Papers, on the other hand, is here illegally and is just leeching off the government."[29] I then asked him if he believed immigrants were a drain on U.S. social services. He groaned, "C'mon, Gamino, are you serious? Of course." He commented that undocumented immigrants are attracted to the United States because they are going to utilize U.S. social services and become dependent on them.

In this conversation with Deputy Andrado, the general racialized trend of equating Latino undocumented immigration status with welfare dependency is once again on full display. He believed Latino immigrants are a burden on the country because U.S. citizens have to foot the bill when it comes to providing assistance to low-income individuals. Evidently, this belief was based on his anti-immigrant sentiment toward Latino immigrants, which illustrates that he viewed welfare dependency through the white racial framing of undocumented immigrants—specifically, that Latino immigrants are dependent on U.S. social services such as food stamps.[30] He also drew on the racialized binary construction of citizen/foreigner at the end of the conversation by making the claim that he would rather have his tax dollars pay for an American soldier's education than an undocumented immigrant's education. Thus, Deputy Andrado adopted the common white framing mechanism for undocumented immigrants by insinuating that "unworthy" Latino undocumented immigrants come to the United States to take from "worthy" American citizens. Even though Deputy Andrado did not use racialized terms when referring to undocumented immigrants, he nonetheless racialized Latino undocumented immigrants by using racially coded language, such as referring to a Latino undocumented immigrant as José No Papers. Like the other officers discussed in this chapter, he is an example of an advocate of the anti-Latino immigrant subframe because of his white-framed ideological stance toward Latino undocumented immigrants.

As mentioned earlier, utilizing racialized terms such as "illegals" and "illegal aliens" when referring to undocumented Latino immigrants is problematic because such terminology only serves to objectify immigrants and thus advocate for the anti-Latino immigrant subframe. Moreover, a new derogatory term that is used to racialize undocumented Latino immigrants has emerged in some police departments, as discussed next.

The New Wetback: The Mojanker

Language plays an instrumental role in defining and guiding individuals to act out certain behaviors such as discriminatory practices. In addition, the usage of certain language, such as racial epithets, by the dominant group suggests that the other group (minorities of color) is not as good. While working as a police officer, I witnessed certain police officers use the racial epithets "mojankers" and "mojados" to racialize undocumented Latino immigrants. As a result of using such derogatory terms when referring to immigrants, these officers were in essence trying to suggest that the Other (undocumented immigrant) was not as good as them. More importantly, the usage of mojanker is synonymous with racial epithets that are associated with the African American community.[31] The following example sheds light on how the term "mojanker" is part of the daily racial dialogue in the police department during roll call whenever some officers talk about undocumented Latino immigrants.

One day while conducting roll call, Sergeant Aviar talked to us about being careful when we responded to assist another officer or law enforcement agency. He provided the example of a deputy who had been involved in an accident days earlier while assisting USBP with a pursuit involving immigrants. The deputy in question ran a red light and T-boned an innocent motorist. Sergeant Aviar said, "To make matters worse, he was assisting BP with a call involving mojankers. . . . And for what? All they [BP agents] wanted him to do was pull over a vehicle so that they could ID the driver." Sergeant Aviar warned us not to rush to calls when USBP agents simply needed our assistance to pull over a vehicle for identification purposes: "There's no need to be killing yourself by trying to catch up to a vehicle to pull it over. Especially if it's to assist BP with mojankers. . . . They're just mojankers, guys. There's no need to endanger other people for mojankers." He continued talking about the situation and mentioned that the innocent motorist was injured because of the careless actions of the deputy.

Several months later, police chases were again a point of emphasis for Sergeant Aviar during roll call. After giving us the quadrant assignment for the day, he reminded us about the departmental pursuit policy. He stressed that we needed to follow the pursuit policy and follow protocol in order to avoid a reprimand. He reminded us about the pursuit policy because two days prior, several deputies were involved in a pursuit with a truck carrying eight undocumented immigrants. The truck eventually crashed, resulting in injury to all occupants aboard the truck.

Sergeant Aviar told us that we needed to be careful whenever we were involved in a pursuit, even though our adrenaline might be running, thereby giving us tunnel vision. He then asked, "If you were involved in a pursuit and saw four or five individuals in the back of the truck, what did you assume it was?" No one replied to his question. He said, "Yeah, exactly. More than likely they're "mojankers," and that's it." He advised us that if we were involved in a pursuit that involved" mojankers," he was going to cancel us, because being an immigrant is not a crime. He then said, "There's nothing wrong with being a mojanker. . . . That's a violation of federal immigration law and not a state criminal violation." Sergeant Aviar reminded us of the dangers of being involved in a pursuit and said he was not going to allow us to endanger ourselves, other motorists, or the immigrants.

Sergeant Aviar also commented about another separate incident several weeks prior in which a deputy was involved in a pursuit. As soon as Sergeant Aviar heard the deputy notify the dispatcher that he was involved in a pursuit, he asked the deputy the reason for the pursuit. The deputy told Sergeant Aviar that he was chasing a truck that had committed a traffic violation and was refusing to stop. The deputy further told Sergeant Aviar that he could see several individuals in the back of the truck. As soon as the deputy advised Sergeant Aviar of the individuals in the back of the truck, Sergeant Aviar ordered the deputy to stop chasing the truck because the driver was more than likely transporting "mojankers." After mentioning this incident, Sergeant Aviar continued with his discussion of police chases involving undocumented immigrants: "It's all fun and games, guys, until someone gets hurt. . . . At the end, is it worth it? No, it's just a vehicle full of mojankers."

The above two examples demonstrate that even though Sergeant Aviar was not explicitly dehumanizing undocumented immigrants, just by the mere usage of the derogatory term "mojankers" he was reinforcing the common white framing of undocumented immigrants and advocating the anti-Latino immigrant subframe. Ironically, in my various encounters with him when I was responding to calls for service dealing with undocumented immigrants, he always treated them with respect (i.e., he did not view them as criminals) and at times purchased food for immigrants who were hungry (a very uncommon practice). However, as noted earlier, racialized terminology is a leading agent of the white racial frame, and although he was empathetic toward undocumented immigrants, Sergeant Aviar was unintentionally an advocate and promoting agent of the anti-Latino immigrant subframe because of his usage of such racialized terms.

In the previous example regarding what was said during roll call, Sergeant Aviar tried to make it clear to police officers that they should not continue a pursuit if they had established that the fleeing vehicle was transporting undocumented immigrants. He did not think it was important enough to continue with a pursuit for such a trivial reason, contrary to a pursuit during which a driver refused to stop because the driver was perhaps transporting drugs or engaged in a serious felony. Sergeant Aviar wanted to make it clear to us that we should not be involved in federal immigration enforcement, especially vehicle pursuits involving undocumented immigrants. The aforementioned roll call examples also illustrate the racialized immigration enforcement practices used by local police in the borderlands. That is, local police in the borderlands are often involved in immigration enforcement practices such as vehicle pursuits involving undocumented immigrants because these pursuits are perceived as an accepted institutionalized practice—Constitution-free policing.

An ongoing debate rages about whether undocumented entry into the United States is actually a crime. According to Title 8, Section 1325 of the U.S. Code, which is the official compilation of the general and permanent federal statutes of the United States, unauthorized entry into the United States is a criminal offense.[32] However, the punishment imposed for this criminal offense is consistent with civil violations. That is, if an undocumented immigrant is caught entering the United States, the immigrant will be fined for such an offense (unauthorized entry) or be imprisoned for not more than six months. Each subsequent unauthorized entry into the United States is subject to additional fines. Therefore, unauthorized entry into the United States is essentially a crime subject to penalty in the form of fines, thus making it a civil matter. According to Sergeant Aviar, police should not be involved in pursuits involving undocumented immigrants both for safety reasons and, more importantly, because no violation of state criminal law has been committed (i.e., the violation is outside the purview of state and local police departments).

A conversation I had one day with a USBP agent clarifies this point and provides insight into the interpretation of the law from an agent's perspective. He said that in essence, clandestine (unauthorized) entry into the United States is an administration violation and not a crime per se. He notified me that the central issue is the method of entry into the United States by the individual. If that individual utilizes unauthorized entry, then he or she has committed an administration violation, which equates to a charge. I was also told that even U.S. citizens can be charged with entering the United States unlawfully if they do not utilize an official port of entry such as a bridge. The USBP agent then told me that if an individual enters the United States through unauthorized means a second time after being charged with an administration violation the first time, he or she will be charged with an expedited removal regardless of the immigrant's country of origin. Thereafter, each subsequent time the individual gets apprehended by USBP, he or she will appear before an immigration judge to receive a formal ban from the United States. As can be noted from the conversation with the USBP agent, a bit of ambiguity exists regarding how agents perceive the law as it is written. According to the aforementioned immigration law, unauthorized entry into the United States is considered a crime. However, the punishment rendered for such a crime is consistent with civil violations. Academic scholarship corroborates this point by noting that most U.S. immigration violations fall into civil as opposed to criminal law.[33]

As noted earlier, language plays an instrumental role in defining and guiding individuals to act out certain behaviors such as discriminatory practices. There were some incidents during which some officers referred to undocumented immigrants as "mojados" and "mojankers," and some of those officers indicated that an officer should not feed undocumented immigrants if the officer encountered them during a call for service. The issue of feeding undocumented immigrants rarely came up during conversations at the department; however, the following illustration describes one incident in which the topic was discussed.

One day I was talking with officers from my shift inside the roll call room about the recent media coverage on the influx of unaccompanied minors and mothers from Central America who had been coming through the RGV. I was standing in front of Deputy Oñate and Deputy Tapanes, while Deputy Calvera was standing to my left. Deputy Oñate made a comment about me providing food for undocumented immigrants as everyone laughed.[34] Deputy Tapanes then asked me, "¿Qué onda, Gamino? [What's up, Gamino?] You're gonna let [Deputy] Oñate talk about you like that?" I laughed and replied, "Well, haters be hating." Again, everyone laughed, and Deputy Oñate then said, "Pos sí, Gamino le da de comer a todos los mojaditos [Well, yes, Gamino gives food to all the wetbacks]."

Deputy Calvera joined the conversation and with an emotionless facial expression said that he had provided food once for "mojankers" on a call for service and would never do it again. He explained that during that call for service he had given the undocumented immigrants packets of tuna that were in the kitchen and that as soon as they finished eating the tuna, they ran away from the stash house. He and the other officers at that call chased after the undocumented immigrants but did not apprehend everyone who ran away from the house. He said that after that incident, whenever he responds to a call for service involving undocumented immigrants, he no longer allows undocumented immigrants to eat the food at the stash house while they are waiting to be transported by USBP agents to the USBP processing center because USBP will eventually feed them there. Deputy Tapanes then stated, "Yeah, poor bastards. All they [USBP] give them are sandwiches and a juice if they're lucky." Deputy Calvera responded, "Well, at least the mojankers get something to eat, but as for me, I won't let them eat."

Aside from the racialized terminology some officers use to describe the immigrant community, some officers see undocumented immigrants as not worthy of being fed should a situation such as the one described above arise. Moreover, "mojankers" was a common term used among some officers whenever they referred to undocumented immigrants. Whether the topic dealt with immigrant criminality or other immigration issues, some officers generally equated undocumented immigration with the terms "mojadito" (wetback) and "mojanker." The above narrative illustrates that contrary to Sergeant Aviar, who made it clear that he believed there was nothing wrong with being a "mojanker" (being one was not a state criminal offense), officers such as Deputy Calvera clearly dehumanized undocumented immigrants by believing that mojankers did not deserve basic human rights such as food. In addition, the above narrative provides yet another example of the problematical but widely accepted institutionalized practice within police departments in the borderlands: immigration enforcement. That is, the narrative illustrates how Constitution-free policing, through collaboration with the USBP, functions as part of everyday routine work activities for local police departments in the borderlands.

In addition to actions, language too has the power to objectify and dehumanize individuals based on the meanings being conveyed through racial epithets. Using derogatory terms (illegals, illegal aliens, mojaditos, mojankers) reinforces the belief that Latino undocumented immigrants are foreign invaders. Therefore, whether officers are involved in racialized immigration enforcement practices (Constitution-free policing) or simply choose not to provide food for immigrants, officers' language has the power to dehumanize individuals just by its utterance.

CHAPTER 6

Civilian Conflict in
the Borderlands

The previous chapter focused on the racialization of undocumented immigrants through the use of racialized dialogue based on racialized ideas, emotions, and speech accents. This chapter focuses on calls for service that I responded to as a police officer during which individuals relied on deportation threats as a means to resolve their disputes. Moreover, all systems of oppression develop oppressors who rationalize and legitimize the oppression of marginalized individuals.[1] This chapter examines the ways some U.S.-born Latinos, in particular, Mexican Americans, rely on deportation threats and at times call the USBP to oppress and marginalize those most vulnerable: undocumented immigrants. That is, some Latinos rationalize and legitimize the oppression of their coracial/coethnic undocumented immigrant counterparts by relying on the USBP to resolve disputes.

Acts such as threats of deportation and reliance on the USBP illustrate that, similar to police officers who utilize racialized language when referring to Latino undocumented immigrants, some Latino civilians are active and promoting agents of the anti-Latino immigrant subframe as a result of such racist practices.[2] The threat of deportation and reliance on the USBP by U.S.-born Latinos reveals that their actions and treatment of undocumented immigrants are influenced by a desire to inflict great emotional pain on undocumented Latino immigrants. Thus, the actions illustrated in this chapter reveal how civilians become enforcers of the racial contract through ideological conditioning by internalizing the white racial frame. The following section illustrates how U.S.-born Latinos rely on USBP threats as a means of resolving disputes that are often trivial in nature.

Border Patrol Threats

One afternoon my partner, Deputy Orlen, and I responded to a civil dispute involving two men at a local flea market. When we arrived at the flea market, we spoke with Javier, who stated that he had taken his television to the flea market to get it fixed by a man named Patricio. Javier said that all he wanted was to get his television back, but Patricio was demanding that Javier pay him for his services before returning his repaired television. I then approached Patricio, who stated in Spanish that he had repaired Javier's television and wanted to get paid for his service. Javier was dissatisfied with Patricio's service and, consequently, refused to pay Patricio for the repair.

After speaking with Patricio for several minutes, I advised him to walk with me to where Deputy Orlen and Javier were standing. Once all four of us were gathered together, Deputy Orlen and I advised Javier that he needed to pay Patricio in order to get his television back, but that if he was dissatisfied with Patricio's service, he needed to file a civil lawsuit with a local court. Javier angrily responded, "You see. Fucking Mexicans, they just come over here to commit crimes! This guy didn't fix my TV right, and now he won't give me back my TV until I pay him. . . . Can't you guys call Border Patrol on his ass so he can be deported?"

To deescalate the situation, Deputy Orlen told Javier to calm down and stop screaming. I then advised Javier that we were not going to call the USBP or get involved in immigration issues. Javier was still irritated and told us, "Well, if you guys won't call them [USBP], then I will!" Javier was adamant about having the USBP involved in his civil dispute with Patricio. Several minutes later, after we advised him again of his legal options, he calmed down and paid Patricio for the services rendered. Javier eventually left the flea market with his television.

Once Javier left, Patricio told us that he understood a little English and knew what Javier was saying about him. He then said in Spanish, "I know I'm Mexican and that I'm not legally here [in the United States], but that does not mean I am a criminal. It is not good that he accuse me of being a criminal if that gentleman does not know me. . . . I don't understand why he wanted to call Border Patrol on me if I haven't done anything bad. . . . I'm just making an honest living to provide for my family" (paraphrased from field notes).

Javier's anti-immigrant sentiment toward undocumented immigrants illustrates that he wanted to have Patricio deported by the USBP as a way to resolve the issue he had with him. According to Javier, Patricio was an undocumented immigrant, which rendered him worthy of being deported from the United States and, conversely, indicated Patricio's unworthiness to belong in the United States. Even though my partner and I provided Javier with information on how to resolve the dispute, his nativistic stance toward undocumented immigrants stipulated that the only way to settle the issue was to have the USBP deport Patricio. Javier's behavior is an example of how some Latinos internalize the white racially framed narrative of Latino undocumented immigrants (in this case, Mexican undocumented immigrants), which was illustrated by his criminalized perceptions of Latino undocumented immigrants such as Patricio. In addition, Javier's actions illustrate how some Latinos in the borderlands become enforcers of the racial contract through ideological conditioning—internalized racism.[3]

The following description of a different call for service illustrates another example of how the threat of deportation is utilized by Latino residents on the South Texas–Mexico border as a method of enforcing order for neighborhood conflicts. One Tuesday morning while working the day shift, I responded to a neighbor dispute call for service: a woman had called the police because of her neighbor's erratic driving behavior. Once at the location, I spoke with an elderly Latina, Minerva, who stated, "I don't know if these people [her neighbors] think they can live the same way over here [the United States] as they did in their home country." She then followed this comment by stating that there were laws in the United States that must be respected. I asked Minerva if she knew the immigration status of her neighbors, and she replied, "Yeah, well, I'm sure they're from Mexico or whatever Latin country because they told me they crossed [clandestinely] to the U.S." Minerva then stated that they did not speak English, and she did not know what to do to keep her neighbors from driving recklessly in the neighborhood.

Minerva's grandson Samuel joined the conversation and stated, "We always call you guys to complain about these illegals, but you never do anything." He then said that they were tired of the neighbors driving fast in the neighborhood and that they always peeled out on the street without any repercussions. Trying to placate them with humor, I informed Samuel that unfortunately I could not be posted in the neighborhood twenty-four hours a day to prevent his neighbors from driving erratically, but I would make note of the issue so that we could patrol the area more frequently.

Minerva then stated that Samuel wanted her to call USBP on their neighbors but that she was unsure what to do and that maybe she would have to call USBP in order to find a resolution herself. I told Minerva that it was not necessary to call the USBP to resolve the issue, since it was a neighborhood problem and not an immigration issue. She informed me that indeed the issue with her neighbors was related to immigration since her neighbors were from a "Latin" country.

Again, the above vignette illustrates how some people utilize the threat of deportation to resolve conflicts with their neighbors. Minerva and Samuel felt that the only way to resolve the issue was to have their neighbors deported from the United States by the USBP. According to them, their neighbors were undocumented immigrants from a Latin-origin country, thus rendering them worthy of being removed from the United States. More importantly, this vignette illustrates the manner in which some Latinos internalize the white racially framed narrative of undocumented immigrants by utilizing racialized language and ultimately wanting their neighbors to be deported by the USBP. Consequently, Latinos such as Minerva and Samuel become agents who promote the anti-Latino immigrant subframe.

The call for service that I describe next illustrates an undocumented immigrant's unfamiliarity with his rights in the United States. The call for service further illustrates a common theme of this chapter: reliance on the USBP to resolve civil disputes.

One morning while I was partnered with Deputy Larrigán, we responded to a civil dispute regarding the purchase of a computer. We both made contact with Mr. Santos, who had called the police because he was having problems with his acquaintance Antonio. Mr. Santos notified us that he performed a favor for Antonio by purchasing a computer from a local department store based on the understanding that Antonio would make the store's monthly payments for the computer. However, after a long time had elapsed, Mr. Santos received a letter from the department store stating that the bill was several months overdue and that no payment had been made for the computer. When Mr. Santos asked Antonio why he had not made any payments for the computer, Antonio's belligerent response was that he was going to call the USBP to have Mr. Santos deported if he called the police to report the issue. Mr. Santos then stated in Spanish, "The fact that I don't have papers to be here doesn't mean that I don't have rights. . . . I don't know, Officers, maybe I'm wrong, but I don't think I should be deported." Deputy Larrigán told Mr. Santos in Spanish that he had nothing to fear since we did not wear green uniforms (he touched his chest with his opened hand while making the comment) or work for the USBP.

Mr. Santos replied that since he and his family members were undocumented immigrants, they were unfamiliar with their rights as residents of the United States.[4] He further stated, "We are constantly being threatened with deportation [by Antonio]. . . . That's why I decided to call the police, even though I was risking being deported by you all." I then told Mr. Santos in Spanish not to worry, because USBP agents only respond to referral calls when they suspect a residence is being used as a stash house.[5] Mr. Santos told us that he was bewildered by Antonio's threats to call the USBP, because Antonio is also of Mexican descent.

Deputy Larrigán replied, "You know, that's something that I've seen here in the [Rio Grande] Valley frequently." Deputy Larrigán went on to comment that he did not know why, but U.S.-born Latinos discriminate more against immigrants than whites do. He noted that this is wrong, because Latinos are not supposed to discriminate against their own, but he then concluded, "But that's not the case in the valley." Mr. Santos agreed with Deputy Larrigán that there were a lot of people in the RGV who discriminate against undocumented immigrants. He continued to discuss this issue and noted, "This [immigrant discrimination] is to be expected from someone who is not your race, but not from someone of your same race."

As evidenced by this call for service, Mr. Santos was being threatened with deportation by his acquaintance Antonio. Antonio took matters into his own hands to dissuade Mr. Santos from filing a police report that would get Antonio in trouble with law enforcement officials by threatening to call the USBP. Thus, Antonio used his citizenship status over Mr. Santos to ensure that Mr. Santos would keep quiet about the situation; in essence, Antonio enforced control over Mr. Santos. Another call for service illustrates how the reliance on the USBP is seen as the be-all and end-all method to resolve a dispute between neighbors.

One gloomy Saturday afternoon, I responded to a call for service involving a neighbor dispute and made contact with a Mr. Manzano, who told me that he had been having problems with his neighbor Ramón for several weeks because Ramón constantly played loud Spanish music at all hours of the day. Mr. Manzano had previously tried to address the issue with Ramón, but every time he broached the subject, Ramón became confrontational. Consequently, Mr. Manzano decided to call the police to see what could be done to resolve the issue.

Mr. Manzano stated that he had been having problems with Ramón for several weeks: "If it's not real early in the morning, it's also late at night that he always has the damn Spanish music real loud." I notified Mr. Manzano that one unfortunate side effect to living in the county (as opposed to inside the city limits) was that no ordinances regarding loud music existed. I advised him that he needed to continue calling the police to document all the incidents of loud music so that eventually he could file a civil lawsuit against Ramón with the local civil court.

Mr. Manzano seemed surprised by my response and said, "So there's nothing you guys can do to him?" I replied that, unfortunately, the only thing I could do regarding the loud music was to advise Ramón to turn it down. I then advised Mr. Manzano again to continue documenting these loud music incidents in case he wanted to pursue a civil lawsuit against Ramón regarding this ongoing loud music issue.

Mr. Manzano said that he would call the police every time Ramón played loud music at his residence, but he figured that we (the police) could have done more by at least giving Ramón a citation for loud music. Mr. Manzano then muttered, "Well, this illegal [pointing in the direction of Ramón's house] doesn't know what he has coming." He then mentioned that he didn't want to call USBP but that he was going to do it in order to resolve the issue with Ramón.

I told Mr. Manzano that there was no need for him to call the USBP to solve the issue, since I had already advised him what to do. He said that me going to talk with Ramón was futile, since he was not home at that time. Mr. Manzano further stated that he was going to call USBP "to see if they deport his illegal ass, because that's the only way to fix this."

It was apparent to me that Mr. Manzano believed that calling the USBP to report Ramón was the most effective method of resolving the issue. He asked me if I could provide him with the phone number to the USBP, but I told him that the only phone number I had was for law enforcement use only. I did tell him, though, that he could find the phone number of the local USBP station by searching for it on his cell phone. As he predicted, I was unable to make contact with anyone at Ramón's residence.

Mr. Manzano was visibly troubled about this loud music situation with Ramón and wanted to utilize the USBP to resolve it. I had a lengthy conversation with Mr. Manzano; however, I've only included here the portion of my conversation that addressed the underlying problem: Ramón's playing of loud music. During my conversation with Mr. Manzano, he constantly utilized the white racially framed narrative of undocumented immigrants by referring to Ramón as an "illegal."[6] Moreover, Mr. Manzano and Ramón's case was not the only call for service that I responded to where neighbors relied on the USBP to enforce order among each other. The following call for service reveals that neighbors rely on the USBP to settle trivial neighborhood issues that have no method of resolution other than the parties in question simply choosing to be amicable to each other.

One hot Friday summer evening, I responded to a disturbance call involving neighbors who lived across the street from each other. I made contact with an older Latina named Mrs. Salinas, who was sitting on a sofa in her living room. Mrs. Salinas had called the police because she wanted to report her neighbor Miguel for being inconsiderate. Mrs. Salinas told me that Miguel continually had guests over to his house for a get-together or some other social event, and the people who visited him always parked in front of her house, sometimes even causing her mailbox to be blocked. According to Mrs. Salinas, the issue had been going on ever since Miguel and his family moved into the colonia. Mrs. Salinas expressed frustration at the situation during our conversation inside her house. She said in

Spanish, "Ever since those illegals moved into the colonia, they've been nothing but problems. . . . They [Miguel's guests] are always parking in front of my house. I hate it." Mrs. Salinas said that she had already addressed the issue once with Miguel's wife, but their guests still parked in front of her house. I notified her that since it was a public roadway, people could park there as long as they parked with the flow of traffic. Mrs. Salinas said that other deputies who had responded regarding this issue had advised her the same way.

Frustrated, Mrs. Salinas complained that she was wasting her time calling the police, since I was providing the same information as the previous deputies. She said that the only thing left to do was to call the USBP, and she asked me how long it would take for the USBP to respond. I told her in Spanish that USBP's response time depended on who called. That is, if a law enforcement agency made the call, the USBP would respond in a timely manner, but if a civilian placed the call, I did not know how long it would take USBP to respond.

Mrs. Salinas then said with excitement, "Can you call them, then?" I smiled and replied that I would not call USBP, since the call for service had nothing to do with immigration. Adamantly, she replied that indeed the call involved immigration, since Miguel and his family were "illegals" and needed to be dealt with accordingly. I told her that if she wanted to call USBP to report Miguel and his family, then she needed to do that on her own.

Mrs. Salinas notified me that as soon as I left, she was going to report Miguel and his family to the USBP, because calling the police to resolve the ongoing issue had not solved the problem. I told her that there was no need to call the USBP, because there was no guarantee that USBP would even respond to the location to deport a family from their residence. I did tell her, however, that I would talk with Miguel about her concerns to ensure that at the very least he instruct his visitors to not block her mailbox during the day.

I walked across the street and talked with Miguel, who was doing maintenance work on his vehicle. Miguel, who was in his late thirties, was changing the oil in his truck, and he rolled out from under the truck when I identified myself. He stood up, grabbed a cloth, wiped his oil-stained hands, and then shook my hand in greeting. He said in Spanish, "How can I help you, Officer?" I replied in Spanish that I needed to talk to him about his neighbor Mrs. Salinas. Miguel replied in a frustrated tone that he more than likely knew what the issue was: Mrs. Salinas's mailbox being blocked. He then said, "She's always bitching for no apparent reason." I told Miguel the reason for her complaint, and he did not seem surprised. Miguel said that Mrs. Salina always complained about him and his family for no apparent reason. He then told me that he wanted to file harassment charges against her: "She's always telling me that I'm an illegal and that she's going to call

Border Patrol so that I can be deported. . . . She doesn't let me live in peace and is always bitching that she's going to have me deported."

I told him that I was going to document what he told me since he wanted to file a report against Mrs. Salinas for the deportation threats.[7] Miguel said that ever since he moved into the colonia with his family, Mrs. Salinas had harassed him by either calling the police or threatening to call the USBP. Miguel further stated that he was happy living in the colonia because it meant he had his own house and property where he could host his friends and family members. He said that Mrs. Salinas was the only neighbor he had problems with on his street. Miguel then stated, "I'm not legal [his immigration status], but I don't think the Border Patrol has time to waste by coming to my house to deport me. . . . You guys come here often, and it's the same thing; you leave after talking with me." As he predicted, after several more minutes of conversation regarding Mrs. Salinas's concerns and getting his side of the story, I left the area and resumed my patrol duties.

Mrs. Salinas is another example of a Latina/o I came in contact with during my routine work activities who relied on the USBP—in particular, deportation threats—to resolve noncriminal neighbor issues. In addition, it depicts the manner in which Mrs. Salinas utilized racialized terminology whenever she referred to her neighbor Miguel. Next, I present another call for service that illustrates how some individuals purposely call the police to inquire about utilizing the USBP as a method of resolving their issue with neighbors.

I responded to a call for service involving a man who wanted information regarding his legal ability to have his neighbors deported. While I was at the residence, I spoke with a middle-aged Latino named Mr. Palomares who said that he called the police because he needed help with his problematic neighbors.[8] Mr. Palomares said that his neighbors had several dogs, and the dogs damaged his fence and kept making their way onto his property. He was annoyed with the dogs and had already filed previous reports regarding the issue. Mr. Palomares notified me that the last time he called the sheriff's office, he was given the information of the local civil court. After calling the civil court, he was instructed regarding what he needed to do in order to bring forward a civil lawsuit against his neighbors for damage to his property. Mr. Palomares told me that he did not want to proceed with the civil lawsuit because it was more expensive to file a civil lawsuit (i.e., it involved paying court fees) than to have his fence repaired.

Mr. Palomares said that he called the police to see what his options were regarding calling the USBP because that was the only method to resolve the dispute: "I've already called you guys in the past because of the illegal aliens [his neighbors] to see what could be done to have my fence fixed. . . . Now I called because I want to see if you can tell me how to have the illegal aliens deported."

I advised Mr. Palomares that I was not familiar with how to deal with USBP from a civilian perspective; therefore, I could not provide assistance regarding his inquiry. He said that he was more interested in knowing if he could make an anonymous call to the USBP to have his neighbors deported without his neighbors knowing that he had called the USBP: "I want to call Border Patrol but do not want to give them any of my information. . . . I just want them to deport the illegal aliens." I asked Mr. Palomares how he knew his neighbors' immigration status. He told me that in a previous conversation he had with his neighbors after they first moved into the colonia, they told him they were immigrants from Mexico. Both Mr. Palomares and his neighbors have lived in the colonia for several years. He told me that even though they had been neighbors for several years, they kept to themselves and did not interact with each other. Mr. Palomares said that he did not like to interact with his neighbors, and that is why he always resorted to calling the police—to let the police express his discontent with his neighbors on his behalf.

I told Mr. Palomares that, in my opinion, I believed it was best for him to talk with his neighbors. I stressed to him that he needed to keep in mind that we, the police, would respond to the location whenever he called; however, at the end of the day, he needed to deal with his neighbors day and night, since the police leave after completion of each call for service. Mr. Palomares had been advised that he needed to file a civil lawsuit to resolve the issue regarding the damaged property. He said to me, "That's exactly why I called today. I don't want to sue them, and I don't want them here anymore. . . . I want those illegal aliens deported."

I advised Mr. Palomares that I would talk to his neighbors about the damaged fence and speak to them regarding the dogs. I told him that it was entirely his decision if he wanted to report his neighbors to the USBP. After speaking for several more minutes with Mr. Palomares, I walked over to his neighbors' property directly next to his house and noticed several vehicles parked on the dirt driveway of the residence. I knocked on the front door, but no one answered. It was clearly evident to me that someone was home but that no one wanted to answer the door, which did not surprise me, because, after I checked the prior history log for the residence, I noticed that we had responded to the residence several times for the same issue: neighbor dispute.[9] They probably assumed that Mr. Palomares had called the police on them again.

Even though neighbors did not call the USBP in the preceding examples, on some calls for service that I responded to, neighbors did call the USBP in an attempt to have undocumented immigrants deported from the United States. The next section illustrates some surprising and alarming examples of the extreme measures people go to in an attempt to resolve noncriminal matters and illuminates how some take advantage of an undocumented immigrant's immigration status. Thus, the following section best illustrates Charles Mills's theoretical conception of how the white supremacist state is reproduced through ideological conditioning by having civilians become enforcers of the racial contract.

Calling the Border Patrol

One hot and humid Wednesday summer evening, I made contact with Mrs. Bonilla in the driveway of her two-story brick home. She stated that she had called the police regarding her ex-husband, Leandro. She and Leandro were married for about ten years but had gotten divorced several weeks prior to our encounter. As a result of their finalized decree of divorce, she was allowed to keep the house, along with the family vehicle. Their decree of divorce also included guidelines regarding the custodial rights of their three children. Mrs. Bonilla stated that ever since their divorce, Leandro had made threats to her that he was going to report her to the USBP if she did not let him see their children whenever he wanted. Mrs. Bonilla told me that she was originally from Mexico and was an undocumented immigrant, whereas Leandro, who was of Salvadoran descent, had been born in the United States.[10] They met and married in Houston but relocated to the RGV after Leandro was given a promotion within his company.

Mrs. Bonilla notified me that she had never called the police before because of her immigration status, but she decided to call the police this time so that she could receive the peace of mind of knowing she would not be deported. She said that she had problems (intimate partner violence) in the past with Leandro, but she never called the police because of her immigration status. Mrs. Bonilla said in Spanish, "Every time he would hit me, he would tell me that if I called the police, I was going to be deported. . . . Earlier today, he called me and said that he had called the Border Patrol so that I could be deported." She was notified by Leandro that he had called USBP because she did not allow him to take the kids from her house to his apartment to spend time with them.

Mrs. Bonilla had paperwork indicating that she had full custodial rights of their children except for every other weekend, which is when Leandro had custodial rights of the children. She further told me that Leandro did not want to abide by the court order because he periodically wanted to take the children from her residence during his noncustodial days (i.e., weekdays) so that they could spend time with him.

Mrs. Bonilla stated that she was worried, because Leandro had finally followed through on his threat to have her deported when she did not comply with his demands: "I think Leandro will have me deported, because all the other days it's just been threats. . . . Today, he actually called the Border Patrol."[11] She went on to state that she was worried USBP was going to take her children away from her, and that is why she finally decided to call the police for help, even though she had been reluctant to call the police in the past due to her immigration status. She said she did not want to continue stressing and fearing that the USBP would deport her.

I told Mrs. Bonilla that she did not have to worry about cooperating with the police, because her immigration status had no bearing on the call for service. I also told her that it was unlikely the USBP would come to her residence, but if for some reason they showed up, she should not open the door or make any contact with the USBP agents. I told her that she had the legal right not to cooperate with any law enforcement agency, such as the USBP, that wanted to enter her residence.

Mrs. Bonilla felt betrayed by Leandro because he wanted her deported even though she was the mother of his children. She could not fathom why he called the USBP, but it did not surprise her, given the fact that he always threatened her with being deported whenever he physically and mentally abused her in the past. Mrs. Bonilla also revealed that she would be on the lookout for the USBP but still felt scared and nervous, even though I had tried to calm her. She said, "I'm going to see if they [USBP] end up coming for me tonight. . . . I'm scared that they'll deport me, but I'm more nervous about what will happen with my kids if the Border Patrol comes."

Before leaving the residence, I provided Mrs. Bonilla with contact information for the local domestic violence and immigrant advocate organizations. My conversation with Mrs. Bonilla reflects the findings in the academic literature, which note that undocumented immigrant victims weigh the costs and benefits of reporting their victimization to the police and at times are reluctant to report their victimization as a result of their immigration status.[12] My call for service with Mrs. Bonilla illustrates how the act of calling the USBP to have someone deported is utilized within a family setting to enforce control over the undocumented individual—in this case, Mrs. Bonilla.

The following call for service illustrates how some Latinos internalize the white racially framed narrative of undocumented immigrants by utilizing racialized language. It is also consistent with the white racial frame because it evokes negative emotions toward undocumented immigrants by reporting undocumented immigrants to the USBP.

One afternoon while working the midday shift, I responded to a call for service from Matias, who stated in Spanish that he called the police because of his landlord, Janet. Matias was renting Janet's house and did not have a landlord-tenant agreement. He told me that he had traveled out of town for the weekend, and when he returned, he was unable to enter the house because the locks to all the doors had been changed. He called Janet to ask her if she had changed the locks to the doors, and she confirmed that she had changed the locks because she no longer wanted him to live there. He told Janet that he was going to call the police, and Janet hung up on Matias and did not answer any subsequent phone calls he made to her. Matias did not know what he had done to upset Janet, since he was always on time with the monthly rent payments. He decided to call the police to see what could be done about this issue, since Janet was not answering his phone calls. While I was talking with Matias in front of the house, Janet arrived and was visibly upset as she got out of her car. I advised Matias to wait by the front door of the residence with his family while I talked to Janet.

Janet confirmed that she did not want Matias and his family to live at her residence anymore, and she had changed the locks on the doors while they were out of town. I notified her that she needed to visit a local justice of the peace in civil court in order to begin the eviction process, since Matias and his family were her tenants. Unhappy with what I told her, she said, "You see, you damn wetbacks! You're going to get what you deserve!" She continued, "Damn wetbacks! You shouldn't even be here. . . . Go back home to your country, wetbacks!"

I told her that she needed to stop referring to the family in a derogatory manner and needed to let me know what was going on. She said that she had called USBP on her way to the residence so the family could be deported. She then pointed at them and said, "You're going to get deported, damn wetbacks!"

At this point, I could see that Janet had become agitated, and I told her that she needed to let me know what the issue was. I asked her why she was annoyed with the family, and she told me that they were spreading rumors to other individuals that she was a bad and inept landlord. Janet then told me that the family members were undocumented Central American immigrants and that she wanted them deported. I advised her that there was no need for her to tell me the immigration status of the family, because their immigration status had no bearing on the outcome of the call for service. She then showed me the call log on her cell phone, which indicated that she had called the USBP prior to arriving at the residence. She said, "Look, I called the Border Patrol, so these wetbacks will get deported."

I told her that she needed to let the family enter the residence, since she had yet to file the proper eviction paperwork in civil court. Janet said she would open the front door for the family, but she was going to go first thing the next morning to civil court to begin the eviction process. I walked back to the front door of the residence to tell Matias that Janet was going to allow them to go inside the house.

He replied in Spanish that he no longer wanted to stay at the residence and was going to call his friend to help him move the family's belongings, since he did not know what Janet was capable of doing to him and his family. He then said, "Besides, she called the Border Patrol, so I don't think it's safe for us to stay here."

I told him that even though she had called the USBP, there was no guarantee that they would respond to the call. Matias was adamant that he wanted to move out, regardless of whether the USBP responded to the call or not, since Janet was evidently upset with him and his family for no reason. Matias denied Janet's accusations after I informed him why she was upset with him.

Unlike the example of Mrs. Bonilla, who was notified by her husband that he had reported her to the USBP, in this incident I made contact with the individual, Janet, who actually called the USBP to resolve a civil issue. Janet is a prime example of how some Latina/os internalize the white racially framed narrative of Latino undocumented immigrants and, in turn, become agents who promote the anti-Latino immigrant subframe.[13] Janet's nativistic hostility toward Matias and his family was evident because she not only berated them with racialized vulgar language—"wetbacks"—but also ultimately notified the USBP of their immigration status with the intent of having them deported. Clearly, Janet's actions reveal a prime example of how individuals become enforcers of the racial contract by maintaining white supremacy. That is, she felt that Matias and his family were unworthy of belonging in the United States and instead were worthy of deportation.

Of all the calls for service that I responded to in which people decided that the USBP was the only arbitrator to resolve their domestic issues, the following call for service was perhaps one of the most alarming. The following illustration demonstrates that even if the issue involves two married individuals, no one is immune from being reported to the USBP.

One afternoon while I was working the midday shift, I responded to a call for service involving a domestic dispute between a man and a woman. Once at the residence, I spoke with Mrs. Jaibo, who stated in Spanish that she had called the police because she had argued with her husband, Nendo, and needed help. Unexpectedly, Mrs. Jaibo revealed some startling information. She said that she was from Mexico and was undocumented and that if I was going to have her deported, then so be it. She then said, "I can't continue to be silent anymore because I don't have papers." I advised her that there was no reason for her to disclose her immigration status to me, since I was not a federal immigration official, that is, a USBP agent.

As I spoke with Mrs. Jaibo in the front yard of the residence, I noticed that she was visibly upset about whatever had just occurred. Mrs. Jaibo revealed that, earlier, she and Nendo were on their way home after running some errands and got into an argument regarding their finances. She told me that she was upset because during the course of the argument, Nendo called USBP and reported her undocumented immigration status. She felt offended and hurt that her husband called the USBP so that she could get deported. She continued by stating, "He knows I'm not here legally, and that's why he called the Border Patrol. . . . If they want to come to pick me up, fine. I don't care anymore."

While I spoke with Mrs. Jaibo, my partner for that call for service, Deputy Nava, spoke with Nendo inside the residence. Nendo advised Deputy Nava that he was going to leave the house to avoid further problems and packed a duffel bag of clothes. After several minutes, Deputy Nava and Nendo walked out of the house and approached Nendo's truck. I then approached Nendo, who was stowing his duffel bag in his truck. I observed that Nendo had already placed a lot of clothes inside the truck prior to our arrival.

While he was arranging his duffel bag and clothes, Nendo conversed with us. I decided to ask him why he had called the USBP on his wife. He said in Spanish, "Well, what could I do? She kept on fucking with me and never shut the hell up." He then admitted that he called USBP so that Mrs. Jaibo would quit nagging him. Surprised that he had called the USBP to report his wife, I asked Nendo what USBP officials had told him after he called. He said that USBP officials notified him that they were going to investigate Mrs. Jaibo by obtaining her information, such as her name, date of birth, country of origin, and home address. I then asked him if he felt bad or remorseful for reporting his wife to USBP, and he quickly replied in Spanish, "I don't feel bad, because she never shut the hell up. If they take her, oh well."[14]

As evidenced by this call for service, Nendo relied on the USBP as an arbitrator to resolve the argument he had with his wife and evidently did not have any qualms about Mrs. Jaibo being potentially deported from the United States by the USBP. Consistent with the other calls for service in this chapter, Nendo relied on the USBP to resolve his issue, even though it did not necessitate federal immigration intervention. Moreover, as noted in this call for service, Nendo was upset with Mrs. Jaibo, which evoked a negative emotion that ultimately resulted in him calling the USBP. It is clearly evident that, based on his actions, Nendo is an active and promoting agent of the anti-Latino immigrant subframe. What was most surprising to me about this call for service—besides Nendo reporting his wife to the USBP—was his carefree, nonchalant attitude regarding the precarious situation he had placed his wife in.

None of the individuals in this chapter who wanted to use the USBP as an arbitrator to resolve their issues had any problem placing their fellow coracial/coethnic counterparts in precarious situations. Their rationale for such behavior seemed to be that in the borderlands, the USBP can and should be utilized as a method to resolve disputes when those disputes involve undocumented immigrants—enforcement of the racial contract. The individuals in this chapter who relied on USBP intervention to solve their dilemmas were clearly operating out of the white racially framed narrative of undocumented immigrants by wanting to have undocumented immigrants deported as a method to enforce control over them.

CONCLUSION

The objective of this book is to extend the scholarship by exploring the racialization of Latino undocumented immigrants and by examining the collaboration between local police and the USBP. Namely, *Enforcing Order on the Border* has two goals. The first is to provide further insight into how the concept of race in a predominantly Latino-origin community, in particular, Mexican American, contextualizes intraracial/intraethnic relations in the South Texas–Mexico borderlands. Second, and most important, it strives to illustrate how the concept of race in regard to police-community relations and immigration enforcement functions in the borderlands and to detail the long-standing history of systemic racism prevalent in law enforcement agencies through racialized institutional practices. That is, from an institutional perspective (that of the local police), this book describes how institutional practices such as immigration enforcement occur in the South Texas–Mexico borderlands as a form of collaborative effort between local police and the USBP. Consequently, this collaborative effort in the South Texas–Mexico borderlands creates a distinctive method of policing that I refer to as Constitution-free policing.

This book explores the central questions of how undocumented Latino immigrants become racialized by their coracials/coethnics, how undocumented Latino immigrants are affected by racialized immigration enforcement practices, and to what extent the racialization process and racialized immigration enforcement practices reveal evidence of racism in the RGV. In order to accomplish this, the study was contextualized theoretically by employing the racial conflict theoretical frameworks of the racial contract, the white racial frame, and racist nativism. Charles Mills argued that the racial contract is another way of theorizing about and critiquing the state and that the white supremacist state was established and is reproduced by two methods of coercion: physical violence and ideological conditioning. Local police participation in immigration enforcement is another form of coercion—institutional violence (race-based immigration enforcement)—although it can also be considered physical violence, since it involves the removal of immigrants from the United States against their will. Further, the white racial frame includes racial images, stereotypes, and emotions, along with distinctive language and imaging tools, that impose the racial hierarchy. In essence, this popular frame involves the common view that purports to the superiority of white individuals and the inferiority of people of color. It is through the white racial frame narrative of people of color and immigrants that poverty, low levels of educational attainment, and oppression are legitimized. Last, racist nativism encompasses racialization and anti-immigrant beliefs that manifest as an ideology that is evidenced within institutional practices such as local police participation in immigration enforcement practices that ultimately serve to ensure white supremacy.

Nativistic hostility has been a central feature of the integration of immigrant groups into the United States. At different periods of time, anti-immigrant sentiment has targeted certain racial and ethnic immigrant groups who have been perceived as posing a threat to the social fabric of U.S. relations. That is, European immigrants (e.g., Irish and Italians), Asian immigrants, and Latino immigrants have each, at one point or another, borne the brunt of nativist hostility. Currently, Latino immigrants continue to be the aim of anti-immigrant and nativistic sentiment, as evidenced by racialized immigration enforcement practices illustrated in the book that are still in practice today.

Enforcing Order on the Border heeds the call of recent scholarship that argues for the need to analyze undocumented immigrants as racialized individuals rather than ethnic people and to include Latinos and immigrants in policing literature.[1] In addition, the objective of the book is to incorporate race perspectives into the examination of Latino immigrants by exploring the various methods by which Latino immigrants are racialized and targeted by racialized immigration enforcement practices.[2] My dual role of academic researcher and, in particular, police officer allowed me to accomplish these goals. As Rogelio Sáenz and Karen Manges Douglas argue, "Race talk and racist actions are most likely to be captured in the field, where race is played out, rather [than] in structured questionnaires."[3] Thus, for this study I employed the qualitative research method of autoethnography and the data collection method of participant observation in order to explore how some Latinos in the RGV become advocates of the anti-Latino immigrant subframe and to illustrate the enforcement of the racial contract in a majority-minority community, the RGV. The findings are illustrated from an autoethnographic context that utilizes the self as both subject and object of research inquiry.

This book also heeds the call of Ronald Weitzer, who noted, "Research is lacking on officers' interactions with or views of Hispanic civilians and on Hispanic officers' behavior and attitudes per se."[4] Several chapters of *Enforcing Order on the Border* provide further insight into this gap in the scholarship.

Racialization throughout the Years

As explained in chapter 2, the autoethnography method established the groundwork for the entire study by providing a chronological recollection of my experiences with the racialization process as a resident on the U.S.-Mexico border, specifically, the RGV. As evidenced in the chapter, my experience with the racialization process dates back to when I was in high school. This chapter includes a discussion of my recollection of how certain students were racialized based on their accent, music preference, dress style, and fondness for playing soccer. These students were subject to racialized terminology such as *mojo*, which is the English slang equivalent of "wetback." In addition, the chapter revealed that I also at different times endured the brunt of racialized terminology. In high school, certain peers and I were seen as foreigners by our classmates because we displayed particular attributes.

Chapter 6 reveals that the use of racialized terminology is widespread not only among police officers but also among community members. This chapter illustrates that in the process of wanting to have their coracials/coethnics deported from the United States, some Latinos utilized racialized terminology whenever they referred to their coracial immigrant counterparts. Alarmingly, the chapter reveals the manner in which some Latinos serve as enforcers of the racial contract by using USBP as an arbitrator to resolve their disputes with the goal of having their coracials/coethnics deported from the United States.

In addition, chapter 4 provides several incidents that illustrate the manner in which police officers utilize racialized terminology when referring to Latino immigrants. As a police officer, I came to realize that no matter how strong the "blue brotherhood bond" of policing was, if certain officers displayed specific foreign attributes, they were susceptible to becoming the subject of racialized dialogue. Indeed, some officers acquired nicknames because of certain characteristics that were deemed worthy of racializing them as foreigners by other officers. Taken together, the aforementioned chapters reveal how some Latinos in the RGV are susceptible to internalizing the white racially framed narrative of Latino undocumented immigrants and thus become advocates of the anti-Latino immigrant subframe.

Police and Race

Chapters 2, 4, and 5 illuminate an alarming aspect of routine police activity on the South Texas–Mexico border: the participation of local police departments in immigration enforcement. Whether through vehicle pursuits or routine calls for service involving stash houses, officers in some local police departments in the RGV have become enforcers of the racial contract that ensures white supremacy. What is noteworthy is the local department's willingness to participate alongside its federal counterparts (e.g., USBP) in everyday immigration enforcement practices when no official agreement among law enforcement agencies—such as the 287(g) program—exists.

In particular, the participation of officers from the Del Monte County Sheriff's Office with USBP agents was partially based on being recipients of the OPSG grant. Since the USBP is the lead agency for operations under this grant, collaboration with USBP is a necessity in order to receive funding. These collaborative efforts on the U.S.-Mexico border between local police agencies such as the DMCSO and the USBP create a distinctive method of policing that I refer to as Constitution-free policing. Moreover, as previously noted, local police participation in immigration enforcement on the U.S.-Mexico border predates the Mexican repatriation campaign, and this research reveals how local police departments are still active participants in racialized police practices that predominantly affect Latino undocumented immigrants. The Constitution-free policing method is not only utilized in the RGV. This distinctive policing method is also utilized in other areas of the Texas-Mexico border, as evidenced by the example of the Maverick County Sheriff's Office deputy in the introduction, and in Arizona and New Mexico, as illustrated with the examples provided in chapter 1. Thus, Constitution-free policing practices are performed throughout the U.S. Southwest borderlands.

One aspect of this book explores how Latino police officers in the RGV racialize their coracial/coethnic immigrant counterparts through everyday conversation and how some local police departments participate in immigration enforcement practices when responding to calls for service. Claudio Vera Sanchez and Dennis Rosenbaum assert that this aspect of police-community relations needs to be addressed: "Police are attuned to race in heterogeneous neighborhoods where different racial and ethnic groups live side by side. But for homogenous minority neighborhoods, a new conceptualization of racialization or biased policing may be needed to understand police interpretations of the environment."[5]

The findings reveal that similar to some Latino civilians in the RGV, some Latino police officers internalize the common white racially framed narrative of Latino undocumented immigrants to racialize immigrants through the use of dehumanizing and objectifying terminology such as "illegals," "illegal aliens," "moja-dos," "IAS," "UAS," and "mojankers." In addition, the results demonstrate that along-side their use of racialized terminology, some local police departments become enforcers of the racial contract as a result of their Constitution-free policing tac-tics, which involve collaboration with the USBP in the apprehension, detention, and deportation of undocumented Latino immigrants.

What Now? Policy Implications

LOCAL POLICE PARTICIPATION IN IMMIGRATION ENFORCEMENT ON THE U.S.-MEXICO BORDER

The findings of *Enforcing Order on the Border* analyze the intersection between race, policing, and immigration enforcement. As a result, one aspect of this book illuminates what occurred in a majority-minority Mexican-origin community in relation to local police participation in immigration enforcement practices with the USBP. These findings can begin to "help clarify the ways in which the policing of Hispanic immigrants [is] both similar to and distinct from that experienced by other racial and ethnic groups."[6] Similar to other scholarship that has documented the hyperpolicing of Black and Latino youths, Black community members, and Latino community members in the interior of the United States, my study found similar patterns of hyperpolicing practices of undocumented Latino immigrants on the U.S.-Mexico border, especially in the form of collaborative policing efforts between local police and the USBP.[7]

The results from the book illustrate that even though the Le Grand Police De-partment and the DMCSO are not official participants in immigration enforcement programs such as the 287(g) program, officers from both departments operate as de facto immigration officials involved in racialized immigration enforcement practices during routine patrol work activities. As explained, local police depart-ments rely on the government funding that they receive for participating in DHS grants such as OPSG as a means of supplementing police officer salaries and the purchase of patrol vehicles, and from an organizational perspective, the depart-ment sees participation in OPSG as just another means of acquiring economic rev-enue for the department. However, local police involvement in federal immigra-tion enforcement can have unintended consequences for both civilians and the police department.

Mistrust and lack of cooperation are two main examples of the negative im-pacts of a local police department's participation in immigration enforcement. If civilians observe local police officers involved in racialized immigration en-forcement practices, they will become wary of the police, which reinforces strained police-community relations.[8] Moreover, civilians will be hesitant to call the police and will not view police officers as individuals on whom they can rely for help or protection because the civilians fear deportation.[9] Mistrust among community members toward the police can in turn hinder the department's efforts to establish trust and address quality-of-life issues such as crime. Crime will go unreported in local communities, which will affect the actual knowledge of crime rate trends affecting immigrants. Cooperation from potential witnesses to a crime will also be negatively affected, because if an immigrant is a witness to a crime, the immigrant might not be as willing to cooperate with police due to fear of deportation. Aside from creating mistrust and lack of cooperation, local police participation in federal immigration has overarching consequences for immigrant communities.[10]

The findings from *Enforcing Order on the Border* should serve as an example to policymakers that it is of the utmost importance that we reanalyze immigration policy, in particular as it relates to DHS-funded grant programs such as OPSG, in order to critically analyze the counterproductive effects of local police participation in federal immigration enforcement on the U.S.-Mexico border. A recent report from the DHS Office of Inspector General provides a critique of OPSG and reveals that the DHS (in particular, FEMA and USBP officials) has not collected reliable program data or developed measures to demonstrate the effectiveness of OPSG.[11] As a police officer who worked the OPSG grant several times, I witnessed firsthand and participated in USBP's requirement to document apprehension statistics when responding to calls for service involving undocumented immigrants (mostly stash house calls for service). However, I never saw how assisting USBP with stash house calls for service and documenting such practices benefit the U.S. polity with border security. In other words, though it is customary to focus on how many immigrants can be apprehended at stash houses, as this book illustrates, most of my encounters with undocumented Latino immigrants reveal that a majority of immigrants come to the United States with the hopes of economic prosperity and the goal of being productive members of the United States. It is no surprise that the Tucson Police Department opted out of OPSG because they knew that participation in OPSG requires the enforcement of federal immigration law, which runs contrary to the local community's mission of being an immigrant-welcoming city. That is why I believe that OPSG and local police participation in federal immigration practices on the U.S.-Mexico border need to be examined closely—similar to interior immigration enforcement programs such as 287(g) and Secure Communities.

DOES LOCAL CONTEXT MATTER?

Due to the rise of strained police-community relations in communities of color, growing concern exists that local police departments are not racially representative of the communities they serve. As a result, residents have demanded that these departments hire more people of color who racially represent their communities. Scholarship has found a growing trend for more employment of people of color in police departments. According to Brian Reaves, a steady increase in the number of people of color working as police officers has occurred; findings reveal an increase of 16 percent in the employment of Latino police officers.[12]

Even though these statistics illustrate a growing trend for people of color to be employed in local police departments, historically, racial composition of police departments has had very little effect on police-community relations. In fact, Jack Kuykendall and David Burns argue that Black police officers are often harder on Black citizens than white police officers are.[13] Likewise, in the 1950s William Kephart found that Black police officers believed they needed to be harsher with Blacks than with civilians of other racial/ethnic groups.[14] Recent scholarship from Jennifer Cobbina regarding police officers in Baltimore, Maryland, documents findings similar to Kephart's.[15]

The aforementioned studies illustrate that despite the widely held belief that hiring more people of color as police officers will promote greater harmony among communities of color, the recruitment and employment of people of color in police departments will do little to repair fragmented police-community relations. As I learned during my tenure as a police officer, I was a small cog in a well-oiled oppressive machine. I do not base this view on the actions of a few bad apples; rather, I base it on an institutional perspective and my outlook on social inequality. As noted by Anthony Bouza, "Most cops enter as altruistic civilians, eager to help others, and then they become acculturated to the real values of a pressurized organizational environment. They finally leave, weary of the human beast and profoundly skeptical about its real nature."[16] Moreover, communities of color suffer from systemic racism related to housing inequality, employment inequality, education inequality, and health care inequality, to name a few. The police, as an extension of a systemically racist criminal justice system, must continue with their primary objective of regulating human behavior, which often disproportionately impacts Black and Latino communities.[17] Thus, it does not matter what the racial makeup of the department is; police officers,

irrespective of racial background, function as agents of social control by enforcing laws that were and continue to be prejudicial toward Blacks and Latinos.[18]

Whose Side Are You On?

When I explained the project and presented my intentions to potential participants, I did not get into specifics about what I was interested in studying within
the DMCSO. I told police officers that I was interested in what it is like to be a deputy for the DMCSO, specifically, a police officer on the South Texas–Mexico border.[19] That is, I was interested in writing a book on policing on the South Texas–
Mexico border in general, not on police officers in particular.[20] I know that the
results of this book cast a negative light on several police officers in the DMCSO
and the department itself. Although some social researchers might have sinister
motives for studying the police, such as the goal of exposing police malpractice,
that was not my intent.[21] I do not even absolve myself from my actions while working as a police officer because I too, like my fellow officers, was a participant in racialized immigration enforcement practices that targeted Latino undocumented
immigrants. Consequently, I also served as an enforcer of the racial contract and
as a participant in the racist nativistic local policing practice of Constitution-
free policing.[22]

Because of my own affiliation with my fellow officers, I cannot help but be
concerned that they will feel a sense of betrayal after learning the results of this
study. According to Didier Fassin, "Writing always means betraying," and I felt
that I betrayed the trust confided in me by my police officer participants, at least
until I accepted Fassin's contention that "not writing is also a betrayal."[23] I had to
remain focused on the fact that "research in police organizations can be a challenging, adventurous undertaking in a sociologically rich environment" and that
the findings serve an important purpose.[24] My work is guided by a racial and
social justice framework, and it is my hope that *Enforcing Order on the Border*
will appeal not only to a general audience interested in the U.S.-Mexico border
but also to policymakers examining immigration policy.

Another alarming aspect of this book is the anecdotal illustrations of some
Latinos in the RGV who utilized racialized language when referring to their cora-
cial/coethnic immigrant counterparts. That is, I illustrate how racialized terminology was common and even normalized among my school peers and other
members of the public. As previously noted in the introduction, the main reason
I chose to conduct this study was that throughout all my years as a resident on
the South Texas–Mexico border, I witnessed and experienced several incidents of
Latinos, in particular, Mexican Americans, denigrating each other through the use

of racialized terminology and other racist behavior. Some readers, based on anecdotes from this book, might develop a generalized view of the RGV as an area
in which intraracial/intraethnic hostility runs rampant on a daily basis. Although
that may not be the case, I cannot ignore the fact that the RGV is not a monolithic
community in which some perceive community relations through a color-blind
lens.[25]

Latinos are always under constant pressure to adopt the white racial framing of
race matters in the hopes of gaining certain social, political, and economic status
in white American culture. In essence, some Latinos are prone to behaving like
elite white men such as Donald Trump. Elite white men do not even need to be
present within a group in order to support the maintenance of white supremacy.
As evidenced in *Enforcing Order on the Border*, some Latinos adopt a white racially framed narrative of undocumented Latino immigrants, and along with the
racialized immigration enforcement practices evidenced in the book, both perspectives serve to ensure the maintenance of white supremacy.

Once that white structure is in place, racial order is maintained. That is, some
Latinos become promoting agents of the white racial frame, while some law enforcement actions, such as the Constitution-free policing method, are carried
out in order to enforce the racial contract. Furthermore, nativism is utilized as
a tool in conjunction with racism, ultimately culminating in racist nativistic actions that target Latino undocumented immigrants.[26] However negative and
alarming, *Enforcing Order on the Border* argues that we must move beyond the
Latino/white binary of race relations in order to address issues of intraracial/
intraethnic conflict among Latinos in a majority-minority community. Thus, we
must first remove the veil from our faces and acknowledge that racial conflict
exists among Latinos as a result of a desire to gain social, political, and economic
status in the white American culture, and we must acknowledge the long-
standing history of systemic racism prevalent in law enforcement agencies on
the U.S.-Mexico border, a racism that is continually reinforced through racialized and institutionalized immigration enforcement practices, if we indeed seek
to live in a just society.

APPENDIX

Reflexivity

As a sociologist interested in racial/ethnic relations, I tend to view societal issues through a racial conflict perspective. This tendency is, of course, a result of my academic graduate school training, which aided me in examining my lived experience through a critical lens as a resident of the South Texas–Mexico border in the Rio Grande Valley and, more importantly, as a police officer. As previously mentioned, as a former resident of the RGV, I have always been curious why some residents, in particular, Mexican Americans, are antagonistic toward Latino immigrants or their fellow coethnics in general, especially since they live within the same majority-minority Latino-origin community. Several examples provided in this book illustrate the process of intraracial/intraethnic conflict in the RGV between Latinos. Moreover, while serving as a police officer, I participated in institutionalized policing practices that at times tended to target immigrants. Therefore, these two lived experiences—witnessing and experiencing intraracial/intraethnic conflict and partaking in racialized immigration enforcement practices—intrigued me and prompted me to research these phenomena further.

It was important for me to engage in and conduct this research because it moves beyond the Black/white binary of race relations and reveals how the concept of race/racism functions within a predominantly Latino-origin community, the RGV. Being raised in a majority-minority Latino-origin community does not preclude one from experiencing and witnessing racism, as evidenced by the findings of this research, which will no doubt be viewed as alarming and disturbing by many.

One contributing factor to the findings in this study is the theoretical framework that guided the study. That is, I utilized racial conflict theories to help me make sense of my lived experiences as a resident and police officer of the South Texas–Mexico border. Thus, this study might have had different findings if I was not interested in examining how the concept of race/racism functions within a predominantly Latino-origin community.

Another contributing factor that must be acknowledged is how my positionality as an academic and police officer influenced the research study. Even though I had a similar working-class background and was a Latino like my fellow police officer colleagues, our education backgrounds differed and, to a certain extent, affected the way our views on our social position as police officers contrasted with each other. Prior to my graduate school training, when I worked as a police officer for the Le Grand Police Department, I was an impressionable and moldable individual who did not question my position within the social institution of the police. I was a primary example of when the police takes working-class individuals and shapes them to its institutional needs. Thus, while working as a police officer for the Le Grand Police Department, I seldom questioned the policing practices I partook in, such as the need to make a high number of arrests during any given shift to illustrate my work productivity for that given workday. As a police officer, I was well aware that I was an agent of social control empowered and entrusted in my capacity as a police officer with the responsibility of regulating human behavior and with the primary duty of police officers: maintenance of order. Even though I possessed a bachelor's degree prior to working as a police officer for the Le Grand Police Department, I can honestly state that I lacked the critical perspective I later gained from my graduate studies, when I learned to question my role and activities performed as a police officer for the Le Grand Police Department.

While working as a police officer for the Del Monte County Sheriff's Office, I was a different police officer than I was during my previous stint as an officer with Le Grand Police Department. I had graduate school training, which allowed me to question and critically analyze my role as a police officer. As noted in the book, my colleagues knew that I was a graduate student working on my doctoral degree while serving as a police officer for the Del Monte County Sheriff's Office. I was still viewed as one of them, but my educational standing clearly differentiated me from them, since most of them just possessed a high school diploma. A few had some college, and even fewer possessed a bachelor's degree. My educational standing at times affected how some of my police officer colleagues addressed me. They would sometimes joke, "What's up, Doc?" or "What's up, Gamino? Or should I say, Dr. Gamino?" On rare occasions, some of my colleagues even confused my academic training with the medical profession.

For example, on one occasion during roll call, the shift supervisor was complaining that officers should not call in sick for several consecutive days without getting a doctor's excuse. The only one who should be able to do that was me, since I was a doctor. He then looked at me and said, "Well, guys, unless you're a doctor; right, Gamino? Only then can you self-diagnose yourself and claim to be sick." My colleague sitting to my left looked at me and stated, "He's right, Dr. Gamino, right?"

Although it was clearly evident and known to my colleagues that I was working on my doctoral degree while serving as a police officer, I never boasted or bragged about my educational attainment, because I felt that I was no better or smarter than they were just because I was attending graduate school. Some of my colleagues and I differed in our worldviews, because they generally tended to have more conservative views than my progressive or Left-leaning worldview, which was influenced by my education. However, aside from our educational differences or worldview perspectives, as cheesy or corny or cliché as it sounds, I knew that at the end of the day, they were willing to take a bullet for me, just like I was willing to do the same for them. Something about the policing profession—such as the ever-present possibility of death—creates a close bond between police officers.

As a result of our various educational levels, some of my colleagues and I differed because some could not critically analyze or question their status as police officers and the policing practices that come with being a police officer. To a certain extent, I know that I was critical of the language utilized to describe immigrants as a result of my parents' immigration history and my educational training. Some of my colleagues had U.S.-born parents and even grandparents. As previously noted, my parents were Mexican immigrants, and I can relate and be empathetic to the immigrant experience, whereas some of my colleagues could not. This outcome does not make me holier-than-thou, but I know from personal experience, whether from my parents or from working alongside immigrants (as previously noted in the book), the hardships of immigrants and their rationales for immigrating to the United States from a foreign country such as Mexico.

As I reflect on this study in which I doubled as a police officer and a researcher at the same time, I want to address the power dynamic between civilians and me. I have been asked when presenting my work in academic settings how I knew that civilians did not feel coerced into participating in the research study. When I described my research study to civilians and other law enforcement officials, my approach was similar to the one I used with police officers: I notified them that aside from serving as a police officer, I was also a sociology graduate student interested in examining police-community relations on the South Texas–Mexico border, and my ultimate goal was to write a book based on this work. I notified civilians that their inclusion in the study had no bearing on the outcome of their call for service during our interaction with each other. Essentially, it is my belief that the civilians who decided to be included in the study did so because they wanted to help me, since it was part of my graduation requirement for graduate school (i.e., my dissertation), and they did not view the study as something problematic. However, in regard to the immigrants in the study, the power differential between them and me was the greatest of all who were involved in the study.

Whenever I interacted with immigrants, I revealed to them that my parents were immigrants from Mexico, that I had previously worked alongside immigrants in a low-wage, labor-intensive job during my adolescence, and that I empathized with their plight. My interactions with immigrants were always sad encounters, because they were often at the end of the road for that particular migration journey. During these encounters, I opened up to them and informed them of how my personal lived experiences shaped the manner in which I viewed the issue of immigration. Thus, I was able to connect with them and humanize myself to them even though they encountered me as a uniformed police officer. Their decision to be included in the study seemed predicated on the hope that I would utilize my position as a social researcher to inform public policymakers and the general public about the immigrant experience. I am not implying that I am the sole vessel of information on the universal immigrant experience; I can, however, represent the experiences of those immigrants I specifically encountered during the course of this study only to all the various stakeholders.

My position as a police officer evidently influenced results, since it is clearly known that civilians rely on the police to relieve an unpleasant situation such as a dispute, whether it is between family members, friends, or strangers. Namely, my encounters with civilians—as noted in the study—involved some form of disagreement, and that disagreement revealed instances of racism and intraracial/intraethnic conflict. The same holds true with my encounters with immigrants. As evidenced in the previous chapters, whenever I encountered immigrants, it was always an unfortunate experience, because my encounters with the immigrants involved their detainment, which began the deportation process and the amply illustrated racialized immigration enforcement practices.

As previously noted, this research was guided theoretically by Charles Mills's racial contract theory, Joe Feagin's white racial frame theory, and Lindsay Perez Huber and colleagues' racist nativism; thus, it should come as no surprise that the results of the study may be alarming and disturbing to some readers. My utilization of these aforementioned theoretical frameworks certainly influenced the findings revealed in this book, since I always viewed my research through a racial conflict perspective. Those theoretical frameworks helped me provide the answers to questions about how the concept of race/racism functions in the area where I was raised—the RGV.

I would also like to reflect on the method utilized for the research. As evidenced in the study, I was already a member of one of the researched groups (I was a police officer); consequently, it was inevitable that I would go native in order to conduct the research. Moreover, I am aware that going native is considered problematic; however, I never lost sight of my researcher role due to the data collection process of writing field notes. Through the process of writing field notes, I was attuned to my other role, that of an academic researcher. Consequently, my positionality within the study, my lived experiences, the power dynamics, the chosen theoretical frameworks, and the chosen methodology for this study ultimately framed the research and its outcomes.

NOTES

<hr />

Introduction

1. Reilly, "Here Are All the Times."

2. Mayra Flores was born in Burgos, Tamaulipas, Mexico, and immigrated to the United States at the age of six. Several years later, at the age of fourteen, she became a U.S. citizen. Her husband is a USBP agent. She won a special election in June 2022 to represent Texas's Thirty-Fourth Congressional District. She served from June 2022 to January 2023. See Harris, "What to Know."

3. Monica De La Cruz made history winning her congressional election for Texas's Fifteenth Congressional District on November 8, 2022, the first Republican and Latina woman to represent the district. See Choi and Neukam, "Monica De La Cruz Becomes First Republican."

4. Boris Sanchez, "Latino Voter Shift."

5. Anzaldúa, *Borderlands / La Frontera*; Juan Jose Bustamante, *Transnational Struggles*; Dowling, *Mexican Americans*; Correa and Thomas, "Rebirth"; Silva and Murga, "Racializing American Authenticity."

6. Gutiérrez, *Walls and Mirrors*; Jiménez, *Replenished Ethnicity*; Ochoa, *Becoming Neighbors*.

7. Unless specifically noted, I use the term "Latino" throughout the book to refer to individuals with Latin American ancestry.

8. Gutiérrez, *Walls and Mirrors*.

9. Ochoa, *Becoming Neighbors*.

10. As noted in the book, the anti-immigrant hostility toward Latino undocumented immigrants (i.e., Mexicans, Central Americans, and South Americans) is derived from Mexican Americans. That is, the nativistic anti-immigrant attitudes displayed in the book by Mexican Americans are twofold: against their coethnic (Mexican) counterparts and against their coracial (Central American and South American) counterparts. Although I do understand that Latino is utilized by some as a panethnic label, Latinos also constitute a racial group similar to all other major racial groupings in the United States. Ultimately, I utilize racial conflict theories to contextualize the racial and ethnic conflict demonstrated in the book.

11. The crimmigration phenomenon entails the intersection between criminal law and immigration law or, simply put, the flow of shared information from local police to federal immigration officials, often resulting in the apprehension, detention, and deportation of undocumented immigrants. See Stumpf, "Crimmigration Crisis."

12. The Illegal Immigration Reform and Immigrant Responsibility Act of 1996 added Section 287(g) to the Immigration and Nationality Act by allowing U.S. Immigration and Customs Enforcement to deputize local and state law enforcement officers to enforce federal immigration law functions under ICE's direction and supervision. See https://www.ice.gov/identify-and-arrest/287g.

13. Armenta, *Protect, Serve, and Deport.*

14. Provine et al., *Policing Immigrants.*

15. Morales and Curry, "Citizenship Profiling."

16. Aranda and Vaquera, "Racism."

17. Menjívar and Abrego, "Legal Violence."

18. Golash-Boza and Hondagneu-Sotelo, "Latino Immigrant Men."

19. Arriaga, "Relationships"; Armenta, *Protect, Serve, and Deport*; Provine et al., *Policing Immigrants*; Bustamante and Gamino, "'La Polimigra'"; Coleman, "Immigration Geopolitics"; Coleman, "The 'Local' Migration State"; Coleman and Kocher, "Detention"; Creek and Yoder, "With a Little Help"; Donato and Rodriguez, "Police Arrests"; Wong, "287(g)."

20. Sandra Sanchez, "WATCH."

21. Sandra Sanchez, quoting Maverick County Sheriff's Office deputy Jesus Sanchez.

22. Omi and Winant, *Racial Formation,* 55.

23. All character names and locations related to the situations described in the text (save my own) are pseudonyms.

24. Jorgensen, *Participant Observation.*

25. Bogdan, *Participant Observation*; DeWalt and DeWalt, *Participant Observation.*

26. Jorgensen, *Participant Observation,* 12.

27. Walker and Katz, *The Police in America.*

28. Jorgensen, *Participant Observation,* 13.

29. Egan, *Dancing for Dollars.*

30. Moskos, *Cop in the Hood.*

31. Jorgensen, *Participant Observation,* 15.

32. Moskos, *Cop in the Hood,* 4.

33. Agar, *The Professional Stranger,* 31.

34. Ellis and Bochner, "Autoethnography"; Marshall and Rossman, *Designing Qualitative Research.*

35. Reed-Danahay, *Auto/ethnography,* 9.

36. Ellis and Bochner, "Autoethnography," 742.

37. Ellis and Bochner, 745.

38. Marshall and Rossman, *Designing Qualitative Research.*

39. Reed-Danahay, *Auto/ethnography*; Marshall and Rossman, *Designing Qualitative Research.*

40. Chang, *Autoethnography as Method,* 49.

41. Warren and Karner, *Discovering Qualitative Methods,* 86.

42. Vera Sanchez and Portillos, "Insiders and Outsiders."

43. Moskos, *Cop in the Hood*, 6.

44. Marquart, "Doing Research in Prison."

45. Marquart, 23.

46. Warren and Karner, *Discovering Qualitative Methods*.

47. Emerson and Pollner, "Constructing," 38.

48. Moskos, *Cop in the Hood*, 8.

49. This is common in ethnographic research when the researcher does not record conversations. See Battle, "'They Look at You.'"

50. An assignment that requires police presence in order to resolve or correct a particular situation.

51. Walker and Katz, *The Police in America*.

52. Walker and Katz, 208.

53. Bouza, *The Police Mystique*; Walker and Katz, *The Police in America*.

54. Briefings involve attendance being taken, quadrant assignments being given to the police officers for the particular workday, and information being provided about previous shift activities. See Pogrebin and Poole, "Humor in the Briefing Room."

55. Goffman, *The Presentation of Self*.

56. Some police departments may grant access to the roll call room as part of a civilian's ride-along process for that particular day.

57. Lofland et al., *Analyzing Social Settings*; Warren and Karner, *Discovering Qualitative Methods*; Friese, *User's Manual*; Bailey, *A Guide*.

58. Mills, *The Racial Contract*, 1.

59. Mills, 7.

60. Omi and Winant, *Racial Formation*; Bonilla-Silva, "Rethinking Racism."

61. Mills, *The Racial Contract*, 13–14.

62. Haney-Lopez, *White by Law*; Gómez, *Manifest Destinies*.

63. Embrick, "Two Nations"; see also Samora, Bernal, and Peña, *Gunpowder Justice*; Collins, *Texas Devils*.

64. Mills, *The Racial Contract*, 84.

65. Bittner, *The Functions of the Police*.

66. Mills, *The Racial Contract*, 84.

67. Bouza, *The Police Mystique*; Bouza, *Bronx Beat*.

68. Bouza, *The Police Mystique*, 4.

69. Personal conversation with Tony Bouza, February 19, 2021.

70. Mills, *The Racial Contract*, 89.

71. For an in-depth discussion regarding internalized racism, see Pyke, "What Is Internalized Racial Oppression?"

72. Feagin, *The White Racial Frame*, 10.

73. Feagin, 15.

74. Pyke and Dang, "'fob' and 'Whitewashed.'"

75. Feagin, *The White Racial Frame*.

76. Molina, "Racializing the Migration Process," 3.

77. Chavez, *The Latina/o Threat*.

78. Santa Ana, *Brown Tide Rising*.

79. Feagin, *The White Racial Frame*, 116.

80. Feagin, 3.
81. Feagin and Cobas, "Latinos/as and White Racial Frame."
82. Feagin, *The White Racial Frame*, 117.
83. Feagin.
84. Lippard, "Racist Nativism."
85. Higham, *Strangers in the Land*; Lippard, "Racist Nativism."
86. Huber et al., "Getting beyond the 'Symptom,'" 43.
87. Lippard, "Racist Nativism."
88. Lippard, 600.
89. Huber et al., "Getting beyond the 'Symptom,'" 47.
90. Singlemann, Slack, and Fontenont, "Race and Place."
91. Singlemann, Slack, and Fontenont, 295.
92. O'Hare and Johnson, "Child Poverty."
93. Ward, *Colonias and Public Policy*, 3.
94. Maril, *The Poorest of Americans*.
95. Maril, 2.
96. Juan Jose Bustamante, *Transnational Struggles*; Castañeda, *Borders of Belonging*.

Chapter 1. Racialized Policing in the U.S.-Mexico Borderlands

1. "Mojankers" is an English slang term for mojados (wetbacks). Mojankers is derived from the Spanish spelling of the word mojados but anglicized in slang; it is pronounced "moe-hankers." I am unfamiliar with its origin.
2. The term is derived from immigrants crossing the Rio Grande from Mexico into South Texas by swimming and wading across the river. See Jorge Bustamante, "The 'Wetback' as Deviant."
3. Bender, *Greasers and Gringos*.
4. Watkins, *Reclaiming the American Revolution*.
5. Hernández, *Migra! A History*.
6. Jorge Bustamante, "The 'Wetback' as Deviant."
7. Jorge Bustamante, 709.
8. Johnson, "'Aliens.'"
9. Johnson, 269.
10. De Genova and Ramos-Zayas, *Latino Crossings*.
11. Johnson, "'Aliens.'"
12. Delgado and Stefancic, "Images"; Johnson, "Fear"; Johnson, "'Aliens'"; De Genova, "Migrant 'Illegality'"; De Genova and Ramos-Zayas, *Latino Crossings*.
13. De Genova, "The Legal Production," 175.
14. Andreas, *Border Games*; Nevins, *Operation Gatekeeper*; Dunn, *Blockading the Border*; Ruben Garcia, "Critical Race Theory"; Ono and Sloop, *Shifting Borders*.
15. Pyke and Dang, "'FOB' and 'Whitewashed,'" 170.
16. Higham, *Strangers in the Land*; Johnson, "'Aliens.'"
17. Blumer, "Race Prejudice."
18. Delgado and Stefancic, "Images"; Scharf, "Tired of Your Masses."
19. Goldsmith et al., "Ethno-racial Profiling"; Johnson, "Race"; Johnson, "'Aliens'"; Romero, "Racial Profiling"; Romero, "Crossing the Immigration"; Romero, "Are Your Papers in Order?"; Sanchez and Romero, "Critical Race Theory."

20. Higham, *Strangers in the Land*.

21. Chang and Aoki, "Centering the Immigrant."

22. Johnson, "'Aliens.'"

23. Juan Ramon Garcia, *Operation Wetback*; Hernández, *Migra! A History*; Lopez, "Undocumented Mexican Migration"; Samora, *"Los Mojados."*

24. Jorge Sanchez, "Face the Nation."

25. Archibold, "Arizona Enacts Stringent Law," A1.

26. Arrocha, "From Arizona's S.B. 1070."

27. Reed, "Senate Bill 4."

28. Kilty and Vidal de Haymes, "Racism, Nativism, and Exclusion," 14.

29. Balderrama and Rodriguez, *Decade of Betrayal*; Hoffman, "Stimulus to Repatriation."

30. Hoffman, "Stimulus to Repatriation," 208.

31. Balderrama and Rodriguez, *Decade of Betrayal*, 70.

32. Hoffman, "Stimulus to Repatriation," 215.

33. Balderrama and Rodriguez, *Decade of Betrayal*; Escobar, *Race, Police*; Hoffman, "Stimulus to Repatriation."

34. Balderrama and Rodriguez, *Decade of Betrayal*, 75.

35. Juan Ramon Garcia, *Operation Wetback*; Hernández, *Migra! A History*.

36. Juan Ramon Garcia, *Operation Wetback*.

37. Juan Ramon Garcia.

38. Juan Ramon Garcia, 189.

39. Romero and Serag, "Violation."

40. Romero and Serag, 95.

41. Romero and Serag; Romero, "Racial Profiling."

42. Romero and Serag, "Violation."

43. Romero, "Racial Profiling," 469.

44. Rodriguez, "Punting."

45. Rodriguez.

46. Rodriguez.

47. Gamino, "Border Splurge."

48. Dunn, *Blockading the Border*.

49. "Governor Abbott, DPS Launch 'Operation Lone Star' to Address Crisis at Southern Border," press release, March 6, 2021, https://gov.texas.gov/news/post/governor-abbott-dps-launch-operation-lone-star-to-address-crisis-at-southern-border.

50. According to the Texas Penal Code, Title 7, chap. 30, §30.05, criminal trespass occurs when "a person commits a crime if the person enters or remains on or in property of another, including residential land, agricultural land, a recreational vehicle park, a building, a general residential operation operating as a residential treatment center, or an aircraft or other vehicle, without effective consent and the person (1) had notice that the entry was forbidden; or (2) received notice to depart but failed to do so. . . . This crime is punishable by a fine not to exceed $2,000 and/or up to 180 days in a county jail" (https://statutes.capitol.texas.gov/docs/pe/htm/pe.30.htm).

51. "Governor Abbott Provides Update on Operation Lone Star in Weslaco," press release, April 1, 2021, https://gov.texas.gov/news/post/governor-abbott-provides-update-on-operation-lone-star-in-weslaco.

52. Sparks, "Operation Lone Star"; Jervis, "Immigration Activists."

53. Sparks, "Operation Lone Star."

54. Jervis, "Immigration Activists," quoting Thomas Sáenz, president and general counsel of the Mexican American Legal Defense and Educational Fund.

55. This "line watch" was different from OSS of 2014, because for OSS, there were fewer law enforcement vehicles, and the vehicles were spaced several yards from each other.

56. Giaritelli, "Texas Troopers."

57. Cepeda and Winkle, "$36.4M Coming."

58. Gamino, "Border Splurge."

59. I stipulate consciously or unconsciously, because some officers who apprehend immigrants while on a routine call for service do not realize that by apprehending and referring the immigrants to USBP custody, they serve as de facto immigration officials.

60. FEMA, Homeland Security Grant Program, https://www.fema.gov/grants/preparedness /homeland-security.

61. Ordóñez, "Modeling the U.S. Border Patrol"; Moscufo, "'Dirty Money.'"

62. Moscufo, "'Dirty Money,'" quoting Ned Norris Jr., chairman of the Tohono O'odham Nation.

63. FEMA, Homeland Security Grant Program, https://www.fema.gov/grants/preparedness /homeland-security. There are no other data provided regarding years prior to 2016.

64. "Final Allocation and Award Announcement Fiscal Year (FY) 2019 State and Local Preparedness Grant Programs," August 2, 2019, https://www.dhs.gov/sites/default/files /publications/19_0801_ola_fy19-allocation-announcement.pdf.

65. Moscufo, "'Dirty Money,'" quoting Sheriff Joe Nole, Jefferson County, Washington.

66. Sayers, "Tucson Police."

67. Sayers.

68. Demers, "Pima County Supervisors."

69. Resendiz, "Border Patrol."

70. McKenney, "'Operation Stone Garden.'"

71. Van Maanen, "Kinsmen in Response," 115.

72. Bouza, *The Police Mystique*.

73. Bouza; Bayley, *Police for the Future*.

74. Bouza, *The Police Mystique*; Bayley, *Police for the Future*; Moskos, *Cop in the Hood*; Van Maanen, "Observations."

75. Van Maanen, "Breaking In."

76. Reiner, *The Politics of the Police*, 144.

77. Reiner, 147.

78. Bouza, *Confessions of a Police Misfit*.

79. Bayley, *Police for the Future*.

80. Bouza, *The Police Mystique*.

81. Bouza, 76.

82. Walker and Katz, *The Police in America*, 134–41.

83. My father's incarceration, coupled with the impoverished community I grew up in, contributed to my desire to become a police officer at a very young age. That is, due to my father's incarceration and my neighborhood conditions (poverty and crime), I knew that involvement in delinquent behavior would lead me to follow in my father's footsteps. My father was incarcerated in a maximum-security prison in Illinois when I was seven years old and was released

when I was eighteen years old. In addition, I wanted to make a difference in my community when I grew older, and one viable option for me to give back to my community was through becoming a police officer.

84. Cortez, "Latinxs in La Migra."

85. Reiner, *The Politics of the Police.*

86. Paoline, *Rethinking Police Culture*, 15.

87. Bouza, *The Police Mystique.*

88. Skolnick, *Justice without Trial*; Van Maanen, "Kinsmen in Response."

89. Skolnick, *Justice without Trial.*

90. Reiner, *The Politics of the Police*, 119.

91. Skolnick, *Justice without Trial.*

92. Reiner, *The Politics of the Police.*

93. Hochschild, "Emotion Work," 561.

94. Bouza, *The Police Mystique*, 75.

Chapter 2. Racialization and Socialization in the Borderlands

1. Reed-Danahay, *Auto/ethnography*; Marshall and Rossman, *Designing Qualitative Research.*

2. Ellis, Adams, and Bochner, "Autoethnography: An Overview."

3. *Mojado* is the Spanish slang term for "wetback." *Mojo* is the anglicized form and is pronounced "moe-joe." I am unfamiliar with its origin. This term is part of the everyday vernacular of residents in the RGV.

4. Some of my football and baseball teammates dressed kicker style—in Justin Roper boots—but were not ridiculed because of their attire.

5. Ochoa, *Becoming Neighbors*, 107–8. Though not noted in *Becoming Neighbors*, *chunties* is Spanish slang for the derogatory term *chuntaros.*

6. Feagin, *The White Racial Frame.*

7. Feagin, 92.

8. As previously noted, *mojo* is such a part of the everyday vernacular of residents within the RGV that a local English radio station uses the racialized term as part of its official title for the morning show, *The Mojo Morning Show* (https://wild104.iheart.com/featured/the-mojo -morning-show/). As noted in Feagin, *The White Racial Frame*, elements of the dominant white frame are learned at home, among peers, and from the media. My peers, similar to most residents in the RGV who utilize "mojo," more than likely learned the meaning and significance of the term through the aforementioned channels.

9. "Border Security," U.S. Customs and Border Protection, last modified October 18, 2024, www.cbp.gov/border-security. Josiah Heyman refers to this area as a "strip" ("'Illegality,'" 125).

10. U.S. Customs and Border Protection (CBP). The USBP has immigration enforcement authority within one hundred miles of a U.S. land or coastal border; in essence, it envelops the entire United States. Interestingly, the Fourth Amendment of the U.S. Constitution protects individuals from random and arbitrary stops and searches; however, these basic constitutional principles do not apply fully within the one-hundred-mile zone, in which the checkpoints are located. For further discussion regarding the one-hundred-mile border zone, see "The Constitution in the 100-Mile Border Zone," August 21, 2014, ACLU, https://www.aclu.org /documents/constitution-100-mile-border-zone.

11. Van Maanen, "Breaking In," 67.

12. Bouza, *Confessions of a Police Misfit*, 74.

13. For an accurate description of the police academy experience from an insider's perspective, see Moskos, *Cop in the Hood*.

14. Standard police procedure when making contact with someone is to ensure that they do not have outstanding warrants with the police department or any other law enforcement agency. Normally, this consists of providing the dispatcher with the name and date of birth of the person or their driver's license number (from any state) if they have a driver's license on hand.

15. At times, not having a driver's license is usually an indicator that the person is an immigrant, which leads to the police malpractice of immigration status questioning.

16. This varied by police officer; some requested USBP, whereas others did not.

17. A concerned citizen is a person who wishes to remain anonymous when reporting an issue to the police via 911.

18. As previously noted, the police department, similar to most departments across the country, did not have federal immigration enforcement authorization.

19. The immigrants at the apartment notified Officer Lablico that they, along with the persons who fled from the scene, were undocumented immigrants from Mexico and Central America.

20. Plascencia, "Where Is 'The Border'?"

21. See the citations listed in note 18 for the introduction.

22. Romero, "State Violence."

23. On repatriation, see Balderrama and Rodriguez, *Decade of Betrayal*; on Operation Wetback, see Hernández, *Migra! A History*; for deterrence strategies, see Dunn, *Blockading the Border*, and Nevins, *Operation Gatekeeper*; and for Proposition 187, see Santa Ana, *Brown Tide Rising*.

24. Saito, "Model Minority," 76.

25. Saito.

26. Vila, "Constructing Social Identities."

27. Dowling, *Mexican Americans*.

28. Aranda and Vaquera, "Racism." This nuance will be analyzed and discussed in further detail in chapters 4, 5, and 6.

29. The dangers experienced by immigrants inside stash houses are the primary focus of chapter 3.

30. U.S. Immigration and Customs Enforcement, "Secure Communities," https://www.ice.gov/secure-communities, accessed October 10, 2024. Secure Communities is a Department of Homeland Security data-sharing program between local, state, and federal law enforcement agencies designed to identify immigrants in U.S. jails who are deportable under U.S. immigration law.

31. Morales, Delgado, and Curry, "Variations in Citizenship Profiling."

32. Morales and Curry, "Citizenship Profiling."

33. These types of domestic violence calls for service vary according to situational factors. That is, if there are visible signs of physical injury, the aggressor will more than likely be arrested. In contrast, if there are no signs of physical injury, even though an assault may have occurred, the police may ask the aggressor to leave the location in order to avoid an arrest being made.

34. This classification system for calls for service is not standard. Police departments utilize different call for service classification systems.

35. An unknown 911 call for service means that an unknown individual has dialed 911, and the dispatch center is unable to make contact with the individual dialing 911 (i.e., the caller decides to remain anonymous). I was the primary officer; therefore, I was responsible for generating the police report.

36. When encountering undocumented immigrants at stash houses, it is department procedure to ask for the following identifying information for documentation purposes: name, date of birth, and country of origin.

37. Depending on the number of immigrants detained, USBP responds to the scene with trucks, fifteen-passenger vans, or a bus.

38. When requesting assistance from another law enforcement agency such as the USBP, estimated time of arrival is requested so that the officer can know how long it is going to take agents to arrive at the scene.

39. Location of call for service was compromised, since USBP was provided the location with the number of undocumented immigrants.

40. The ten-code for "repeat" is 10-9. My call sign was 17 Adam 62.

41. Sergeant Ontario was a patrol shift supervisor on my shift. The ten-code for "location" is 10-20.

42. Bourdieu, *Outline*, 82–83.

43. Bourdieu, 86.

44. MacLeod, *Ain't No Making It*, 15.

45. MacLeod, 15.

46. MacLeod, 15.

47. Even though I had a bachelor's degree, it was not until I began my graduate studies at Texas A&M University that I was able to obtain crucial and specific knowledge allowing me to view my position as a police officer through a critical lens. That is, I benefited immensely from my graduate academic training because I was provided with the tools to view societal issues and, more importantly, my role as a member of the policing institution through a critical perspective. While in college, I also experienced a divided self as my personal (working-class) habitus competed with the middle-class culture of the academic field. For further discussion regarding habitus conversion between working-class/first-generation college students and academia, see Lehmann, "Habitus Transformation"; and Ivemark and Ambrose, "Habitus Adaptation."

48. Detasseling corn entails the removal of pollen-producing flowers (the tassel) from the tops of corn plants.

Chapter 3. Immigrant Vulnerabilities in the Borderlands

1. In the summer of 2014, the South Texas–Mexico border became the epicenter of a humanitarian crisis when thousands of unaccompanied minors and mothers seeking asylum traveled from Central America to the RGV.

2. It is not known whether Alfonso was deported because unaccompanied minors were transported to a reunion with their relatives residing in the United States after being processed by the USBP. Since Alfonso came to the United States to be with his uncle in South Carolina, it is plausible that he was reunited with him.

3. Later on during this particular workday, I conversed with Deputy Sayago (see chapter 5)

about this call, and he expressed his anti-Latino immigrant sentiment when he was made aware that I purchased food for Alfonso.

4. Further insight regarding the actual day-to-day operations of OPSG will be illustrated in chapter 4.

5. The 911 caller called from a Houston area code. Several of us later made the connection between the phone calls made to the sheriff's office. We noted a theme—several of the calls for service involving stash houses were made by someone using a Houston area code.

6. Sergeant Aquino's comment is consistent with the sexual assault academic literature that notes that sexual assault survivors are often blamed for their victimization. See Eigenberg and Garland, "Victim Blaming"; Lonsway and Fitzgerald, "Rape Myths"; Russel and Hand, "Rape Myth."

7. According to Texas Penal Code, Title 5, chap. 20, §20.05, "smuggling of persons" is considered a state felony punishable by imprisonment between two and ten years and a fine not to exceed $10,000. See https://statutes.capitol.texas.gov/Docs/PE/htm/PE.20.htm.

8. Those who paid less were Mexican immigrants, whereas those who paid higher prices were Central American immigrants. For further discussion regarding Central American crossing rates, see Coutin, *Nations of Emigrants*; Vogt, "Crossing Mexico."

9. Central American immigrants told me they paid between $5,000 and $7,000. Mexican immigrants were charged lower rates.

10. This is one officer's view of the USBP's inability to arrest human smugglers. It is unknown if the driver was arrested later on.

11. For further discussion regarding the commodification of undocumented immigrants see Coutin, *Nations of Emigrants*. In addition to profitability derived from human smuggling, human smuggling is just as lucrative as drug smuggling because the punishment imposed for human smuggling pales in comparison to that for drug smuggling.

Chapter 4. Latino Immigrant Criminalization in the Borderlands

1. Mills, *The Racial Contract*.

2. Mills; Huber et al., "Getting Beyond the 'Symptom.'"

3. After our roll call session that day, Lieutenant Obrero told some of us that prior to roll call, he had a meeting with his supervisor regarding our response to calls for service involving stash houses. He was scolded by his supervisor because deputies were taking too much time while on stash house calls for service when instead they could be available for calls for service that were within our purview. In essence, Lieutenant Obrero was berated by his supervisor for logistical purposes.

4. This discussion during roll will be illustrated further in chapter 5.

5. Mills, *The Racial Contract*; Huber et al., "Getting Beyond the 'Symptom.'"

6. Sometimes if a police officer is parked in the parking lot of a business, a civilian will take advantage of the opportunity to report an incident that already occurred. That is, if someone sees a police vehicle parked in a public space, they will notify the officer(s) that they wish to file a report on an incident that occurred several days, weeks, or months ago. The individual will then notify the officer(s) that he or she did not file a report when the incident occurred, but upon seeing the police vehicle parked in a public space, he or she wanted to take advantage of the opportunity to report the incident that already occurred.

7. Report writing is a time-consuming task, because generally police officers are expected to write a report for most of the calls for service to which they respond. A report can document a noncriminal incident such as a neighbor dispute or a criminal incident such as an assault.

8. I could have pulled over the driver of the van for a nonmoving traffic violation, but I decided not to pull the driver over until he committed a moving violation.

9. Before they left the location, I was able to speak privately with the man, who notified me that he was indeed the caretaker (the human smuggler) of the stash house.

10. Mills, *The Racial Contract*.

11. Each officer working an overtime detail for OPSG fills out a form (a work activity sheet) that summarizes the work activity for that particular shift, such as apprehension statistics of undocumented immigrants and traffic stops conducted during the shift. The work activity sheet is then forwarded to DHS in order to demonstrate work productivity for OPSG. I was never able to obtain apprehension statistics from the sheriff's office, even though I was a member of that institution. Additionally, DHS does not publish statistics regarding OPSG related to law enforcement.

12. Sometimes when working OPSG, the shift supervisor has the autonomy of deciding what area of the county the OPSG officers will be working that day. Unless otherwise noted by high-ranking sheriff's office personnel, the OPSG shift supervisor for the certain day and shift can randomly assign the OPSG officers to wherever he or she decides.

13. Heyman, "Why Caution Is Needed"; Martinez, Cantor, and Ewing, "No Action Taken"; Phillips, Hagan, and Rodriguez, "Brutal Borders?"; Phillips, Rodriguez, and Hagan, "Brutality at the Border?"; Sarabia, "Migrants, Activists."

14. Fideo is a short and golden type of noodle that is thin like vermicelli.

15. The Spanish translation of an Aztec word for a coarse flour made from ground, toasted maize kernels, often in a mixture with a variety of herbs and ground seeds, that can be eaten by itself or be used as the base for a beverage.

16. Sergeant Camarena knew the sheriff's office had no immigration enforcement authority but circumvented this issue by having OPSG deputies respond to the location, since immigration enforcement was within the purview of OPSG overtime grant detail.

17. Sometimes stash houses are located in rural areas of the county; however, this house was situated within the multifamily neighborhood. Thus, it blended in with the other houses in the neighborhood.

18. Deputy Archuleta and Sergeant Toscano notified the rest of us that they could see at least twenty individuals inside who were sitting down in the unfurnished living room. All of the individuals inside the house were later confirmed to be undocumented immigrants from Mexico and Central America.

Chapter 5. Police Officers' Voices on Immigrant Racialization

1. Johnson, "'Aliens.'"

2. Jorge Bustamante, "The 'Wetback' as Deviant"; Ngai, *Impossible Subjects*; Chavez, *The Latina/o Threat*.

3. Johnson, "'Aliens'"; Ngai, *Impossible Subjects*; De Genova, "Migrant 'Illegality'"; De Genova, "The Legal Production."

4. Johnson, "'Aliens'"; Ngai, *Impossible Subjects*.

5. Chavez, *The Latina/o Threat*, 25.

6. Feagin, *The White Racial Frame*, 3.

7. Molina, *Racializing the Migration Process,* 108.

8. De Genova, "The Legal Production," 161.

9. The official use of the term "alien" when describing undocumented immigrants can be traced back to the Alien and Sedition Acts of the late 1700s (Watkins, *Reclaiming the American Revolution*).

10. Johnson, "'Aliens.'"

11. Johnson, 272.

12. Molina, *Racializing the Migration Process*, 110.

13. "Illegal floater" and "floater" are the preferred terms in the police department whenever officers refer to undocumented immigrant drowning victims.

14. Basila is a small town located within the county that has a large concentration of undocumented immigrants.

15. See Chavez, *The Latina/o Threat*; and Santa Ana, *Brown Tide Rising*.

16. Huntington, *Who We Are*.

17. Huntington, 247–56.

18. For further discussion regarding the English-only movements of the 1990s, see Jorge Sanchez, "Face the Nation."

19. Fory-Fay is pronounced "foe-rē fi."

20. Feagin, *The White Racial Frame*, 14.

21. This particular call for service was explained in detail in chapter 3.

22. Chavez, *The Latina/o Threat*.

23. Clearly, Deputy Guidero was erroneously assuming and generalizing that most, if not all, individuals residing in Colonia Díaz Ordaz receive monthly food stamp assistance.

24. See Food and Nutrition Service, U.S. Department of Agriculture, Supplemental Nutrition Assistance Program, page updated July 1, 2024, https://www.fns.usda.gov/snap/supplemental-nutrition-assistance-program.

25. See Social Security, Disability, https://www.ssa.gov/disability. Children must meet the Social Security Administration's definition of disability for children.

26. Deputy Guidero was born in Mexico but became a naturalized U.S. citizen.

27. Later on, it was established that he was referring to early twentieth-century white European immigrants (e.g., Italian, Irish, Polish) when discussing "immigrants from the past."

28. DREAMers (referring to the Development, Relief and Education for Alien Minors [DREAM] Act) are undocumented immigrants who can benefit from the Obama administration's Deferred Action for Childhood Arrivals (DACA) Initiative as a result of being brought to the United States as children.

29. His use of the name José No Papers is analogous with the English equivalent, John Q. Public or John Q. Citizen.

30. Feagin and Cobas, "Latinos/as and White Racial Frame"; Feagin, *The White Racial Frame*.

31. Personal conversation with Joe R. Feagin, February 13, 2015.

32. "Improper Entry by Alien," 8 U.S. Code §1325, Legal Information Institute, Cornell Law School, https://www.law.cornell.edu/uscode/text/8/1325, accessed October 22, 2024.

33. Eagly, "Prosecuting Immigration"; Martin, "The Geopolitics of Vulnerability"; Menjívar and Kanstroom, *Constructing Immigrant "Illegality"*; Noferi, "Cascading Constitutional Deprivation."

34. Deputy Oñate was referring to the call for service discussed in chapter 3 when Sergeant Aviar purchased hamburgers for the immigrants. They were squad mates, and they erroneously thought I was the person who purchased the food for the immigrants.

Chapter 6. Civilian Conflict in the Borderlands

1. Feagin, *The White Racial Frame*, 10, 141–61.
2. Feagin, 113–17.
3. For an in-depth discussion regarding internalized racism, see Pyke, "What Is Internalized Racial Oppression." See also Pyke and Dang, "'FOB' and 'Whitewashed.'"
4. As noted here, Mr. Santos voluntarily disclosed his immigration status to us; we did not elicit that information from him.
5. Border Patrol generally responds to referral calls made to them only after confirming that a residence is being utilized as a stash house. That is, if a civilian calls the USBP to have someone deported, the USBP will first send an intel group of undercover agents to conduct an investigation into the house in question. If agents determine that the residence is being used as a stash house, they will then conduct a raid at the residence to deport the immigrants.
6. Feagin, *The White Racial Frame*.
7. Threatening to have someone deported is not considered a crime in Texas.
8. During our conversation, he told me that he was born in the United States.
9. The prior history log reveals all the calls for service made to the police from a certain address. The prior history log can be accessed by using the mobile data terminal, a computerized device that is inside police vehicles.
10. Mrs. Bonilla voluntarily divulged her immigration status to me without me asking her about it.
11. Mrs. Bonilla showed me a screenshot of a message Leandro sent her indicating in his cell phone call log that an outgoing call had been made to a local USBP station. Even though she was not aware of the particulars about Leandro's phone call to the station, the mere fact that he made a phone call was enough for Mrs. Bonilla to suspect he had called the USBP with the intention of having her deported, unlike previous threats that were just verbal.
12. Fussell, "The Deportation Threat Dynamic"; Hautala, Dombrowski, and Marcus, "Predictors of Police Reporting"; Menjívar and Bejarano, "Latino Immigrants' Perceptions"; Rennison, "Reporting to the Police"; Rennison et al., "Reporting Violent Victimization."
13. I was at this call for service for about forty-five minutes. Janet eventually calmed down while I was at the call for service, and during my conversation with her, I learned she was a third-generation Mexican American who was a lifelong resident of the RGV.
14. While conversing with Deputy Nava and me, Nendo showed us his cell phone call log, which confirmed that he had made an outgoing call to the USBP station.

Conclusion

1. For a discussion of viewing immigrants as racialized individuals, see Sáenz and Douglas, "A Call"; for including immigrants in policing literature, see Martinez, "Incorporating Latinos."
2. Romero, "Crossing the Immigration"; Goldsmith et al., "Ethno-racial Profiling."
3. Sáenz and Douglas, "A Call," 176.
4. Weitzer, "The Puzzling Neglect," 2000.
5. Vera Sanchez and Rosenbaum, "Racialized Policing," 173.
6. Weitzer, "The Puzzling Neglect," 2009.

7. For Black and Latino youths, see Rios, *Punished*; for Black community members, see Moskos, *Cop in the Hood*, and Cobbina, *Hands Up, Don't Shoot*; and for Latinos in the U.S. interior, see Armenta, *Protect, Serve, and Deport*, and Golash-Boza, *Deported*.

8. Menjívar et al., "Immigration Enforcement."

9. Menjívar and Bejarano, "Latino Immigrants' Perceptions"; Messing et al., "Latinas' Perceptions"; Theodore and Habans, "Policing Immigrant Communities."

10. Golash-Boza, *Deported*.

11. DHS Office of Inspector General, "FEMA and CBP Oversight."

12. Reaves, "Local Police," 5–6.

13. Kuykendall and Burns, "The Black Police Officer."

14. Kephart, *Racial Factors*, 116–17.

15. Cobbina, *Hands Up, Don't Shoot*, 60–64.

16. Bouza, *How to Stop Crime*, 274.

17. Bouza, *Confessions of a Police Misfit*; Durán, *The Gang Paradox*.

18. Personal conversation with Tony Bouza, April 12, 2022.

19. Van Maanen, "On Watching."

20. Moskos, *Cop in the Hood*.

21. Van Maanen, "On Watching."

22. Huber et al., "Getting Beyond the 'Symptom.'"

23. Fassin, *Enforcing Order*, 33.

24. Van Maanen, "On Watching," 312.

25. Bonilla-Silva, *Racism without Racists*.

26. Huber et al., "Getting Beyond the 'Symptom.'"

BIBLIOGRAPHY

Agar, Michael H. *The Professional Stranger: An Informal Introduction to Ethnography.* 2nd ed. San Diego: Academic Press, 1996.

Andreas, Peter. *Border Games: Policing the U.S.-Mexico Divide.* 2nd ed. Ithaca, N.Y.: Cornell University Press, 2009.

Anzaldúa, Gloria. *Borderlands / La Frontera: The New Mestiza.* 4th ed. San Francisco: Aunt Lute Books, 2012.

Aranda, Elizabeth, and Elizabeth Vaquera. "Racism, the Immigration Enforcement Regime, and the Implications for Racial Inequality in the Lives of Undocumented Young Adults." *Sociology of Race and Ethnicity* 1, no. 1 (2015): 88–104. https://doi .org/10.1177/2332649214551097.

Archibold, Randal C. "Arizona Enacts Stringent Law on Immigration." *New York Times,* April 23, 2010, A1.

Armenta, Amada. *Protect, Serve, and Deport: The Rise of Policing as Immigration Enforcement.* Oakland: University of California Press, 2017.

Arriaga, Felicia. "Relationships between the Public and Crimmigration Entities in North Carolina: A 287(g) Program Focus." *Sociology of Race and Ethnicity* 3, no. 3 (2017): 417–31. https://doi.org/10.1177/2332649217700923.

Arrocha, William. "From Arizona's S.B. 1070 to Georgia's H.B. 87 and Alabama's H.B. 56: Exacerbating the Other and Generating New Discourses and Practices of Segregation." *California Western Law Review* 48, no. 2 (2012): 245–78.

Bailey, Carol A. *A Guide to Qualitative Field Research.* Thousand Oaks, Calif.: Pine Forge Press, 2007.

Balderrama, Francisco E., and Raymond Rodriguez. *Decade of Betrayal: Mexican Repatriation in the 1930s.* Albuquerque: University of New Mexico Press, 2006.

Battle, Brittany Pearl. "'They Look at You Like You're Nothing': Stigma and Shame in the Child Support System." *Symbolic Interaction* 42, no. 4 (2019): 640–88. https://doi.org/10.1002/symb.359.

Bayley, David H. *Police for the Future.* New York: Oxford University Press, 1994.

Bayley, David H., and Harold Mendelsohn. *Minorities and the Police: Confrontation in America.* New York: Free Press, 1969.

Bender, Steven W. *Greasers and Gringos: Latinos, Law, and the American Imagination.* New York: New York University Press, 2003.

Bittner, Egon. *The Functions of the Police in a Modern Society.* Bethesda, Md.: National Institute of Mental Health, 1970.

Blumer, Herbert. "Race Prejudice as a Sense of Group Position." *Pacific Sociological Review* 1, no. 1 (1958): 3–7. https://doi.org/10.2307/1388607.

Bogdan, Robert. *Participant Observation in Organizational Settings.* Syracuse, N.Y.: Syracuse University Press, 1972.

Bonilla-Silva, Eduardo. *Racism without Racists: Color-Blind Racism and the Persistence of Racial Inequality in the United States.* 6th ed. Lanham, Md.: Rowman & Littlefield, 2021.

Bonilla-Silva, Eduardo. "Rethinking Racism: Toward a Structural Interpretation." *American Sociological Review* 62, no. 3 (1997): 465–80. https://doi.org/10.2307/2657316.

Bourdieu, Pierre. *Outline of a Theory of Practice.* New York: Cambridge University Press, 1977.

Bouza, Anthony V. *Bronx Beat: Reflections of a Police Commander.* Office of International Criminal Justice, University of Illinois at Chicago, 1990.

Bouza, Anthony V. *Confessions of a Police Misfit.* Self-published memoir, 2021.

Bouza, Anthony V. *How to Stop Crime.* New York: Plenum Press, 1993.

Bouza, Anthony V. *The Police Mystique: An Insider's Look at Cops, Crime, and the Criminal Justice System.* New York: Plenum Press, 1990.

Bustamante, Jorge A. "The 'Wetback' as Deviant: An Application of Labeling Theory." *American Journal of Sociology* 77, no. 4 (1972): 706–18. https://doi.org/10.1086/225196.

Bustamante, Juan Jose. *Transnational Struggles: Policy, Gender, and Family Life on the Texas-Mexico Border.* El Paso, Tex.: LFB Scholarly Publishing, 2013.

Bustamante, Juan Jose, and Eric Gamino. " 'La Polimigra': A Social Construct behind the 'Deportation Regime' in the Greater Northwest Arkansas Region." *Humanity and Society* 42, no. 3 (2018): 344–66. https://doi.org/10.1177/0160597617748165.

Castañeda, Heide. *Borders of Belonging: Struggle and Solidarity in Mixed-Status Immigrant Families.* Redwood City, Calif.: Stanford University Press, 2019.

Cepeda, Paola, and Kate Winkle. "$36.4M Coming to Support Operation Lone Star as Thousands of Pounds of Drugs Seized Since March." *Border Report,* October 14, 2021. https://www.borderreport.com/hot-topics/border-crime/live-texas-dps-holds-third-briefing-on-operation-lone-star/.

Chang, Heewong. *Autoethnography as Method.* Walnut Creek, Calif.: Left Coast Press, 2008.

Chang, Robert S., and Keith Aoki. "Centering the Immigrant in the Inter/National Imagination." *California Law Review* 85, no. 5 (1997): 1395–1447. https://doi.org/10.2307/3481063.

Chavez, Leo R. *The Latina/o Threat: Constructing Immigrants, Citizens, and the Nation.* 2nd ed. Stanford, Calif.: Stanford University Press, 2013.

Choi, Matthew, and Stephen Neukam. "Monica De La Cruz Becomes First Republican to Win in 15th Congressional District in South Texas." *Texas Tribune,* November 9, 2022. https://www.texastribune.org/2022/11/08/monica-de-la-cruz-michelle-vallejo-texas-15/.

Cobbina, Jennifer E. *Hands Up, Don't Shoot: Why the Protests in Ferguson and Baltimore Matter, and How They Changed America*. New York: NYU Press, 2019.

Coleman, Mathew. "Immigration Geopolitics beyond the Mexico-U.S. Border." *Antipode* 39, no. 1 (2007): 54–76. https://doi.org/10.1111/j.1467-8330.2007.00506.x.

Coleman, Mathew. "The 'Local' Migration State: The Site-Specific Devolution of Immigration Enforcement in the U.S. South." *Law and Policy* 34, no. 2 (2012): 159–90. https://doi.org/10.1111/j.1467-9930.2011.00358.x.

Coleman, Mathew, and Austin Kocher. "Detention, Deportation, Devolution and Immigrant Incapacitation in the U.S., post 9/11." *Geographic Journal* 177, no. 3 (2011): 228–37. https://doi.org/10.1111/j.1475-4959.2011.00424.x.

Collins, Michael L. *Texas Devils: Rangers and Regulars on the Lower Rio Grande, 1846–1861*. Norman: University of Oklahoma Press, 2008.

Correa, Jennifer G., and James M. Thomas. "The Rebirth of the U.S.-Mexico Border: Latina/o Enforcement Agents and the Changing Politics of Racial Power." *Sociology of Race and Ethnicity* 1, no. 2 (2015): 239–54. https://doi.org/10.1177/2332649214568464.

Cortez, David. "Latinxs in La Migra: Why They Join and Why It Matters." *Political Research Quarterly* 74, no. 3 (2021): 688–702. https://doi.org/10.1177/1065912920933674.

Coutin, Susan. *Nations of Emigrants: Shifting Boundaries of Citizenship in El Salvador and the United States*. Ithaca, N.Y.: Cornell University Press, 2007.

Creek, Heather M., and Stephen Yoder. "With a Little Help from Our Feds: Understanding State Immigration Enforcement Policy Adoption in American Federalism." *Policy Studies Journal* 40, no. 4 (2012): 674–97. https://doi.org/10.1111/j.1541-0072.2012.00469.x.

De Genova, Nicholas P. "The Legal Production of Mexican/Migrant 'Illegality.'" *Latina/o Studies* 2 (2004): 160–85.

De Genova, Nicholas P. "Migrant 'Illegality' and Deportability in Everyday Life." *Annual Review of Anthropology* 31 (2002): 419–47. https://doi.org/10.1146/annurev.anthro.31.040402.085432.

De Genova, Nicholas P., and Ana Y. Ramos-Zayas. *Latino Crossings: Mexicans, Puerto Ricans, and the Politics of Race and Citizenship*. New York: Routledge, 2003.

Delgado, Richard, and Jean Stefancic. "Images of the Outsider in American Law and Culture: Can Free Expression Remedy Systemic Social Ills?" *Cornell Law Review* 77 (1992): 1258–97. https://doi.org/10.4324/9780429037627-2.

Demers, Jasmine. "Pima County Supervisors Reject Operation Stonegarden Grant Funding 3–2." *Arizona Daily Star*, February 4, 2020. https://tucson.com/news/local/pima-county-supervisors-reject-operation-stonegarden-grant-funding-3-2/article_e4417766-477d-11ea-a0d4-dff6d7de104a.html.

DeWalt, Kathleen Musante, and Billie R. DeWalt. *Participant Observation: A Guide for Fieldworkers*. New York: Altamira Press, 2002.

DHS Office of Inspector General. "FEMA and CBP Oversight of Operation Stonegarden Program Needs Improvement." November 9, 2017. https://www.oig.dhs.gov/sites/default/files/assets/2017-11/OIG-18-13-Nov17.pdf.

Donato, Katharine M., and Leslie Rodriguez. "Police Arrests in a Time of Uncertainty: The Impact of 287(g) on Arrests in a New Immigrant Gateway." *American Behavioral Scientist* 58, no. 13 (2014): 1696–722. https://doi.org/10.1177/0002764214537265.

Dowling, Julie A. *Mexican Americans and the Question of Race*. Austin: University of Texas Press, 2014.

Dunn, Timothy J. *Blockading the Border and Human Rights: The El Paso Operation That Remade Immigration Enforcement*. 2nd ed. Austin: University of Texas Press, 2009.

Durán, Robert J. *The Gang Paradox: Inequalities and Miracles on the U.S.-Mexico Border*. New York: Columbia University Press, 2018.

Eagly, Ingrid V. "Prosecuting Immigration." *Northwestern University Law Review* 104, no. 4 (2010): 1281–359.

Egan, R. Danielle. *Dancing for Dollars and Paying for Love: The Relationship between Exotic Dancers and Their Regulars*. New York: Palgrave Macmillan, 2006.

Eigenberg, Helen, and Tammy Garland. "Victim Blaming." In *Controversies in Victimology*, 2nd ed., edited by Laura J. Moriarty, 21–36. Cincinnati: Anderson Publishing, 2003.

Ellis, Carolyn, Tony E. Adams, and Arthur P. Bochner. "Autoethnography: An Overview." *Historical Social Research* 36, no. 4 (2011): 273–90.

Ellis, Carolyn S., and Arthur Bochner. "Autoethnography, Personal Narrative, Reflexivity: Researcher as Subject." In *The Handbook of Qualitative Research*, edited by Norman Denzin and Yvonna Lincoln, 733–68. Thousand Oaks, Calif.: Sage, 2000.

Embrick, David G. "Two Nations, Revisited: The Lynching of Black and Brown Bodies, Police Brutality, and Racial Control in 'Post-Racial' Amerikkka." *Critical Sociology* 41, no. 6 (2015): 835–43. https://doi.org/10.1177/0896920515591950.

Emerson, Robert M., and Melvin Pollner. "Constructing Participant/Observation Relations." In *Qualitative Approaches to Criminal Justice: Perspectives from the Field*, edited by Mark R. Pogrebin, 27–43. Thousand Oaks, Calif.: Sage, 2003.

Escobar, Edward J. *Race, Police, and the Making of a Political Identity: Mexican Americans and the Los Angeles Police Department, 1900–1945*. Berkeley: University of California Press, 1999.

Fassin, Didier. *Enforcing Order: An Ethnography of Urban Policing*. Malden, Mass.: Polity Press, 2013.

Feagin, Joe R. *The White Racial Frame: Centuries of Racial Framing and Counter-Framing*. 2nd ed. New York: Routledge, 2013.

Feagin, Joe R., and Jose A. Cobas. "Latinos/as and White Racial Frame: The Procrustean Bed of Assimilation." *Sociological Inquiry* 78, no. 1 (2008): 39–53. https://doi.org/10.1111/j.1475-682x.2008.00220.x.

Friese, Susanne. "User's Manual for ATLAS. ti 6.0." Berlin: ATLAS. ti Scientific Software Development GmbH, 2011. https://images10.newegg.com/UploadFilesForNewegg/itemintelligence/Antec/miniManual_v6_20111470284726873.pdf.

Fussell, Elizabeth. "The Deportation Threat Dynamic and Victimization of Latino Migrants: Wage Theft and Robbery." *Sociological Quarterly* 52, no. 4 (2011): 593–615. https://doi.org/10.1111/j.1533-8525.2011.01221.x.

Gamino, Eric. "Border Splurge to Deter Border Surge: An Auto-ethnographic Examination of Border Security Operations on the South Texas–Mexico Border." *Humanity and Society* 45, no. 2 (2021): 247–72. https://doi.org/10.1177/0160597621991544.

Garcia, Juan Ramon. *Operation Wetback: The Mass Deportation of Mexican Undocumented Workers in 1954*. Westport, Conn.: Greenwood Press, 1980.

Garcia, Ruben J. "Critical Race Theory and Proposition 187: The Racial Politics of Immigration Law." *Chicano-Latino Law Review* 17 (1995): 118–54. https://doi
.org/10.5070/C7171021069.

Giaritelli, Anna. "Texas Troopers Credited with Retaking Control of Del Rio Border."
Washington Examiner, September 20, 2021. https://www.washingtonexaminer.com
/news/texas-troopers-credited-retaking-control-del-rio-border.

Goffman, Erving. *The Presentation of Self in Everyday Life*. New York: Anchor Books, 1959.

Golash-Boza, Tanya M. *Deported Immigrant Policing, Disposable Labor and Global Capital-
ism*. New York: NYU Press, 2015.

Golash-Boza, Tanya M., and Pierrrette Hondagneu-Sotelo. "Latino Immigrant Men and
the Deportation Crisis: A Gendered Racial Removal Program." *Latino Studies* 11, no. 3
(2013): 271–92. https://doi.org/10.1057/lst.2013.14.

Goldsmith, Pat R., Mary Romero, Raquel Rubio-Goldsmith, Manuel Escobedo, and Laura
Khoury. "Ethno-racial Profiling and State Violence in a Southwest Barrio." *Aztlan: A
Journal of Chicano Studies* 34, no. 1 (2009): 93–123.

Gómez, Laura E. *Manifest Destinies: The Making of the Mexican American Race*. New York:
New York University Press, 2007.

Gutiérrez, David G. *Walls and Mirrors: Mexican Americans, Mexican Immigrants, and the
Politics of Ethnicity*. Oakland: University of California Press, 1995.

Haney-Lopez, Ian. *White by Law: The Legal Construction of Race*. 10th anniversary ed. New
York: New York University Press, 2006.

Harris, Cayla. "What to Know about Texas Republican Mayra Flores, the First Congress-
woman-Elect Born in Mexico." *Houston Chronicle*, June 16, 2022. https://www
.houstonchronicle.com/politics/texas/article/Five-things-to-know-about-Texas
-Republican-Mayra-17243470.php.

Hautala, Dane, Kirk Dombrowski, and Anthony Marcus. "Predictors of Police Reporting
among Hispanic Immigrant Victims of Violence." *Race and Justice* 5, no. 3 (2015): 235–58.
https://doi.org/10.1177/2153368714554717.

Hernández, Kelly Lytle. *Migra! A History of the U.S. Border Patrol*. Berkeley: University of
California Press, 2010.

Heyman, Josiah McC. "'Illegality' and the U.S.-Mexico Border: How It Is Produced and
Resisted." In *Constructing Immigrant "Illegality,"* edited by Cecilia Menjívar and Daniel
Kanstroom, 111–35. New York: Cambridge University Press, 2014.

Heyman, Josiah McC. "Why Caution Is Needed before Hiring Additional Border Patrol
Agents and ICE Officers." American Immigration Council special report,
April 24, 2017. https://www.americanimmigrationcouncil.org/research
/why-caution-needed-hiring-additional-border-patrol-agents-and-ice-officers.

Higham, John. *Strangers in the Land: Patterns of American Nativism 1860–1925*. New Bruns-
wick, N.J.: Rutgers University Press, 1955.

Hochschild, Arlie Russell. "Emotion Work, Feeling Rules, and Social Structure." *American
Journal of Sociology* 85, no. 3 (1979): 551–75. https://doi.org/10.1086/227049.

Hoffman, Abraham. "Stimulus to Repatriation: The 1931 Federal Deportation Drive and the
Los Angeles Mexican Community." *Pacific Historical Review* 42, no. 2 (1973): 205–19.
https://doi.org/10.2307/3638467.

Huber, Lindsay Perez, Corina Benavides Lopez, Maria C. Malagon, Veronica Velez, and
    Daniel G. Solorzano. "Getting beyond the 'Symptom,' Acknowledging the 'Disease':
    Theorizing Racist Nativism." *Contemporary Justice Review* 11, no. 1 (2008): 39–51.
    https://doi.org/10.1080/10282580701850397.
Huntington, Samuel P. *Who We Are: The Challenges to America's National Identity*. New
    York: Simon and Schuster, 2004.
Ivemark, Biörn, and Anna Ambrose. "Habitus Adaptation and First-Generation University
    Students' Adjustment to Higher Education: A Life Course Perspective." *Sociology of Ed-
    ucation* 94, no. 3 (2021): 191–207. https://doi.org/10.1177/00380407211017060.
Jervis, Rick. "Immigration Activists: Texas Program Violates Constitution." *USA Today*,
    September 29, 2021. https://www.usatoday.com/story/news
    /nation/2021/09/29/border-crossers-texas-arrested-state-initiative-police
    -border/5911692001/?gnt-cfr=1.
Jiménez, Tomás R. *Replenished Ethnicity: Mexican Americans, Immigration, and Identity*.
    Oakland: University of California Press, 2009.
Johnson, Kevin R. "'Aliens' and the U.S. Immigration Laws: The Social and Legal Construc-
    tion of Nonpersons." *University of Miami Inter-American Law Review* 28, no. 2 (1996):
    263–92.
Johnson, Kevin R. "Fear of an 'Alien Nation': Race, Immigration, and Immigrants." *Stanford
    Law & Policy Review* 7, no. 2 (1995): 111–26.
Johnson, Kevin R. "Race, the Immigration Laws, and Domestic Race Relations: A 'Magic
    Mirror' into the Heart of Darkness." *Indiana Law Journal* 73, no. 1 (1998): 1111–60.
Jorgensen, Danny L. *Participant Observation: A Methodology for Human Studies*. Newbury
    Park, Calif.: Sage, 1989.
Kephart, William M. *Racial Factors and Urban Law Enforcement*. Philadelphia: University
    of Pennsylvania Press, 1957.
Kilty, Keith M., and Maria Vidal de Haymes. "Racism, Nativism, and Exclusion: Public Pol-
    icy, Immigration, and the Latino Experience in the United States." *Journal of Poverty* 4,
    no. 1 (2000): 1–25. https://doi.org/10.1300/j134v04n01_01.
Kuykendall, Jack L., and David E. Burns. "The Black Police Officer: An Historical Perspec-
    tive." *Journal of Contemporary Criminal Justice* 1, no. 4 (1980): 4–11.
Lehmann, Wolfgang. "Habitus Transformation and Hidden Injuries: Successful Working-
    Class University Students." *Sociology of Education* 87, no. 1 (2013): 1–15. https://doi
    .org/10.1177/0038040713498777.
Lippard, Cameron D. "Racist Nativism in the 21st Century." *Sociology Compass* 5, no. 7
    (2011): 591–606. https://doi.org/10.1111/j.1751-9020.2011.00387.x.
Lofland, John, David A. Snow, Leon Anderson, and Lyn H. Lofland. *Analyzing Social Set-
    tings: A Guide to Qualitative Observation and Analysis*. 4th ed. New York: Thomson and
    Wadsworth, 2006.
Lonsway, Kimberly A., and Louise F. Fitzgerald. "Rape Myths in Review." *Psychology
    of Women Quarterly* 18 (1994): 133–64. https://doi.org/10.1111/j.1471-6402.1994.
    tb00448.x.
Lopez, Gerald P. "Undocumented Mexican Migration: In Search of a Just Immigration Law
    and Policy." *UCLA Law Review* 615, no. 28 (1981): 641–72.

MacLeod, Jay. *Ain't No Making It: Aspirations and Attainment in a Low-Income Neighborhood*. 3rd ed. New York: Routledge, 2009.

Maril, Robert L. *The Poorest of Americans: The Mexican Americans of the Lower Rio Grande Valley of Texas*. Notre Dame, Ind.: University of Notre Dame Press, 1989.

Marquart, James W. "Doing Research in Prison: The Strengths and Weaknesses of Full Participation as a Guard." *Justice Quarterly* 3, no. 1 (1986): 15–32. https://doi.org/10.1080/07418828600088771.

Marshall, Catherine, and Gretchen B. Rossman. *Designing Qualitative Research*. Thousand Oaks, Calif.: Sage, 2006.

Martin, Lauren. "The Geopolitics of Vulnerability: Children's Legal Subjectivity, Immigrant Family Detention and U.S. Immigration Law and Enforcement Policy." *Gender, Place, and Culture* 18, no. 4 (2011): 477–98.

Martinez, Daniel E., Guillermo Cantor, and Walter A. Ewing. "No Action Taken: Lack of CBP Accountability in Responding to Complaints of Abuse." American Immigration Council special report, May 2014. https://www.americanimmigrationcouncil.org/sites/default/files/research/No%20Action%20Taken_Final.pdf.

Martinez, Ramiro. "Incorporating Latinos and Immigrants into Policing Research." *Criminology & Public Policy* 6, no. 1 (2007): 57–64. https://doi.org/10.1111/j.1745-9133.2007.00421.x.

McKenney, David Haller. " 'Operation Stone Garden': A Case Study of Legitimation of Violence and the Consequences for Mexican Immigrants in Chaparral, New Mexico." M.A. thesis, University of Texas at El Paso, 2013.

Menjívar, Cecilia, and Leisy Abrego. "Legal Violence: Immigration Law and the Lives of Central American Immigrants." *American Journal of Sociology* 117, no. 5 (2012): 1380–421. https://doi.org/10.1086/663575.

Menjívar, Cecilia, and Cynthia Bejarano. "Latino Immigrants' Perceptions of Crime and Police Authorities in the United States: A Case Study from the Phoenix Metropolitan Area." *Ethnic and Racial Studies* 27, no. 1 (2004): 120–48. https://doi.org/10.1080/759053711.

Menjívar, Cecilia, and Daniel Kanstroom, eds. *Constructing Immigrant "Illegality": Critiques, Experiences, and Responses*. New York: Cambridge University Press, 2014.

Menjívar, Cecilia, William Paul Simmons, Daniel Alvord, and Elizabeth Salerno Valdez. "Immigration Enforcement, the Racialization of Legal Status, and Perceptions of the Police: Latinos in Chicago, Los Angeles, Houston, and Phoenix in Comparative Perspective." *Du Bois Review: Social Science Research on Race* 15, no. 1 (2018): 107–28. https://doi.org/10.1017/S1742058X18000115.

Messing, Jill Theresa, David Becerra, Allison Ward-Lasher, and David K. Androff. "Latinas' Perceptions of Law Enforcement: Fear of Deportation, Crime Reporting, and Trust in the System." *Journal of Women and Social Work* 30, no. 3 (2015): 328–40. https://doi.org/10.1177/0886109915576520.

Mills, Charles. *The Racial Contract*. Ithaca, N.Y.: Cornell University Press, 1997.

Molina, Hilario, II. "Racializing the Migration Process: An Ethnographic Analysis of Undocumented Immigrants in the United States." PhD dissertation, Texas A&M University, 2011.

Morales, Maria Cristina, and Theodore R. Curry. "Citizenship Profiling and Diminishing Procedural Justice: Local Immigration Enforcement and the Reduction of Police Legitimacy among Individuals and in Latina/o Neighbourhoods." *Ethnic and Racial Studies* 44, no. 1 (2021): 134–53. https://doi.org/10.1080/01419870.2020.1723669.

Morales, Maria Cristina, Denise Delgado, and Theodore R. Curry. "Variations in Citizenship Profiling by Generational Status: Individual and Neighborhood Characteristics of Latina/os Questioned by Law Enforcement about Their Legal Status." *Race and Social Problems* 10, no. 2 (2018): 293–305. https://doi.org/10.1007/s12552-018-9235-3.

Moscufo, Kiki. "'Dirty Money': Key Border Communities Are Rejecting $2.5 Million in Federal Money over Trump's Wall and Extreme Immigration Policies." *Business Insider*, October 28, 2020. https://www.businessinsider.com /border-communities-reject-25-million-over-trumps-extreme-policies-2020-10.

Moskos, Peter. *Cop in the Hood: My Year Policing Baltimore's Eastern District*. Princeton, N.J.: Princeton University Press, 2008.

Nevins, Joseph. *Operation Gatekeeper: The Rise of the "Illegal Alien" and the Making of the U.S.-Mexico Boundary*. New York: Routledge, 2002.

Nevins, Joseph. *Operation Gatekeeper and Beyond: The War on "Illegals" and the Remaking of the U.S.-Mexico Boundary*. 2nd ed. New York: Routledge, 2010.

Ngai, Mae M. *Impossible Subjects: Illegal Aliens and the Making of Modern America*. Princeton, N.J.: Princeton University Press, 2004.

Noferi, Mark L. "Cascading Constitutional Deprivation: The Right to Appointed Counsel for Mandatorily Detained Immigrants Pending Removal Proceedings." *Michigan Journal of Race and Law* 18, no. 1 (2012): 63–129.

Ochoa, Gilda L. *Becoming Neighbors in a Mexican American Community: Power, Conflict, and Solidarity*. Austin: University of Texas Press, 2004.

O'Hare, William P., and Kenneth M. Johnson. "Child Poverty in Rural America." *Population Reference Bureau Reports on America* 4, no. 1 (2004): 1–20.

Omi, Michael, and Howard Winant. *Racial Formation in the United States: From the 1960s to the 1990s*. New York: Routledge, 1994.

Ono, Kent A., and John M. Sloop. *Shifting Borders: Rhetoric, Immigration, and California's Proposition 187*. Philadelphia: Temple University Press, 2002.

Ordóñez, Karina J. "Modeling the U.S. Border Patrol Tucson Sector for the Deployment and Operations of Border Security Forces." M.A. thesis, Naval Postgraduate School, 2006.

Paoline, Eugene A., III. *Rethinking Police Culture: Officers' Occupational Attitudes*. New York: LFB Scholarly Publishing, 2001.

Phillips, Scott, Jacqueline Maria Hagan, and Nestor Rodriguez. "Brutal Borders? Examining the Treatment of Deportees during Arrest and Detention." *Social Forces* 85, no. 1 (2006): 93–109. https://doi.org/10.1353/sof.2006.0137.

Phillips, Scott, Nestor Rodriguez, and Jacqueline Maria Hagan. "Brutality at the Border? Use of Force in the Arrest of Immigrants in the United States." *International Journal of the Sociology of Law* 30, no. 4 (2002): 285–306. https://doi.org/10.1016 /S0194-6595(03)00003-0.

Plascencia, Luis F. B. "Where Is 'The Border'? The Fourth Amendment, Boundary Enforcement, and the Making of an Inherently Suspect Class." In *The U.S.-Mexico Transborder Region: Cultural Dynamics and Historical Interactions*, edited by Carlos G. Vélez-Ibañez and Josiah Heyman, 244–80. Tucson: University of Arizona Press, 2017.

Pogrebin, Mark R., and Eric D. Poole. "Humor in the Briefing Room: A Study of the Strategic Uses of Humor among Police." In *Qualitative Approaches to Criminal Justice: Perspectives from the Field*, edited by Mark R. Pogrebin, 80–93. Thousand Oaks, Calif.: Sage, 2003.

Provine, Doris Marie, Monica W. Varsanyi, Paul G. Lewis, and Scott H. Decker. *Policing Immigrants: Local Law Enforcement on the Front Lines*. Chicago: University of Chicago Press, 2016.

Pyke, Karen. "What Is Internalized Racial Oppression and Why Don't We Study It? Acknowledging Racism's Hidden Injuries." *Sociological Perspectives* 53, no. 4 (2010): 551–72. https://doi.org/10.1525/sop.2010.53.4.551.

Pyke, Karen, and Tran Dang. "'FOB' and 'Whitewashed': Identity and Internalized Racism among Second Generation Asian Americans." *Qualitative Sociology* 26, no. 2 (2003): 147–72. https://doi.org/10.1023/A:1022957011866.

Reaves, Brian A. "Local Police Departments, 2013: Personnel, Policies, and Practices." Bureau of Justice Statistics, U.S. Department of Justice, Washington, D.C., 2015. https://static1 .squarespace.com/static/5eb5d3a0c609106d0d7ecd08/t/62452511058cf24a3764b0b3 /1648698642832/BJS_USDOJ_2013_local_police_study.pdf.

Reed, Megan. "Senate Bill 4: Police Officers' Opinions on Texas's Ban of Sanctuary Cities." *Chicanx-Latinx Law Review* 36, no. 1 (2019): 67–112. https://doi.org/10.5070 /C7361042814.

Reed-Danahay, Deborah. *Auto/ethnography: Rewriting the Self and the Social*. Oxford: Berg Publishers, 1997.

Reilly, Katie. "Here Are All the Times Donald Trump Insulted Mexico." Time.com, August 31, 2016. https://time.com/4473972/donald-trump-mexico-meeting-insult/.

Reiner, Robert. *The Politics of the Police*. 4th ed. New York: Oxford University Press, 2010.

Rennison, Callie Marie. "Reporting to the Police by Hispanic Victims of Violence." *Violence and Victims* 22, no. 6 (2007): 754–72. https://doi.org/10.1891/088667007782793110.

Rennison, Callie Marie, Angela R. Gover, Stacey J. Bosick, and Mary Dodge. "Reporting Violent Victimization to the Police: A Focus on Black, White, Asian, and Hispanic Adolescent Victims." *Open Families Studies Journal* 4, no. 1 (2011): 54–67. https://doi .org/10.2174/1874922401104010054.

Resendiz, Julian. "Border Patrol, Small New Mexico Town Forge Strong Bond amid Migrant Crisis." *Border Report*, September 17, 2021. https://www.ktsm.com/news/border-report /border-patrol-small-new-mexico-town-forge-strong-bond-amid-migrant-crisis/.

Rios, Victor. *Punished: Policing the Lives of Black and Latino Boys*. New York: NYU Press, 2011.

Rodriguez, Adrian J. "Punting on the Values of Federalism in the Immigration Arena? Evaluating Operation Linebacker, a State and Local Law Enforcement Program along the U.S.-Mexico Border." *Columbia Law Review* 108, no. 5 (2008): 1226–67.

Romero, Mary. "Are Your Papers in Order? Racial Profiling, Vigilantes, and 'America's Toughest Sheriff.'" *Harvard Latino Law Review* 14, no. 1 (2011): 337–58.

Romero, Mary. "Crossing the Immigration and Race Border: A Critical Race Theory Approach to Immigration Studies." *Contemporary Justice Review* 11, no. 1 (2008): 23–37. https://doi.org/10.1080/10282580701850371.

Romero, Mary. "Racial Profiling and Immigration Law Enforcement: Rounding Up of Usual Suspects in the Latino Community." *Critical Sociology* 32, nos. 2–3 (2006): 447–73. https://doi.org/10.1163/156916306777835376.

Romero, Mary. "State Violence, and the Social and Legal Construction of Latino Criminality: From El Bandito to Gang Member." *Denver Law Review* 78, no. 4 (2001): 1081–118.

Romero, Mary, and Marwah Serag. "Violation of Latino Civil Rights Resulting from INS
and Local Police's Use of Race, Culture and Class Profiling: The Case of the Chandler
Roundup in Arizona." *Cleveland State Law Review* 52, no. 1 (2005): 75–96.

Russel, Kristin J., and Christopher J. Hand. "Rape Myth Acceptance, Victim Blame Attribution and Just World Beliefs: A Rapid Evidence Assessment." *Aggression and Violent Behavior* 37 (2017): 153–60. https://doi.org/10.1016/j.avb.2017.10.008.

Sáenz, Rogelio, and Karen Manges Douglas. "A Call for the Racialization of Immigration
Studies: On the Transition of Ethnic Immigrants to Racialized Immigrants." *Sociology of
Race and Ethnicity* 1, no. 1 (2015): 166–80. https://doi.org/10.1177/2332649214559287.

Saito, Natsu Taylor. "Model Minority, Yellow Peril: Functions of 'Foreignness' in the Construction of Asian American Legal Identity." *Asian Law Journal* 4, no. 6 (1997): 71–94.

Samora, Julian. *"Los Mojados": The Wetback Story.* South Bend, Ind.: University of Notre
Dame Press, 1971.

Samora, Julian, Joe Bernal, and Albert Peña. *Gunpowder Justice: A Reassessment of the Texas
Rangers.* Notre Dame, Ind.: University of Notre Dame Press, 1979.

Sanchez, Boris. "The Latino Voter Shift Comes into Focus in South Texas." *CNN*, October
15, 2022. https://www.cnn.com/2022/10/14/politics/latino-voters-texas-15th/index
.html.

Sanchez, Gabriella, and Mary Romero. "Critical Race Theory in the U.S. Sociology of Immigration." *Sociology Compass* 4, no. 9 (2010): 779–88. https://doi
.org/10.1111/j.1751-9020.2010.00303.x.

Sanchez, Jorge T. "Face the Nation: Race, Immigration, and the Rise of Nativism in Late
Twentieth Century America." *International Migration Review* 31, no. 4 (1997): 1009–30.
https://doi.org/10.1177/019791839703100409.

Sanchez, Sandra. "WATCH: Migrants in Eagle Pass, Texas, Try to Outrun Border Law Enforcement." Borderreport.com, June 14, 2023. https://www.borderreport.com
/immigration/border-crime/watch-migrants-in-eagle-pass-texas-try-to-outrun-border
-law-enforcement/.

Santa Ana, Otto. *Brown Tide Rising: Metaphors of Latinos in Contemporary American Public
Discourse.* Austin: University of Texas Press, 2002.

Sarabia, Heidy. "Migrants, Activists, and the Mexican State: Framing Violence, Rights, and
Solidarity along the U.S.-Mexico Border." *Citizenship Studies* 24, no. 4 (2020): 512–29.
https://doi.org/10.1080/13621025.2020.1755175.

Sayers, Justin. "Tucson Police to Quit Taking Funds from Federal Border-Security Grant."
Arizona Daily Star, January 18, 2020. https://thisistucson.com/news/local
/tucson-police-to-quit-taking-funds-from-federal-border-security-grant
/article_a7e5d96e-ee26-5a40-a136-eb16ae47bbd5.html.

Scharf, Irene. "Tired of Your Masses: A History of and Judicial Responses to Early 20th
Century Anti-Immigrant Legislation." *University of Hawaii Law Review* 21 (1999):
131–68.

Silva, Angela J., and Aurelia L. Murga. "Racializing American Authenticity: Mexican Americans' Perceptions of the Foreign *Other*." *Humanity and Society* 45, no. 2 (2021): 202–24.
https://doi.org/10.1177%2F0160597621993408.

Singlemann, Joachim, Tim Slack, and Kayla Fontenont. "Race and Place: Determinants of Poverty in the Texas Borderland and the Lower Mississippi Delta." In *International Handbook of Rural Demography*, edited by L. J. Kulcsar and K. J. Curtis, 293–306. New York: Springer, 2012.

Skolnick, Jerome H. *Justice without Trial: Law Enforcement in Democratic Society.* New York: John Wiley & Sons, 1966.

Sparks, Hayden. "Operation Lone Star Has Seized Thousands of Pounds of Narcotics as Border Crisis Persists, per Abbott." *The Texan*, August 26, 2021. https://thetexan.news /operation-lone-star-has-seized-thousands-of-pounds-of-narcotics-as-border-crisis -persists-per-abbott/.

Stumpf, Juliet. "The Crimmigration Crisis: Immigrants, Crime, and Sovereign Power." *American University Law Review* 56, no. 2 (2006): 367–419.

Theodore, Nik, and Robert Habans. "Policing Immigrant Communities: Latino Perceptions of Police Involvement in Immigration Enforcement." *Journal of Ethnic and Migration Studies* 42, no. 6 (2016): 970–88. https://doi.org/10.1080/1369183X.2015.1126090.

Van Maanen, John. "Breaking In: Socialization to Work." In *Handbook of Work, Organization, and Society*, edited by Robert Dubin, 67–130. Chicago: Rand McNally, 1976.

Van Maanen, John. "Kinsmen in Response: Occupational Perspectives of Patrolmen." In *Policing: A View from the Street*, edited by Peter K. Manning and John Van Maanen, 115–28. Santa Monica, Calif.: Goodyear Publishing Company, 1978.

Van Maanen, John. "Observations on the Making of Policemen." In *Qualitative Approaches to Criminal Justice: Perspectives from the Field*, edited by Mark R. Pogrebin, 66–79. Thousand Oaks, Calif.: Sage, 2003.

Van Maanen, John. "On Watching the Watchers." In *Policing: A View from the Street*, edited by Peter K. Manning and John Van Maanen, 309–49. Santa Monica, Calif.: Goodyear Publishing Company, 1978.

Vera Sanchez, Claudio G., and Edwardo L. Portillos. "Insiders and Outsiders: Latino Researchers Navigating the Studying of the Police." *Race and Justice* 11, no. 4 (2018): 384–406. https://doi.org/10.1177/2153368718802410.

Vera Sanchez, Claudio G., and Dennis P. Rosenbaum. "Racialized Policing: Officers' Voices on Policing Latino and African American Neighborhoods." *Journal of Ethnicity in Criminal Justice* 9, no. 2 (2011): 152–78. https://doi.org/10.1080/15377938.2011.566821.

Vila, Pablo. "Constructing Social Identities in Transnational Contexts: The Case of the Mexico-U.S. Border." *International Social Science Journal* 51, no. 159 (1999): 75–87. https://doi.org/10.1111/1468-2451.00178.

Vogt, Wendy. "Crossing Mexico: Structural Violence and the Commodification of Undocumented Central American Migrants." *American Ethnologist* 40 (2013): 764–80. https:// doi.org/10.1111/amet.12053.

Walker, Samuel, and Charles Katz. *The Police in America: An Introduction.* 8th ed. New York: McGraw-Hill, 2013.

Ward, Peter M. *Colonias and Public Policy in Texas and Mexico: Urbanization by Stealth.* Austin: University of Texas Press, 1999.

Warren, Carol A. B., and Tracy X. Karner. *Discovering Qualitative Methods: Field Research, Interviews and Analysis.* Los Angeles: Roxbury Publishing Company, 2005.

Watkins, William J., Jr. *Reclaiming the American Revolution: The Kentucky and Virginia Resolutions and Their Legacy.* New York: Palgrave Macmillan, 2004.

Weitzer, Ronald. "The Puzzling Neglect of Hispanic Americans in Research on Police-Citizen Relations." *Ethnic and Racial Studies* 37, no. 11 (2014): 1995–2013. https://doi.org/10.1080/01419870.2013.790984.

Wong, Tom K. "287(g) and the Politics of Interior Immigration Control in the United States: Explaining Local Cooperation with Federal Immigration Authorities." *Journal of Ethnic and Migration Studies* 38, no. 5 (2012): 737–56. https://doi.org/10.1080/1369183X.2012.667983.

INDEX

www.ingramcontent.com/pod-product-compliance
Lightning Source LLC
Chambersburg PA
CBHW020534270326
41927CB00006B/565